# The Pesher of Christ

*The true story of Jesus and his Church*

by Dylan Stephens

Copyright © 2017 Dylan Stephens.
All rights reserved.
Based on site pesherofchrist.com ©
2009-2017 Dylan Stephens.
Pesher of Christ™ Dylan Stephens. All rights reserved.
Publisher: Infinite SOULutions™ - pesherofchrist.com
All rights reserved under international and
Pan-American Copyright Conventions

Infinite SOULutions
9 Sanwick Point Ct
Bellingham, WA. 98229
USA

## RECOMMENDATION

*"Somewhere in 2000 onward Dylan Stephens came into my discussion group, taking a very strong, intelligent, and well-informed interest in the Nag Hammadi and Apocrypha, when the group was dissolved, he offered to build me a site (663 megabytes) and this collaboration was immensely successful."* Dr Barbara Thiering, author of "Jesus the Man"/Jesus & The Riddle of The Dead Sea Scrolls.

## ACKNOWLEDGEMENT

*Above all the joys of my life: my songs, and my spiritual studies is my dear wife, WendyBird, sharing this spiritual path with me and our three children of the astral plane, of the heavenly, and of prophecy: Kesdjan, Nirvana, and Tarot, and the three grandchildren of Nirvana: Isis, Llyr, and Atira and the three grandchildren of Tarot: Lucie, Tilka, and Maïa.*

## BIOGRAPHY

With a Jesuit education from Fordham Prep School and Georgetown University earning a Bachelor of Science degree (having graduated in the same class of 68 with a U.S. President), I pursued a career in computer systems and GIS programming while also songwriting, having had a recording contract with Columbia Records in 1967 (oldiesbutdillies on YouTube). I was part of three inner circles of
 Mr. Nyland, a direct student of G. I. Gurdjieff;
 the Native American 'Man with Ravens'; and
 Dr. Barbara Thiering, author of "Jesus the Man", (having built and maintaining her website, hosted on my non-profit website: infinitesoulutions.com since her death). My uncle, Richard Waring, was a Hollywood actor (1944) and my grandfather, Thomas E. Stephens, was friend and portrait painter of Eisenhower (Smithsonian). My half-brother Anton Holden and my father Peter John Stephens are published authors. I am self-published with books: "Magnetic Disturbance", "Paulina's Promise to her Grandfather, Jesus", "The Seven Sisters and the Apocalypse", "Arthur:King and Saint" and soon "Simon Magus: The Grear 666".

# 50+ Answers to the following questions in this book

- Was Jesus married to Mary Magdalene?
- Did he and Mary Magdalene have children?
- Who was Mary Magdalene's mother?
- Who was the prostitute that Jesus rescued?
- Was Mary Magdalene the daughter of Martha?
- What was Martha's real name?
- Were Peter and Andrew freedmen of the Herod court?
- Was Thomas the banished son of Herod the Great?
- Were Philip's sisters merely the nuns who included Mary Magdalene?
- Was the second John of the twelve the same as Bartholomew and the "disciple that Jesus loved"?
- Were James son of Alphaeus and Matthew the sons of the High Priest Ananus?
- Was the disciple Simon, the Zealot/Canaanite the same as Simon Magus, actually the step-father, Zebedee, of James and John?
- Were James and John the illegitimate children of Augustus Caesar's daughter and Mark Antony's son?
- Was Thaddaeus/Theudas the Prodigal Son and the leader Zadok who fought with Judas the Galilean?
- Are Barsabbas and Barnabas just corruption of Jesus' last name: Sabbas ('Bar'=son of)?
- Was Barabbas, son of Abba, Theudas?
- Was Susanna the betrothed of James the Just?
- Who was Joseph of Arimathea?
- Who was Nicodemus?
- Was James the Just, Jesus' younger brother?
- Was Joses, Jesus' second brother, the same as Barnabas and Matthias?
- Were Jude and Simon-Silas, also brothers of Jesus?
- Was Judas Iscariot the man on the cross who rebuked Jesus?
- Was Simon the Cyrene really the same as Simon Magus carrying his own cross to be crucified?
- Did Jesus survive the Crucifixion by taking poison on the cross that made him appear to be dead?
- Did Jesus live in secret to an old age of 78 in Rome?

- What was the mysterious three-hour time difference between the Synoptic Gospels and that of John at the Crucifixion
- Was the Crucifixion at Qumran and not at Jerusalem?
- Was Bethlehem the same as the Queen's house, just south of Qumran?
- Was Mazin on the Dead Sea really Capernaum on the Sea of Galilee?
- Was Ein Feshkha the location of Galilee?
- Was Egypt just the wilderness of Mird, near Qumran?
- Was Mary Magdalene pregnant with Jesus' daughter when he was on the cross?
- Was Jesus' daughter the same as Tamar/Phoebe who was married to Paul?
- Was Jesus Justus the elder son of Jesus and Mary Magdalene?
- Was Mary Magdalene pregnant with Jesus' second son (Joseph) when Peter knocked?
- Did Mary Magdalene divorce Jesus and did Jesus remarry and have another son?
- What was Jesus's second wife's name?
- Did Paul have two daughters (the first called Paulina)?
- Was Bernice called the "Harlot of Babylon" because of her affair with Emperor's son: Titus?
- Who is the Beast 666 and what does it stand for?
- Were 'Michael' and 'Gabriel' just Essene titles and not angels?
- Was Satan just another word for Tester or Zealot?
- Did Luke make a mistake saying that Jesus' birth was twelve years late or was it his Bar Mitzvah?
- Did Joseph force himself on Mary and cause Jesus to be illegitimate?
- Were the shepherds in Luke really the Therapeuts, who influenced Jesus in the creation of his Church?
- Was Salome the daughter of Herodias and the disciple Thomas?
- Was Thomas really the dispossessed Herod associated with Esau with Jacob?
- Did Salome dance to remove John's head or did the consort of Simon Magus and Mary Magdalene's mother dance?
- Did Jesus take over from John the Baptist after he was killed, rather than create his own following?
- Was Paul really a Jew as he claimed or was he a Roman citizen being the son of Herod Antipas?
- Was Timothy, who was Paul's trusted leader, the son of Salome?
- Is the birth of Jesus' great-grandson (Jesus IV) shown at the end of Revelation in Sept 112?

# CONTENTS

PREFACE
Family relationships of Jesus ... 000
I. Dead Sea Scrolls reveal The Pesher of Christ ... 002
II. Jesus Survived the Crucifixion say two Pre-Nicean Fathers ... 004
III. Gospel of Matthew - the Winged Man (angel) ... 006
IV. Gospel of Mark - the Lion, the symbol of kingship ... 008
V. Gospel of Luke - the Bull, the symbol of monasticism ... 010
VI. Gospel of John - the Eagle also the zodiacal sign Scorpio ... 012

SECTION 1 **(8BC to 28AD)**
**The Early Years: Birth, Coming of Age, joining the monastery of Qumran ... 014**
Chapter 1 - The Age of Wrath ... 016
Chapter 2 - Taxation of Cyrenius; Revolt of Judas the Galilean ... 018
Chapter 3 - The Rebellion Finds Religion ... 020
Chapter 4 - Matthew's Bethlehem Story ... 022
Chapter 5a - The Sins of the Father ... 024
Chapter 5b - Mary's Sorrow ... 026
Chapter 6 - Jesus, an acolyte under Eleazar Annas ... 028
Chapter 7 - Jesus' Bar Mitzvah ... 030
Chapter 8 - Therapeuts are Shepherds ... 032
Chapter 9 - At age 23 Jesus is accepted into Qumran ... 034
Chapter 10 - Joseph is killed by Pilate leaving Mary a widow ... 036
Chapter 11 - John the Baptist becomes Pope in 26AD ... 038
Chapter 12 - The Rise of the Beast 666 ... 040

SECTION 2 **(March 29AD (Jesus' 35th birthday) to Sept 30AD)**
**Jesus leaves the monastery of Qumran for Marriage; Assembles the Twelve Disciples ... 042**
Chapter 13 - John refuses to baptize Jesus ... 044
Chapter 14 - Jonathan Ananus aligns with Jesus ... 046
Chapter 15 - Aligning with Simon Magus ... 048
Chapter 16 - A Secret Meeting with Helena by the Well ... 050
Chapter 17 - The Overthrow of John the Baptist ... 052
Chapter 18 - Peter and Andrew, Fishers of Men, and Philip ... 054
Chapter 19 - Absolution of Peter's mother-in-law ... 056
Chapter 20 - The twins James and John of Royal Lineage ... 058
Chapter 21 - Centurion's Servant (John Mark) is recruited) ... 060
Chapter 22 - Gadarenes demonic (Theudas) is recruited) ... 062
Chapter 23 - Thomas the Twin, the disinherited Esau ... 064
Chapter 24 - Judas Sicarii (Iscariot) the Tester ... 066
Chapter 25 - The Tax Collectors complete the Twelve ... 068
Chapter 26 - The Twelve Disciples ... 070

SECTION 3 **(29AD to 30AD)**
**The Marriage of Jesus and Mary Magdalene** ... 072
Chapter 27 - Mother of Mary Magdalene convinces Jesus ... 074
Chapter 28 - The Bat Mitzvah of Mary Magdalene ... 076
Chapter 29 - Water into Wine ... 078
Chapter 30 - The Sins of the Mother ... 080
Chapter 31 - The Marriage - Song of Solomon ... 082

SECTION 4 **(September 30AD to December 32AD)**
**Miracles are Metaphors** ... 084
Chapter 32 - Father Ananus, a paralytic, let down from the roof ... 086
Chapter 33 - Jesus Commands the Sea and Walks on Water ... 088
Chapter 34 - Impotent Man (James) at the Pool of Bethesda ... 090
Chapter 35a - The Mission: Parable of the Sower ... 092
Chapter 35b - The Mission: The Five and Four Thousand ... 094
Chapter 36 - Transfiguration of Jesus ... 096
Chapter 37 - Healing the Deaf man, Blind man, and Epileptic ... 098 Chapter 38a - The Excommunication of Simon as Lazarus ... 100
Chapter 38b - Removing the Excommunication of Lazarus ... 102

SECTION 5 **(March 33AD) Month before the Last Supper** ... 104
Chapter 39 - Rock of Peter; James and John in Glory ... 106
Chapter 40 - Judas and the 30 pieces of silver ... 108
Chapter 41 - Jesus rides a donkey into Jerusalem ... 110
Chapter 42 - Mary Magdalene announces their child ... 112

SECTION 6 **(8AM to 10PM Thursday, April 2, 33AD) The Last Supper (Sacrament 8PM to 9PM)** ... 114
Chapter 43a - Finding the location ... 116
Chapter 43b - Washing the feet of the disciples ... 118
Chapter 43c - The Sacrament; Judas leaves ... 120
Chapter 43d - Musical Chairs at Discussion Time ... 122
Chapter 43e - The cock will crows twice, three hours denied ... 124

SECTION 7 **(10PM, Thursday to 8:15AM, Friday, April 3, 33AD)**
**Counter-plot, Arrest, and Trial** ... 126
Chapter 44 - Garden of Gethsemane ... 128
Chapter 45 - The Arrest ... 130
Chapter 46 - Trial of Jesus before Ananus and Caiaphas ... 132
Chapter 47 - Peter Weeps ... 134
Chapter 48 - Trial before Pilate (What is Truth?) ... 136
Chapter 49 - Trial before Agrippa ... 138
Chapter 50 - Trial before Pilate (Release Barabbas!) ... 140
Chapter 51 - Judas repents too late ... 142

SECTION 8 **(8:15AM to 3:05PM (crucified 9AM (3rd hour/6th hour)), Friday, April 3, 33AD)**
**The Crucifixion** ... 144
Chapter 52 - Carrying the Cross ... 146
Chapter 53 - Postponing the Poison ... 148
Chapter 54a - Placed on the Cross; King of the Jews... 150
Chapter 54b - Two criminals talk to Jesus ... 152
Chapter 54c - Four Marys and a possible son ... 154
Chapter 54d - Darkness (time moves 3 hrs) ... 156
Chapter 54e - Jesus: Requesting the poison ... 158

SECTION 9 **(3:05PM to midnight, Friday, April 3, 33AD)**
**The Rescue** ... 160
Chapter 55 - Ask for the body, test for death, Sabbath excuse ... 162
Chapter 56 - Taking down the bodies ... 164
Chapter 57 - Wrapping the bodies; put in the tomb ... 166
Chapter 58 - Guarding the tomb ... 168
Chapter 59 - Jesus' dream ... 170

SECTION 10 **(Saturday, April 4 to May 6, 33AD)**
**The Resurrection** ... 172
Chapter 60 - Magdalene gets Peter and John Mark ... 174
Chapter 61 - Mary mistakes Jesus for James, the Gardener ... 176
Chapter 62 - The women visit the tomb. Jesus is gone. ... 178
Chapter 63 - Judas dies in a Field of Blood ... 180
Chapter 64 - Emmaus, Thomas, and Broiled fish ... 182
Chapter 65 - Ascension to Monastery ... 184

SECTION 11 **(May 24, 33AD to 37AD)**
**The New Mission** ... 186
Chapter 66 - Choosing a replacement for Judas ... 188
Chapter 67 - Peter heals James; Jesus has a daughter ... 190
Chapter 68 - Peter and John Mark are arrested by Caiaphas ... 192
Chapter 69 - Pentecost 34AD ...194
Chapter 70 - Ananias & Sapphira excommunicated by Peter ... 196
Chapter 71 - Agrippa is imprisoned; released by Caligula ... 198
Chapter 72 - Jonathan is martyred as Stephen ... 200
Chapter 73 - Magdalene has given birth to a son: Jesus Justus ... 202
Chapter 74 - Philip sent to the Ethiopian of Ham ... 204

SECTION 12 **(37AD to 44AD)**
**Ascendency of Peter & Paul;**
**the rise and fall of Herod Agrippa 40 to 44AD** ... 206
Chapter 75 - Paul is blinded, Jesus speaks to him ... 208
Chapter 76 - Paul escapes from Damascus; Agrippa ascendant ... 210
Chapter 77 - James appointed to bishop of Jerusalem ... 212
Chapter 78 - Peter comforts Mother Mary: Tabitha ... 214
Chapter 79 - Jesus out of monastery to renew his marriage ... 216
Chapter 80 - Peter is to give equal standing to Gentiles ... 218
Chapter 81 - Herod Agrippa insanity; Peter is archbishop ... 220
Chapter 82 - King Herod Agrippa poisoned by Simon Magus ... 222
Chapter 83 - To Jesus a second son; Magdalene asks divorce ... 224
Chapter 84 - In Antioch, Syria first called Christians ... 226

SECTION 13 **(44AD to 46AD)**
**Paul's First Missionary Journey with Barnabas** ... 228
Chapter 85 - Paul, Barnabas, John Mark & Jesus sail to Cyprus ... 230
Chapter 86 - Acts of Paul - Paul and Thecla ... 232
Chapter 87 - Barnabas and Paul are mistaken for gods ... 234
Chapter 88 - The Council of Jerusalem ... 236

SECTION 14 **(46AD to 48AD)**
**John Mark and Barnabas Mission to Cypress; Paul's Second Missionary Journey (47-48(54))** ... 238
Chapter 89 - Antioch; Magdalene's divorce papers ... 240
Chapter 90 - Acts of Barnabas; the Gospel of Matthew ... 242
Chapter 91 - Paul's Second Missionary Journey begins ... 244

SECTION 15 **(47AD to 48AD)**
**Canonizing of the Gospels** ... 246
Chapter 92 - Jesus' Letters to the Seven Churches ... 248
Chapter 93 - Matthew intends to canonize the Four Gospels ... 250
Chapter 94 - The bitterness of the Gospel of John is removed ... 252
Chapter 95 - Worthy is the Lamb to unseal the Gospels ... 254

SECTION 16 **(49AD to September 51AD)**
**Jesus Second Marriage to Lydia** ... 256
Chapter 96 - Paul to baptize Lydia, then betrothed to Jesus ... 258
Chapter 97 - Bernice Confronted; Jesus' marriage begins ... 260
Chapter 98 - Lydia presents Jesus with a son ... 262

SECTION 17 **(November 51AD to March 54AD)**
**Paul and Phoebe meet; betrothed, married, and with child** ... 264
Chapter 99 - Speech on the Unknown God; Meets Seneca ... 266
Chapter 100 - Paul betrothed to Phoebe ... 268
Chapter 101 - Felix marries Drusilla; The Acts of Philip ... 270
Chapter 102 - Paul released by Gallio ... 272
Chapter 103 - Paul's Nazarite vow; Phoebe 3 months pregnant ... 274

SECTION 18 **(September 54 to May 58AD)**
**Paul's Third Missionary Journey** ... 276
Chapter 104 - Paul at Paulina's birth; Third Journey begins ... 278
Chapter 105 - Paul is bishop of Ephesus; Apollos is removed ... 280
Chapter 106 - Felix kills Jonathan; Paul sends Phoebe to Rome ... 282
Chapter 107 - (Vercelli) Acts of Peter; Travel to Rome ... 284
Chapter 108 - Magdalene dies; Simon sells silver icons ... 286
Chapter 109 - Joyous reunion of John Mark (Eutychus) ... 288
Chapter 110 - Paul insists on going to Jerusalem ... 290

SECTION 19 **(June 58AD to 61AD)**
**Paul imprisoned in Jerusalem** ... 292
Chapter 111 - Paul enters the Temple; saved by guards ... 294
Chapter 112 - Paul leaves with Jesus for Felix's Trial in Rome ... 296
Chapter 113 - Shipwreck and a Viper ... 298

SECTION 20 **(61AD to 65AD)**
**Jesus, Paul, & Peter in Rome** ... 300
Chapter 114 - Paul in Prison; Simon Magus on the Ropes ... 302
Chapter 115 - Ananus kills James; Paul visits Spain 62AD ... 304
Chapter 116 - Jesus meets Peter fleeing Rome (Quo Vadis) ... 306
Chapter 117 - Phoebe hears that Paul has been beheaded ... 308

SECTION 21 **(70AD to 112AD)**
**Church survives the death of Peter and Paul** ... 310
Chapter 118 - Bernice almost saves Jerusalem ... 312
Chapter 119 - Paulina's promise; Jesus dies in June 72AD ... 314
Chapter 120 - Betrothal of Jesus' grandson; 6 Sacraments ... 316
Chapter 121 - Jesus IV is born in 112; First & Last ... 318

Abbreviations:
SM - Secret Gospel of Mark; GP - Gospel of Peter
Antiq & War - Antiquities of the Jews & The Jewish War by Flavius Josephus AD93
R. & H. - Clementine Recognitions & Homilies using writings of Pope Clement I and "The Memoirs of Agrippina the Younger"
Eccl Hist - Church History, Eusebius
NT text is from Young's Bible modernized;
"italic parenthesis" indicates inductive reasoning

# Family relationships of Jesus
## (the key to his actions and alliances)

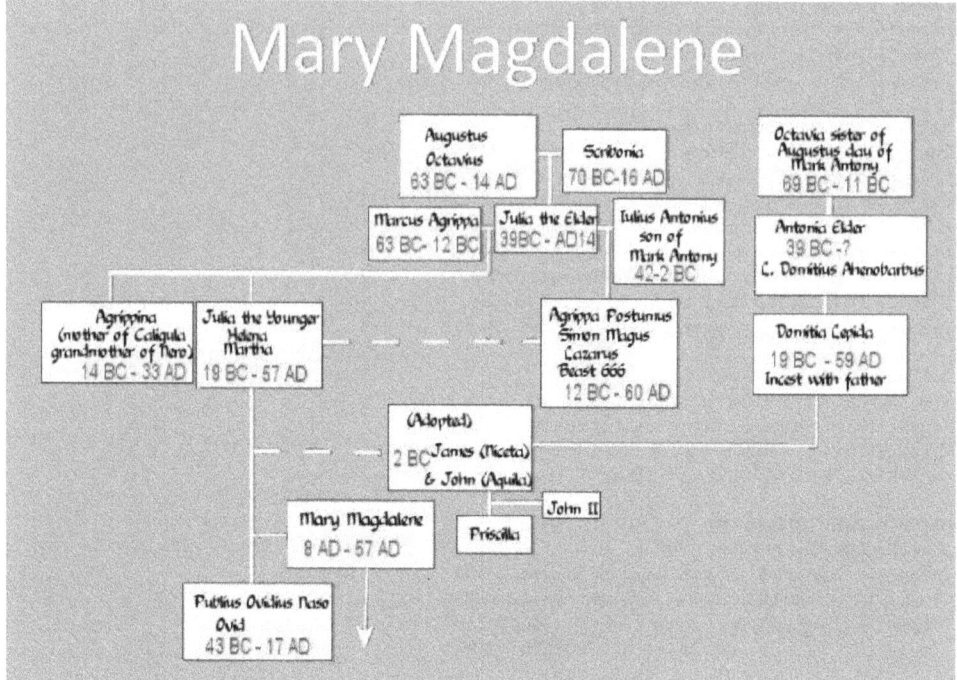

Julia the Elder, daughter of Augustus, had an affair with Iulius Antonius, son of Mark Antony, and the child was Agrippa Postumus who can be linked to Simon Magus from the "Clementines". She is exiled to an island. His sister Julia the Younger (Martha/Helena), daughter of Julia the Elder, had a brief affair with Ovid who is exiled to a Black Sea town. She is exiled to an island where Mary Magdalene was born.

Agrippa Postumus was supposed to have been killled by Tiberius, Julia the Younger was left to supposedly die on the island and her baby ordered to be killed at birth but: see my book: "Simon Magus, the Great 666").

James and John were twins Niceta and Aquila born from Domita Lepida from incest with her father and cast out (Clementines). Being relatives they were rescued and adopted by Helena (Martha) and Simon Magus (Zebedee).

# Jesus Children & Grandchildren

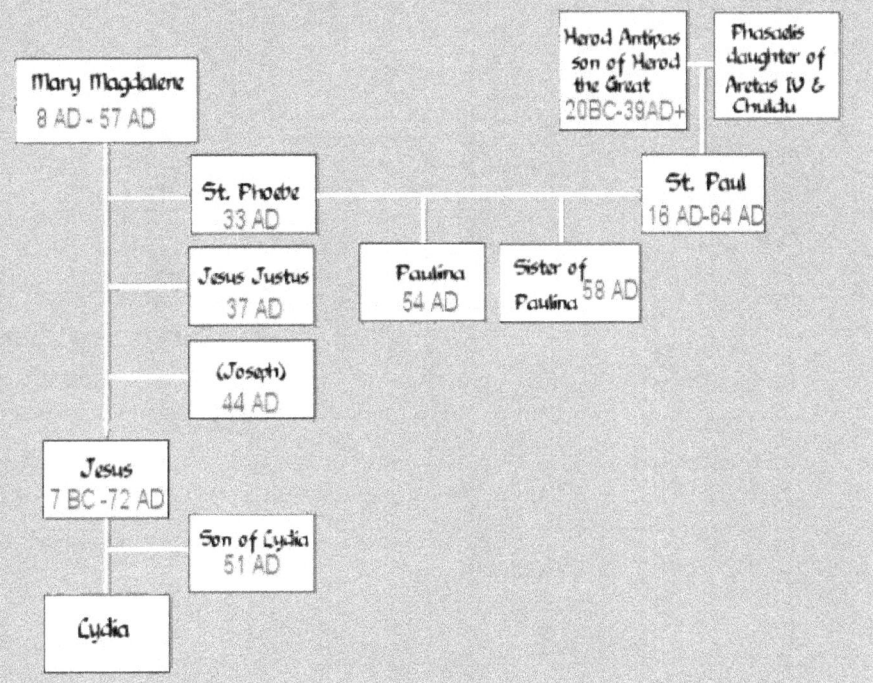

Mary Magdalene was pregnant with Jesus' child when he was on the cross. Mary Magdalene's mother is the Syro-Phoenician woman (Helena). Helena was part of John the Baptist's group: Luna or Joanna (feminine of John) as the head of Magdalene's convent: Martha). Paul is the son of Herod Antipas by his first wife Phasaelis, daughter of king Aretas IV of Nabatea. (Remember Paul and the bucket). When Herod Antipas divorced her, he got in trouble with John the Baptist and King Aretas by marrying his brother (Herod)'s wife Herodias. The daughter of Herodias and Herod was Salome and you know how that ended for John the Baptist. The clue was a slip by Luke in Acts, saying "Paul's sister's son" (the sister is Salome, Antipas' step-daughter).

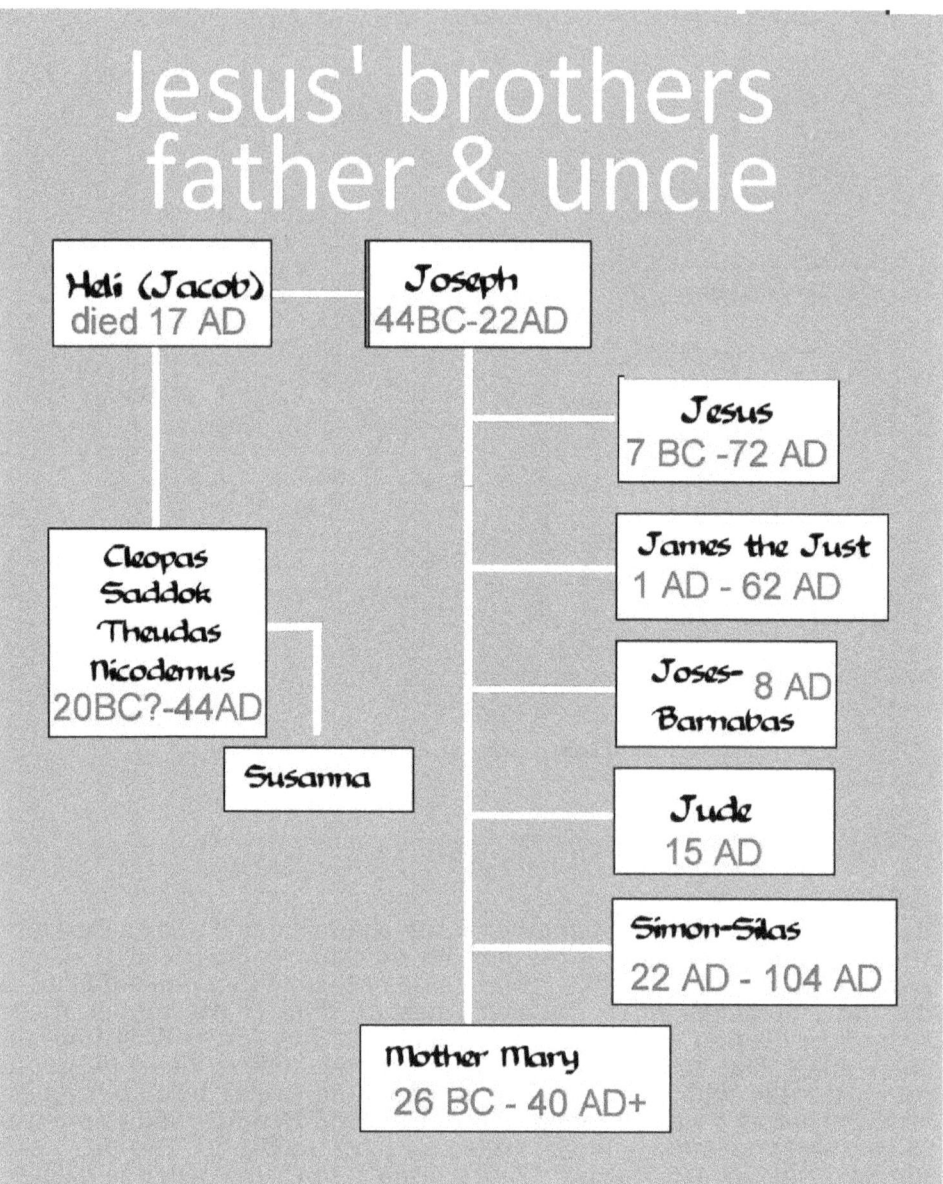

Brothers are in Mark 6:3. Sabbas is Jesus' father's name ('bar' is son of) such as in Simon Barsabbas, and and Joses (Barnabas corrupted from Barsabbas). Barabbas is also corrupted (uncle Cleopas, Thaddeus, Nicodemus).

# Introduction

Religion is usually grounded in a belief of a super-human God or Gods that need to be appeased by certain prescribed actions or dress code in order to gain favor or at least to avoid the God's wrath against them. Of the religions today (Christianity, Islam, Hinduism, Buddhism, Judaism, Sikhism, Bahaism, Confucianism, Jainism, Shintoism, Taoism, etc.), there are few that would be recognizable to their founders, having been usurped by narcissists who distorted them for personal gain. Most religions consider their religion, and thus their God or founder, to be the true one and seem to be obsessed with annihilating the other's religion. Even within each religion, there are factions that war with each other such as Protestant vs. Catholic, Shia vs. Sunni, Vaishnavism vs Shaivism, Hinayana vs. Mahayana, etc. Many lives and cultures have been annihilated in the name of religion.

There are still those who claim that there is no proof from non-Christian historians living around the time of Jesus that he existed, but here they are:

- Josephus (7AD-100AD) mentions Jesus, his brother James, and John the Baptist
- Tacitus (56AD-120AD) "Christ, the founder of the name, had undergone the death penalty in the reign of Tiberius, by sentence of the procurator Pontius Pilate"
- Suetonius (69AD-122AD) Claudius: "disturbances at the instigation of Chrestus" & Nero: "punishment was inflicted on the Christians"

It is the winner who forces their new religion on the losers and Christianity is no exception for without the Roman Emperor Constantine and the Frankish King Clovis, it would not be a major religion today. The creation of Christianity, which is different from what Jesus intended, began with the Council of Nicaea in 325AD. The main discussion revolved around whether Jesus was the 'Son of God' or 'equal to God'. The absurdity of this is that careful study reveals Jesus never saying he was the 'Son of God', but rather the 'Son of Man'. The 'Jesus is God' faction won out, in this chess game, because they had the most bishops!

No doubt this God duplication was an improvement because Jesus' personality was more gentle than the vindictive Jewish God, especially if he would be judging those alive ('quick') and dead. Sadly, Jesus' concept of 'agapé' love was forgotten and thus its foundation in the universal law of reciprocity: "To avoid doing to others, what you would not want to be done unto you."

Aside from the problem of making Jesus a God, the current erosion of belief in Christianity comes from the doubt about Jesus' miracles and resurrection. The Gospel of Thomas and the Gospel of Philip uncovered in 1945 in Nag Hammadi tell of a Jesus without these miracles and, as to resurrection, they claim that resurrection from the physical realm comes from freeing oneself from the world of illusion. Since the Church requires its followers to accept these miracles of Jesus and his resurrection on faith, it dismissed these works long ago as heresy and ironically calling them 'gnostic' as having 'knowledge' ('gnostikos', a term used by Irenaeus).

With science continuing to create greater miracles than the gods could ever perform, it has been tempting to install the God of Science, but there is no ethics in science. It is also not a time to dread the future that has been tainted by an incorrect reading of Revelation that tells of an apocalypse of evil and destruction, which was merely a telling of past history with imaginative images. And thus it comes to the purpose of this book that by 'revealing' the true story of Jesus and the early Church, that humankind can move more rapidly towards a new paradigm, that will become our 'Revelation':

- all people as brothers and sisters
- unfettered by tired religious dogma
- joined together with hearts and minds
- reflecting the purity and truth of our Being
- as Christ and all religious leaders hoped for us.

I pray that this book can be the focal point for proofs of the hidden story in the Gospels and Acts and Revelation and the foundation of a new paradigm: Pesher of Christ™. "You shall know the truth, and the truth shall make you free!" (John 8:32)

*Here will be revealed the secret knowledge by the method of*
*The Pesher of Christ™*
*Revealing the true history of Jesus and his Church. (8BC - 112AD)*
*The paradigm shift is beginning!*

*(A Novella with left-hand pages of referenced Truth)*

*The Qumran Pesher on Habakkuk (1QpHab) (extracts only; translated by B.T.)*
*1:12-13 [For the wicked one surrounds] the righteous one (Habakkuk 1:4)*
*[Its pesher, the wicked one is the Wicked Priest (Jesus), and the righteous one] is the Teacher of Righteousness (John the Baptist)*
*5:8-11 Why do you stare, traitors, and remain silent when the wicked one swallows up one more righteous than he? (Habakkuk 1:13) Its pesher refers to the House of Absalom (David)and the men of its Council who kept silent when the Teacher of Righteousness was punished and did not help him against the Man of a Lie (Jesus) who flouted the Law in the midst of their whole congregation. (Transfiguration - Luke 9:28–36.).*

*Luke 10:21-24 In that hour was Jesus glad in the Spirit, and said, "I do confess to you, Father, Lord of the heaven and of the earth, that You did hide these things from wise men and understanding, and did reveal them to babes; yes, Father, because so it became good pleasure before You. All things were delivered up to me by my Father, and no one does know who the Son is, except the Father, and who the Father is, except the Son, and he to whom the Son may wish to reveal Him."*
*And having turned unto the disciples, he said, by themselves, "Happy the eyes that are perceiving what you perceive; for I say to you, that many prophets and kings did wish to see what you perceive, and did not see, and to hear what you hear, and did not hear."*

## I. (1946 -1956)
### Dead Scrolls reveal The Pesher of Christ

When the Dead Sea Scrolls were discovered in the ten years following 1947, it was discovered (but, at first, purposefully hidden because they were related to early Christianity) that some fragments of the Scrolls would interpret past passages from Scripture as if they were related to the present, using the phrase: "The pesher is". This was an important clue in deciphering the New Testament since it suggested that a hidden narrative could be found within! This novel idea of applying the concept of the pesher to the New Testament was first the 'Pesher Technique' of Dr. Barbara Thiering; then followed by 'The Pesher of Christ™', which was developed by Dylan Stephens, the author of this book. Both relied on Inductive Reasoning, however, when Dr. Barbara Thiering attempted to prove her hypothesis scientifically by developing complicated rules, such as the Rule of the Last Referent, this latter phase of her career was shown to be inconsistent by the author of this book.

> *St. Paul and Jesus hint at the concept of hiding things from initiates until they are ready to receive it. This is a well-known esoteric fact that knowledge is a substance that should not be diluted by giving it to everyone and not even to initiates (babes) until they are ready:*
> *1 Cor 3:2 Paul, "With milk, I fed you, and not with meat, for you were not yet able, but not even yet are you now able."*
> *Matt 13:13-17 "Because of this, in parables do I (Jesus) speak to them, because seeing they do not see, and hearing they do not hear, nor understand, and fulfilled on them is the prophecy of Isaiah, that said, 'You will be ever hearing, but never understanding; you will be ever seeing, but never perceiving. This people's heart has become calloused; they hardly hear with their ears, and have closed their eyes lest they might see with the eyes, and with the ears might hear, and with the heart understand, and turn back, and I might heal them.'*
> *And blessed are your eyes because they see, and your ears because they hear, for verily I say to you, that many prophets and righteous men did desire to see that which you look on, and they did not see, and to hear that which you hear, and they did not hear."*

## IRENAEUS    EUSEBIUS
## 130 - 202 AD   260 - 340 AD

*Irenaeus was Bishop of Lugdunum in Gaul (Lyon, France). He was an early Church Father and apologist, and his writings were formative in the early development of Christian theology. Irenaeus is recognized as a saint in both Roman Catholicism and Eastern Orthodoxy. His most famous of his writings is 'Against Heresies', which was aimed against the Gnostics. He considered himself to be superior to them because as a student of Polycarp, who was in touch with John the Evangelist (son of John, the brother of James, therefore John II), he had a direct connection with Jesus. He is one of the preeminent early Christian Fathers, venerated in the following Churches: Roman Catholic, Lutheran, Eastern and Oriental Orthodox, Anglican Communion, and Eastern Assyrian.*

*(Quotes on right are from Against Heresies" (c. 180AD), The Ante-Nicene Fathers. translations of the writings of the fathers down to A.D. 325 Vol 1 edited by Roberts and Donaldson - paraphrased)*

*Eusebius succeeded Agapius as Bishop of Caesarea soon after 313AD. Being a learned man and famous author, and thus enjoying the favor of Emperor Constantine, he played a prominent role at the Council of Nicaea in 325AD. When he wrote his Church History, he must have had the works of Papias before him, but they have since been lost. Papias of Hierapolis (died c. 100AD) is described by Irenaeus (previously quoted above) as "an ancient man who was a hearer of John and a companion of Polycarp". Polycarp (69-155AD) was a Christian bishop of Smyrna, one of the Seven Churches of Revelation in 48AD. With Clement of Rome (the first Pope) and Ignatius of Antioch, Polycarp is regarded as one of three chief Apostolic Fathers. His sole surviving work attributed to his authorship is his Letter to the Philippians (first recorded by Irenaeus). Polycarp must have had strong connections with Papias at Hierapolis which is where the Apostle Philip lived and whose bones are said to be buried. (Quotes on right are from Church History Fragments of Papias 3.39.8-10 Eusebius)*

## II. (April 33AD)
## Jesus Survived the Crucifixion say two
## Pre-Nicean Fathers

Irenaeus writes, "Jesus, in his thirties, being in fact still a young man, suffered on the cross, but this was merely the first stage of his early life that would extend onwards past his fortieth year. Even though a man begins to decline towards **old age towards his fiftieth year**, Jesus continued to fulfill his role as a Teacher as the Gospel and all the elders testify. These elders in Asia were conversant with the son of John, the disciple of Jesus, who remained among them up to the times of Trajan (98AD)."

Eusebius records the fragmented words of Papias that tell of wonderful events that have come down to him by tradition. Papias was a contemporary of Philip the Apostle who resided in Hierapolis with his daughters (Acts 21:08). He relates a marvelous tale from the daughters of Philip:

"that in his time a man rose from the dead[1], and again how Justus[2] who was surnamed Barsabbas[3] drank a deadly poison, and yet, by the grace of the Lord, suffered no serious harm."

*(1) This is obviously Lazarus (shown to be Simon Magus)*
*(2) This is Jesus, although Eusebius has mistaken him for James the Just in the next phrase from Papias: **"And they put forward two, Joseph, called Barsabbas, who was surnamed Justus, and Mathias."** The Clementines says that Mathias is Joses. Justus means crown prince used by James, younger brother of Jesus and later by Jesus' son: Jesus Justus, the true crown prince (Colossians 4:11).*
*Thus the choice is between Jesus' brothers: James and Joses.*
*(3) The prefix 'Bar' in Barsabbas means "son of", thus "son of Sabbas." It is used in Acts 1:23 for James (Joseph Barsabas), in Acts 4:36 Joses (called by the corrupted Bar-nabas) and in Acts 15:22 for Jude (Judas called Barsabas) with Silas (Simon). (Brothers of Jesus: Mark 06:03 'Is not this the carpenter, the son of Mary, and brother of James, and Joses, and Jude, and Simon?' Barabbas is son of Abbas, another name for Theudas.)*

# The White Horse

*Rev 6:1,2 And I saw when the Lamb opened one of the seals, and I heard one of the four living creatures saying, as it were a voice of thunder, 'Come and behold!' and I saw, and lo, a white horse, and he who is sitting upon it is having a bow, and there was given to him a crown, and he went forth overcoming, and that he may overcome.*

***Author: Matthew*** *(written last)*
*Matthias, High Priest 43AD, a Sadducee, younger brother of Theophilus (dedicated in Luke and Acts), Matthew, disciple of Jesus. His father, Ananus (Ananus: John 18:13; Alphaeus in disciple list) was High Priest (6–15 A.D.) and had 5 sons who were High Priests: Eleazar, Jonathan, Theophilus, Matthias, Ananus. His daughter was the wife of Caiaphas.*

## III. (48AD)
### Gospel of Matthew associated with the Winged Man (angel)

In Revelation, the Lamb is Jesus, who breaks the seal of each book in turn. The four living creatures are from the first chapter of Ezekiel, having four faces, that of a man, a lion, an ox and an eagle.

This is the canonizing of the Book of Matthew. White is symbolic of the white robe that was worn by the Sadducee Priest acting as God. Thus the horse, representing the priest who carries the Gospel of Matthew is white because it was written by the Sadducee Priest Matthew Ananus. The crown is from his older brother Jonathan Ananus who called himself Stephen *('stephanos' is Greek for 'crown')*. The bow is symbolic of Artemis, the goddess of Ephesus where the cathedral is located and also symbolic of the spiritual war of non-violence.

> *Matthew, who was also presiding, wanted to build an epic story similar to Luke so he added the Sermon on the Mount from the Jewish sages such as Hillel, whose grandson is Gamaliel (Acts 5:34-40), and added more parables (Luke's concept of explaining new and old history). Most importantly he added the Bethlehem Birth with the Magi who were the only ones who recognized Jesus as the true descendant of David because Joazar Boethus, Pharisee High Priest, had rejected him as illegitimate using Essene rules of marriage. (The shepherds are from Luke which only has Jesus' symbolic birth: Bar Mitzvah.) As a Sadducee, he disparages the Pharisees and the scribes (those who only apply the strict interpretation of the law without regard to circumstances).*

# The Red Horse

*Rev 6:3,4 And when he opened the second seal, I heard the second living creature saying, 'Come and behold!' and there went forth another horse fiery red, and to him who is sitting upon it, there was given to him to take the peace from the land, and that one another they may slay, and there was given to him a great sword.*

**Author: Peter, scribed by Mark (not John Mark)** *(written second)*
*(Fragments Of Papias, Eccl Hist 3.39.15 "Mark, having become the interpreter of Peter, wrote down accurately, though not indeed in order, whatsoever he remembered of the things said or done by Christ."*

## IV. (48AD)
### Gospel of Mark associated with the Lion, the symbol of kingship

This is the canonizing of the Book of Mark. Red is symbolic of the red robes that were worn by the cardinal acting for the "Son of God". Thus the horse, representing the priest who carries the Gospel of Mark, is red because it was written by Peter, Jesus' cardinal. (Shown in Acts 13:1 as Simeon called Niger wearing the black of an monastic archbishop interchangeable with the abbey cardinal red.) The sword is symbolic of the angels at the Garden of Eden. Peter used this sword to defend his position as the 'Ear' (& mouth) of Jesus against James in the Garden of Gethsemane.

Peter set out to write a no-nonsense commentary with no virgin birth, seven miracles, and no resurrection. The miracles are merely changes of doctrine that brought him from a 'fisher' of converts in the Noah ceremony to Pope of the Christian Church. Peter ends it abruptly with:

*Mark 16:08 "And, having come forth quickly, they fled from the sepulcher, seized with trembling and amazement, and saying nothing to anyone, for they feared."*
*(It is clear that Peter intended this ending due to his disdain for the Resurrection story, evidenced by the absence of verses 16:9-20 in Codex Sinaiticus and Vaticanus. Aside from the forged ending, there were clearly more edits, in order to make it correspond to the Luke and Matthew narrative, as can be seen by the remnants of the original version in the "Gospel of Peter" and the "Secret Gospel of Mark".)*

## *The Black Horse*

*Rev 6:5,6 And when he opened the third seal, I heard the third living creature saying, 'Come and behold!' and I saw, and lo, a black horse, and he who is sitting upon it is having a balance in his hand, and I heard a voice in the midst of the four living creatures saying, 'A measure of wheat for a denary, and three measures of barley for a denary,' and 'The oil and the wine you may not treat unjustly.'*

**Author: Jesus, scribed by Luke** *(written third)*
*Dedicated to Theophilus, son of Ananus, High Priest 37- 41AD*

*Colossians 4:14 - Paul: Our dear friend* **Luke***, the doctor*

*Phil.4.3 - Paul: And I ask you also, true yoke-fellow* **(ox)** *(Phoebe - his wife), help these women, for they have labored side by side with me in the gospel together with Clement and the rest of my fellow workers, whose names are in the book of life.*

## V. (48AD)
### Gospel of Luke associated with the Ox, the symbol of bearing the yoke of the monastic or Nazarite.

This is the canonizing of the Book of Luke. Black is symbolic of the black robes that were worn by the monastic archbishop John Mark. Thus the horse, representing the apostle who carries the Gospel of Luke, is black. The three groups are "wheat" for the 4000 celibate followers; "barley" for the 5000 married followers; (The miracles of the Feeding the 4000 and the 5000"); and oil and wine for the monastics, like Jesus when in monastery, who did not use oil or fermented wine. (Antiq 18.1 on the Essenes: "Oil they consider defiling".)

The Schism of the Churches after the Council of Jerusalem in June 46AD, created a problem with the acceptance of the Gospel of John that Jesus had written with Simon Magus because now he was on the opposing side. Jesus saw the need to write a more complete gospel that would tell his side of the story, leaving out Simon Magus. He dedicated it to Theophilus Ananus (37- 41 AD), the High Priest, a Sadducee, brother of Matthew, High Priest in 43AD, both sons of Ananus giving a clue as to when it was written. He also used parables or seemingly simple moral stories to illustrate the past and present history. Matthew would copy this in his Gospel.

*(A proof of the primacy of the Gospel of John, which scholars refute, is in the dedication of Luke 1:2 "servants of the 'Word'" which, having been used in the first verse of John, established it as code for Jesus.)*

# *The Green (Pale) Horse*

*Rev 6:7,8 And when he opened the fourth seal, I heard the voice of the fourth living creature saying, 'Come and behold!'*
*and I saw, and lo, a pale horse, and he who is sitting upon him -- his name is Death, and Hades does follow with him, and there was given to them authority to kill, (over the fourth part of the land,) with sword, and with hunger, and with death, and by the beasts of the land.*

**Author: Jesus and Simon Magus, scribed by John Mark**
*(written first, but revised later)*
*The section below about its revision alludes to Simon Magus' poisoning of King Herod Agrippa:*
*Rev 10:7-11: "I took the little book out of the angel's hand, and ate it up. It was as sweet as honey in my mouth. When I had eaten it, my belly was made bitter."*

*Simon's philosophy contained in it is shown in "Refutations of All Heresies", Hippolytus of Rome (170 – 235AD) book 6.7 on the philosophy of Simon Magus and in Ptolemaeus (late 2nd century), disciple of Valentinius in "Ptolemy's Letter to Flora".*

## VI. (48AD)
### Gospel of John associated with the Eagle also the zodiacal sign Scorpio, the symbol of the Crucifixion and Resurrection of Jesus

This is the canonizing of the Book of John. Green is symbolic of the green robes of the clergy and of the tradition of the Sower to the Diaspora (the Jews who lived abroad) which began with Jesus' grandfather Heli and was continued by Joseph and Jesus. Thus the horse, representing the priest who carries the Gospel of John, is green (changed to pale since no horse is green). Green is also representative of the time Jesus was out of the monastery for the conception of an heir with Mary Magdalene and the continued dynasty of David. For this was when he taught the initiates who sat on the green grass in the Feeding of the Multitudes.

The indication of joint authorship are the symbols of "Death" *(Simon Magus who had the power to excommunicate)* and of "Hades" *(Jesus being revived from that state between life and death in the Cave after the Crucifixion)*. The powers are: Sword *(angels at the Garden of Eden who protect the monasteries from outside contamination)*, "Hunger" is the Nazarite practice that Jesus followed when out of monastery *(Jesus tempted by Satan in the Wilderness)*, Death *(excommunication)*, and "Wild Beasts" *(Zealots)*.

The Gospel of John is essentially Jesus' words with some of Simon Magus' philosophy. Although the first to be written, in its revisions by James Niceta, Pope Simon Magus' presence is hidden by using nicknames for him such as Simon of Cyrene, Lazarus, ... and his consort Helena: "the woman at the well"; "the menstruous woman", ...) made it the last to be canonized. However, Simon's philosophy is clearly contained at the beginning:

*GOD is made of three aspects "Hidden" and "Manifest" and "Spirit". The "Hidden" (passive force) and the "Manifest" (active force) are joined together by "Spirit" (reconciling force). The act of Creation, as in Genesis, is when the Spirit separates the "Hidden" and "Manifest" giving us existence by means of "Spirit".*

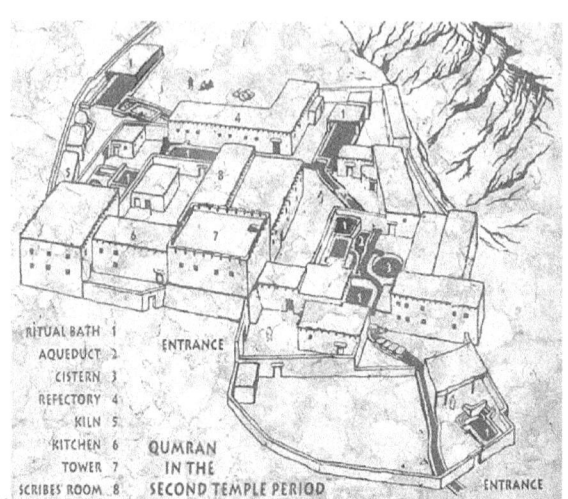

RITUAL BATH 1
AQUEDUCT 2
CISTERN 3
REFECTORY 4
KILN 5
KITCHEN 6
TOWER 7
SCRIBES ROOM 8
ENTRANCE
QUMRAN IN THE SECOND TEMPLE PERIOD
ENTRANCE

*The Essenes having been excluded by Herod in the Restoration of the Temple established Qumran (Jerusalem plural: Ἱεροσόλυμα) as the mirror image of Jerusalem (Jerusalem singular: Ἱερουσαλὴμ). All other places were also moved so that Capernaum, Bethsaida, Nazareth, Nain became Ein Feshkha; Bethlehem: the Queen's House (just south of Qumran); Gennesaret, the Sea of Tiberias (Galilee) became Mazin. The convents of Dan and Asher (Bethany) were at Mird. Therapeuts were there also in the wilderness (Egypt). Thus Jesus entered the monastery of Qumran and walked and sailed along the Dead Sea and walked the paths to Mird and Emmaus (the halfway point of the path to the Jerusalem Temple). His crucifixion was on the grounds of Qumran marked as the latrine with a skull.*

## SECTION 1 (8BC to 28AD)
## *The Early Years: Birth, Coming of Age, joining the monastery of Qumran*

Leonardo da Vinci (1452-1519)

*"And in the Age of Wrath (6AD)... they perceived their iniquity and recognized that they were guilty men" (Cairo-Damascus Document chapter 1.5) Pontius Pilate is made Prefect in 26AD.*

Daniel 9:24 "Seventy weeks (490 years) are determined concerning your people and concerning your holy city to finish the transgression and to make an end of sins, and to make reconciliation for iniquity, and to bring in everlasting righteousness, and to seal up the vision and prophecy, and to anoint the Most Holy. Restoration of the Temple 527BC- 490 = 37 BC (start of Herod's reign). Menahem the Essene prophesies Herod's reign in the 8th week of Enoch. (Antiq 15.10.5)

T.Levi 5:11-12 "And in the seventh week (107 BC: 7th jubilee) shall become priests, who are idolaters, adulterers, lovers of money, proud, lawless, lascivious, abusers of children and beasts. And after their punishment shall have come from the Lord, the priesthood shall fail."

Age 1 Creation 0-490 Anno Mundi
Age 2 Noah & the Flood 490-980 Anno Mundi
Age 3 Abraham 980-1470 Anno Mundi
Age 4 Moses & Exodus 1470-1960 Anno Mundi
Age 5 First Temple Built 1960-2450 Anno Mundi
Age 6 Fall of Jerusalem and Captivity 2450-2520 Anno Mundi
Age 7 Restoration of the Temple 2520-3010 Anno Mundi (597BC)
"390 years after he had given them into the hand of King Nebuchadnezzar of Babylon, He visited them, and He caused a plant root to spring from Israel and Aaron to inherit His Land and to prosper on the good things of His earth." (Damascus Document CD 1:6-9)
Age 8 Birth of the Anointed One 3010-3080 Anno Mundi starting with the reign of Herod the Great (37/38BC)
Age 9 Restoration of the Priests and line of David Kings 3080-3150 Anno Mundi (34AD) The inauguration of the new Christian Era, but sadly also the destruction of the Temple 70AD

John 2:19,20 Jesus answered and said unto them, "Destroy this temple, and in three days I will raise it up." The Jews (followers of John the Baptist), therefore, said, "46 years was this sanctuary building, and wilt thou in three days raise it up?" 27AD is the 46th year from of the rebuilding of the Temple by Herod in 20BC. Thus one Jubilee (49 years later) brings the Restoration of the Jewish Kingdom to 30AD. Jesus is saying that the Restoration should be three and a half years later at 33AD because the Great Jubilee of 29AD needed to be moved forward three years and a half years to account of the desecration of the Temple in 167BC by Antiochus. (The word 'day' means 'year'. The literalists used it to pretend that Jesus was 'three days in the tomb'.) (This prophecy also failed with the Crucifixion, but was declared a win because Jesus survived. More predictions would also fail like 64AD: the great fire of Rome and 70AD: the Destruction of the Temple of Jerusalem.)

# Chapter 1. (6AD - 34AD:Pentecost)
## The Age of Wrath

*The year 6AD was declared by Daniel as the Age of Wrath, saying that "seventy weeks (490 years) are determined to make reconciliation for iniquity, and to bring everlasting righteousness." In the 8th Age, God's promise was to take an active role to bring his kingdom on earth and thus upheavals were to be expected. Subtracting 490 years from the Restoration of the Temple in 527BC, equaled the start of Herod's reign at 37BC. Menahem the Essene had prophesied this date to Herod the Great, which made him partial to the Essenes. Although Herod had rebuilt the Temple, he 'slaughtered the innocents', thus the original date was moved forward two jubilees to exclude Herod's reign thus 2\*(49+1)=100 years from Enoch's original 8th week of 107BC is 7BC, the birth of John the Baptist (8BC) or Jesus (7BC)).*

> "Then the Lord shall raise up a new priest. And to him all the words of the Lord shall be revealed, and he shall execute a righteous judgment upon the earth for a multitude of days. And his star shall arise in heaven as of a king. Lighting up the light of knowledge as the sun the day, and he shall be magnified in the world. He shall shine forth as the sun on the earth, and shall remove all darkness from under heaven, and there shall be peace in all the earth. And in his priesthood, the Gentiles shall be multiplied in knowledge upon the earth, and enlightened through the grace of the Lord. In his priesthood shall sin come to an end, and the lawless shall cease to do evil. And he shall open the gates of paradise, and shall remove the threatening sword against Adam, and he shall give to the saints to eat from the tree of life, and the spirit of holiness shall be on them." (T.Levi 5:11-29)

> *A crisis would occur when John the Baptist was imprisoned before March 30AD (his predicted day) and removed as Pope by Herod Antipas, later beheaded by Herod Agrippa. Jesus, who was out of monastery for marriage, was convinced to join with Simon Magus, who replaced him as Pope.*

## Judea after Herod the Great

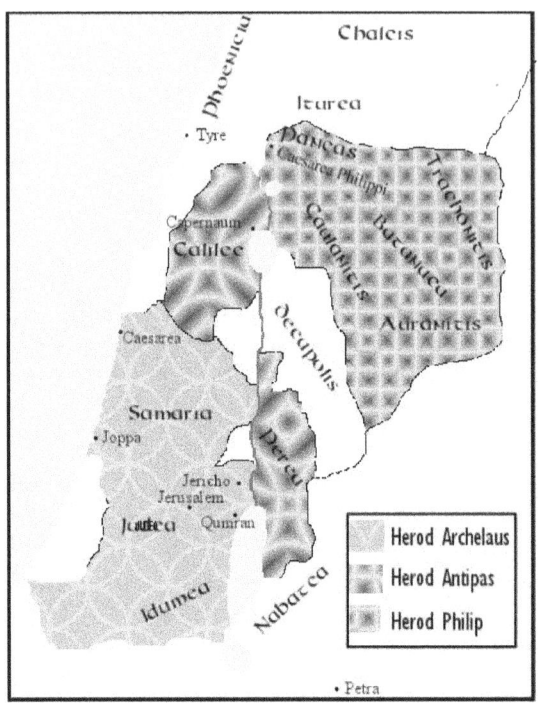

***Judas' Fourth Jewish Philosophy***
*(Antiq 18.1.6) "There was yet another philosophy, founded by Judas the Galilean, agreeing in all other things with the Pharisaic notions; but having an inviolable attachment to liberty, and saying that God is to be their only Ruler and Lord. They also do not value dying any kinds of death, nor indeed do they heed the deaths of their relations and friends, nor can any such fear make them call any man lord."*

## Chapter 2. (January 6AD)
## Taxation of Cyrenius;
## Revolt of Judas the Galilean

Joseph greets Theudas "Hail my brother, the Zadok, I am confident that we will prevail against Cyrenius' tax collections. Our leader Judas the Galilean will succeed like the Maccabees of old."

Theudas replies, "Yes, dear brother Joseph, the Star of David, we are to assemble with the other Zealots on the plains of Armageddon for the final stand."

"With the fatted calf, King Archelaus, banished, I am glad that you, the Prodigal Son, and Glaphyra have come to your senses and left that Qumran fort that was a brothel of Roman swine. Its conversion to a monastery is now complete."

"Father Simeon granted me contrition and I have repented of wasting my share of the Church fortune on wine, women, and song. I am sorry that I betrayed you, dear brother."

Joseph says, "It was a mistake that Augustus Caesar awarded Archelaus the kingdom of Judea upon the death of his father Herod the Great. His half-brother, Antipas, who also petitioned Caesar, but received merely a tetrarchy, would have been a better ruler."

"Philip, the son of Herod's fifth wife who was given areas north of these lands was also a better choice. But now we are at war." *They ride off.*

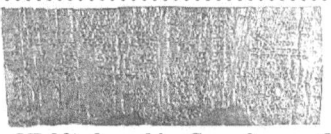

*Copper Scroll (3Q15 Column VI 29) found in Cave 3 near Qumran "In the **Dwelling of the Queen** on the western side dig twelve cubits: 27 talents." (Conveniently this 'inn at Bethlehem' is just one hour's walk south of Qumran; Ein Feshkha ('Galilee') 3 hours along the Dead Sea; and Mazin (Capernaum) 6 hours, closer by boat.)*

## Ein Feshkha (Nazareth)
## Mazin (Capernaum)

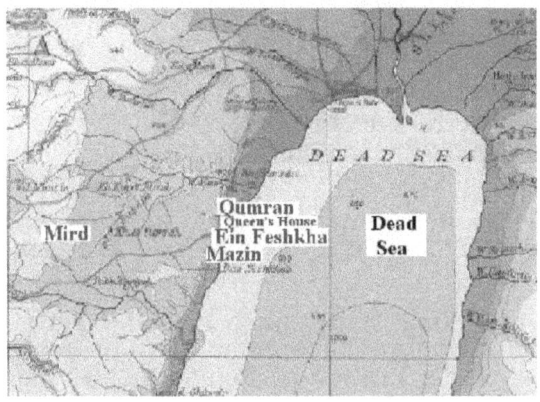

### Essene Third Jewish Philosophy

*(Antiq 18.1.5) "The Essenes believed that all things are best ascribed to God. They teach the immortality of souls, and esteem that the rewards of righteousness are to be earnestly striven for. They share the wealth and do not marry or keep servants. They minister one to another. They also appoint certain stewards to receive the incomes of their revenues, and of the fruits of the ground; such as are good men and priests."*

*Pesher on Nahum (4Q169) (tr. B.T.)(Nahum 2:12):*
*Its pesher refers to the Young Lion of Wrath (Pilate) [who fills a cave with a mass of corpses to wreak revenge on the seekers-of-smooth-things (Jesus), who hangs men alive [from the tree, to perform an abomination which was not done] in Israel since earlier times.*

## Chapter 3. (March 6AD)
## The Rebellion Finds Religion

The Queen's House

Ananas, the new High Priest, greets Joseph at the entrance of Qumran (Jerusalem), saying "Joseph, your son Jesus is now the rising star of the West! Many are planning to attend his Bar Mitzvah."

Joseph says, "Thank you Father Ananus for absolving my son Jesus who has suffered from my indiscretion."

"Now that Zealots have been removed from the fort that Judas the Galilean established at Qumran, let us hope that we can remain at peace with Rome so that the promised Restoration can occur. This monastery, having been abandoned by the Essenes after the earthquake of 31BC, now houses your group of less strict Essenes who can act as the focal point of secret opposition to the Romans."

Joseph says, "Yes, the 'Seekers of Smooth Things'; that derogatory term for our Essene sect. Obviously, marriage had to be allowed for the priests and the descendants of David or these important lines would die out. There is already a massive amount of gold coins, collected from pilgrims, which are hidden in the buildings around here listed in the Copper Scroll. In fact, I have been made the designated gardener for one of two caves on the south edge of Qumran, which is a latrine and a hiding place for these coins."

"It was a fortunate happenstance that twelve years ago when you were chastised for your actions, the monastery lent you and Mary a small birthing room, south of here, now called the Queen's house in her honor. This room, being next to a stable where the ceremonial donkey and the oxen are housed, would symbolize that your firstborn son of the David line was firstly a man of the people rather than a king."

*Matt 02:07-10 Then Herod (Herod the Great died in 4BC), "privately having called the Magi, did inquire exactly from them the time of the appearing star (the star stands for the six-point star of David), and having sent them to Bethlehem (really the Queen's house, south of Qumran), he said, "Having gone -- inquire you exactly for the child, and whenever you may have found, bring me back word, that I also having come may bow to him." And they, having heard the king, departed, and lo, the star, that they did see in the east (note: east of Jerusalem, not south), did go before them, till, having come, it stood over where the child was. And having seen the star, they rejoiced with exceeding great joy, and having come to the house, they found the child with Mary his mother, and having fallen down they bowed to him, and having opened their treasures, they presented to him gifts, gold (book of sayings); and frankincense (to wash the Essene linens white); and myrrh (perfume used in marriage in the Song of Solomon). (They were the only ones to recognize him as the legitimate David king, eligible to be an Essene, and allowed to marry. For twelve years from his birth in 7BC, Jesus would be treated as illegitimate by the High Priest Joazar Boethus. Remember there was no 0 between 7BC and 6AD because the Moslems had not invented it yet.)*

*(The Nabataeans traded in frankincense, thus King Aretas IV of Petra would have been that wise man. His and Chuldu's daughter was Phasaelis, the first wife of Herod Antipas who would be St. Paul's mother.) (2 Clues:)*
*Acts 13:1 And there were certain in Antioch of Syria, in the assembly there, prophets and teachers ... (σύντροφος (reared) (καὶ removed))* **Saul reared by Herod the tetrarch.**

*Acts 23:16 And* **the son of Paul's sister** *.... told Paul, (This sister would be Salome, the daughter of Herodias. Her three sons with Aristobulus are Herod, Agrippa, and Aristobulus; their Christian names were Timothy, Tychicus, and Trophimus (Paul's cousins). Salome is the daughter of Herodias the second wife of Herod Antipas, the son of Herod that Great with Mathace, but she is also the daughter of Herod Thomas (sometimes called Philip), who is also the son of Herod the Great with Mariamme (the daughter of the High Priest Boethus). Both have Herod the Great as a grandfather, but also* **Herod Antipas is Paul's father and Salome's step-father.***)*

## Chapter 4. (March 7BC<--)
## Matthew's Bethlehem Story

*The year was 6AD. Jesus bowed before Herod Antipas and his wife Phasaelis as they approached him.*

"Congratulations, you are legitimate again," says Herod Antipas. I see that Joazar Boethus, the deposed High Priest, is here. He foolishly supported the taxation of Cyrenius. It is fitting that this symbolic birth of your Bar Mitzvah is now being held at your birthplace at the Queen's House."

Jesus says, "His opposition was nothing compared to your father, Herod the Great, whom the wise men deceived by means of a calendar error in his slaughter of the innocents."

"Even I could have been one of his executions like my half brothers: Alexander and Aristobulus. But let me introduce my wife Phasaelis, the daughter of King Aretas IV of the Nabataeans, our neighbors to the west and south." Then, beckoning to a couple dressed like an Arabian King and Queen, he continues with a smile, "Let me introduce my father-in-law King Aretas IV and his Queen Huldu of the Nabataeans. He has met you before."

Thinking quickly and remembering how that country was famous for a certain spice, Jesus says, "Could it really be that you were the wise man who brought me frankincense!"

"I am that very one. I brought you frankincense because it is the cleaning agent of the white linen garments of the Essenes of whom I believe you will be part of one day. Hillel brought you a golden book of his sayings; your grandfather Heli-Jacob brought you myrrh to use with your bride of Solomon to continue the David line."

War 2.8.13 - retranslated "There is yet another order of Essenes, who, while at one with the rest in their mode of life, customs and regulations, differ from them in their views on marriage. They think that those who decline to marry cut off the chief function of life - that of transmitting it - and furthermore that, were all to adopt the same view, the whole race would very quickly die out. They give their wives, however, a three month's probation, and only marry them after they have thrice undergone purification (no menstruation), in proof of fecundity (of pregnancy to term). But they do not accompany their wives when they are with child, as a demonstration that they do not marry out of regard to pleasure, but for the sake of posterity. Now the women go into the baths with some of their garments on, as the men do with somewhat girded about them." (This special Essene marriage for priests and kings is revoked if the woman cannot conceive after three years or aborts during the first three months. Clearly 'virgin' is just a word for young woman who is a nun.)

More detailed rules, not explicitly shown, are that "betrothal" means that the couple has been chosen to be a mother and father, but while in this state they are not allowed to have sexual relations except for November thru January (problem for Jesus conceived in June), when there are no holy days. After conception, they enter back into the betrothal state and must wait six years after the birth of a son or three years after a daughter (a girl being worth half a man) before entering the marriage state again.(These rules can be surmised since September is the month of the birth of kings and in Mary and Joseph's case (allowing a 9 months for pregnancy): Jesus born 7BC (in March; the rest in September), James the Just born 1AD, Joses 8AD, Jude born 15AD, and Simon born 22AD. Jesus and Mary Magdalene's daughter Phoebe was born in 33AD; his son Jesus Justus born 37AD (3+ year span): "And the Word of God increased" (Acts 06:07); his 2nd son (Joseph) born in 44AD: "But the word of God grew and multiplied" (Acts 12:24); and his 3rd son with his new wife Lydia: born 51AD: "the word of God declared by Paul" (Acts 17:13).

Matt 01:19 and Joseph her husband being righteous (Joseph Justus, crown prince to Heli), and not willing to make her an example, did wish privately to send her away.

A Nazarite vow is a substitute for permanent celibacy, thus a specified time (40 days), usually before marriage, that includes a fasting retreat.

Luke 6:6,9,10 And it came to pass also, on another Sabbath, that he goes into the synagogue, and teaches, and there was there a man, and his right hand was withered. (Even masturbation is forbidden.) Then said Jesus unto them, "I will question you something: Is it lawful on the Sabbaths to do good, or to do evil? life to save or to kill?" And having looked around at them all, he said to the man, "stretch forth your hand;" and he did so, and his hand was restored whole as the other;

## Chapter 5a. (June 8BC<--)
## The Sins of the Father

Seeing Simeon and Anna, Jesus says, "Esteemed ones, I need your help to explain why my mother has greater love for my younger brother James? Have I not attended to my mother and helped her with her tasks in the female convent? What is it that James offers her that I do not? At five years old, people are already calling him James the Just because he is legitimate and I am not?"

Anna kissed Jesus on his forehead and said to him. "A mother's love should always be equal. Do not blame yourself that you remind her of a traumatic incident concerning your conception. It was a technical violation of an Essene rule of marriage that was involved, but it caused her much shame."

Simeon explains, "Joseph and Mary were betrothed in June 8BC and betrothal means that they have been chosen to beget children, but while in this state sexual relations are disallowed. The state of marriage is allowed to be consummated between November and January when there are no holy days. This adjustment to the Essene celibacy rule was to allow for the continuation of the priestly and kingly lines. After conception, they abstain from sexual relations and must wait six years after the birth of a son before they can be married again. For a daughter, it is three years because girls are worth half a man."

Jesus doing the calculation in his head, clearly distraught, "So that is why James is seven years younger than me. I see now that his birth in September is also significant!"

"Yes, you have surmised the truth because your birthday March 7BC does show that rules were broken. The birthday of priests and kings is meant to be the special month of September."

*Luke 1:28-32 And the angel, having come in unto her, said, "Hail, favored one, the Lord is with you; blessed are you among women;" and she, having seen, was troubled at his word, and was reasoning of what kind this salutation may be. And the angel said to her, "Fear not, Mary, for you have found favor with God; and lo, you shall conceive in the womb, and shall bring forth a son and call his name Jesus;*
*he shall be great, and Son of the Highest he shall be called, and the Lord God shall give him the throne of David his father."*
*Matt 01:18 And of Jesus Christ, the birth was thus: For his mother Mary having been betrothed to Joseph, before their coming together she was found to have conceived from the* **Holy Spirit** *(Joseph's title in third position.)*

*War 2.8.3 The Essenes think that oil is a defilement; and if anyone of them be anointed without his own approbation, it is wiped off his body; for they think to be sweaty is a good thing, as they do also to be clothed in white garments.*
*War 2.8.7 These are the oaths by which they secure their proselytes to themselves: to swears to communicate their doctrines to no one any otherwise than as he received them himself; that he will abstain from robbery, and will equally preserve the books belonging to their sect, and the names of the angels.*

*Rev 12:07,08 And there came war in the heaven; Michael (High Priest Ananus) and his angels (Essenes) did war against the dragon (Joazar Boethus), and the dragon did war, and his angels, and they did not prevail, nor was their place found anymore in the heaven;*

*The Second Seven Years of the Mission 13-19AD: Death of Augustus in 14AD, Tiberius succeeded. Rev 8:8-10 And the second angel (Eleazar Ananus High Priest 16-17AD) did sound, and as it were a great mountain with fire burning was cast into the sea (Tiber Island Mission in Rome is shut down), and a third of the sea became blood (spilled wine) and die did the third of the creatures that are in the sea, those having life (monastics), and the third of the ships (missionaries) were destroyed.*
*Antiq 18.3.5 "There was a man who was a Jew (Simon Magus), but had been driven away from his own country by an accusation laid against him for transgressing their laws. He, then living at Rome, professed to instruct men in the wisdom of the laws of Moses. He procured also three other men to be his partners. These men persuaded Fulvia, a woman of great dignity, and one that had embraced the Jewish religion, to send purple and gold to the temple at Jerusalem; and when they had gotten them, they employed them for their own uses. Whereupon Tiberius ordered all the Jews to be banished out of Rome; at which time the consuls listed 4,000 men sent o the island Sardinia; but a greater number of them punished, who were unwilling to become soldiers, on account of keeping the laws of their forefathers.(19AD)*

## Chapter 5b. (July 8BC<--)
## Mary's Sorrow

Mary preserved all pondering in her heart

Anna taking a deep breath to control her anger, "Mary was the most faithful to God of any woman that I have known. I am sorry to tell you, Jesus, that Joseph forced himself on her. He had no remorse, only the thought that he should have her put away to hide his sin, being as he is called a just man!"

Simeon replied, "Anna, as a prophetess and a widow of 84 years you know that the term 'just' is used for the David crown prince whether they are just or not. Further, his sin is exposed in the expression that the 'Holy Spirit came upon her' because his title is Holy Spirit at third position, like mine in second position of Gabriel. I had to work hard to prevent their expulsion from the Essene order."

Jesus exclaims, "Was Mary just coddling me, saying I was going to be great? She said you told her that I would be called the Son of the Highest and be given the throne of David, but I was just a bastard son!"

Simeon in a calming voice, "The expression 'Son of the Highest', as you know, means the position second to the High Priest who is 'God'. This was my position as 'Man' being the expression of God in human form. It will be yours one day. The third position is already yours as the descendent of David being the 'Son of Man' as the representative of the people. That you are not responsible for the sins of your father is reflected in your name Jesus, the Joshua of Moses. Your brother bears his name. The Sadducee Ananus has agreed, knowing where his power rests."

*This philosophical discussion in September 32AD between the Pharisees and Jesus reveals their view that Jesus is illegitimate.*

*John 08:31-43 Jesus then said to the Jews who had believed in him, "If you continue in my word, you are truly my disciples, and you will know the truth, and the truth will make you free."*

*They answered him, "We are descendants of Abraham, and have never been in bondage to anyone. How is it that you say, `You will be made free'?"*

*Jesus answered them, "Truly, truly, I say to you, everyone who commits sin is a slave to sin. The slave does not continue in the house forever; the son continues forever. So if the Son makes you free, you will be free indeed. I know that you are descendants of Abraham, yet you seek to kill me because my word finds no place in you. I speak of what I have seen with my Father, and you do what you have heard from your earthly father."*

*They answered him, "Abraham is our father."*

*(Abraham is being used for Hillel the Elder) who said:*
*"What is hateful to you, do not do to your fellow: this is the whole Torah; the rest is the explanation; go and learn".*

*Jesus said to them, "If you were Abraham's children, you would do what Abraham did, but now you seek to kill me, a man who has told you the truth which I heard from God; this is not what Abraham did. You do what your earthly father did."*

*They said to him,* **"We were not born of fornication; we have one Father, even God."**
*(They are saying, 'We are born of legitimate births, but you were born of a woman yet unmarried, like the bastards born of whores. - This is a direct reference to the betrothal problem - the concept of a virgin birth would be invented later.)*

*Jesus said to them, "If God were your Father, you would love me, for I proceeded and came forth from God; I came not of my own accord, but he sent me. Why do you not understand what I say? It is because you cannot bear to hear my word.*

*War 2.8.11 The Theological Views of the Essenes concerning the Soul:*
*It is a fixed belief of theirs that the body is corruptible and its constituent matter impermanent, but that the soul is immortal and imperishable. Emanating from the finest ether, these souls become entangled, as it were, in the prison-house of the body, to which they are dragged down by a sort of natural spell; but, once released from the bonds of the flesh, then, as though liberated from a long servitude, they rejoice and are borne aloft. The soul is immortal, so, by doing good, the soul is rewarded after death; but, if wicked, the soul will undergo never-ending punishment.*

## Chapter 6. (March 6AD)
## Jesus, to become an acolyte under Eleazar Ananus

*Jesus stood there dazed. He could not shake the revelation of the sin of his not so-called righteous father and vowed right then and there to be chaste until his marriage. He had always rejected the Essene teaching that claimed the women were the seducers and now he had greater respect for all women and even prostitutes who must live under the tyranny of men. He was now appreciating his mother's strength, especially in this day of his Bar Mitzvah when she would give him up, like a baby from her womb. His eyes watered up, but he held them back knowing that he must be brave today and forever.*

Anna, sensing his pain, "Jesus, the difficult path makes you stronger. John, the son of Zechariah and Elizabeth, was born six months before you according to the rules. As the son of a Priest, his life will be easy. He is to be the 'Teacher of Righteousness' and will baptize many, but it will not be given to him on a silver platter (she was a seer); he will have to seek it in the wilderness. Remember when John's mother Elizabeth and your mother were in the wilderness from June to September to hide their pregnancy and commune with God, Elizabeth said to your mother to comfort her, 'Blessed are you among women; blessed is the fruit of your womb'."

Simeon says, "Shall I recommend you to Eleazar Ananus, the eldest son of the High Priest, so that you can become an acolyte. It is important that you reject your father's Zealot ways." "Yes, I would like that."

Simeon says "May you find redemption in Jerusalem." Anna adds, "And a worthy wife."

*Luke 2:6,7 And it came to pass, in their being there, the days were fulfilled for her bringing forth, and she brought forth her son, the first-born, and wrapped him up, and laid him down in the manger, because there was not for them a place in the guest-chamber.*
*Luke 2:19 and Mary was preserving all these things, pondering in her heart.*

*Rev 12:1-6 And a great sign was seen in the heaven, a woman arrayed with the sun, and the moon under her feet, and upon her head a crown of twelve stars, and being with child she does cry out, travailing and pained to bring forth. And there was seen another sign in the heaven, and, lo, a great red dragon, having seven heads and ten horns, and upon his head seven diadems, and his tail does draw the third of the stars of the heaven, and he did cast them to the earth; and the dragon did stand before the woman who is about to bring forth, that when she may bring forth, her child he may devour; and she brought forth a male child, who is about to rule all the nations with a rod of iron, and caught away was her child unto God and His throne, and the woman did flee to the wilderness, where she has a place made ready from God, that there they may nourish her -- days a thousand, two hundred, sixty. (The three and half years of Daniel: 3.5 years\*360 (12 months of 30 day months) or 42 months. This is an expression to say that as in the time of the Maccabean revolt, God will bring the restoration of the Jewish Kingdom.)*

*Matt 13:24-26,37-43,51 Parable of the weeds of the field*
*"The kingdom of heaven was likened to a man sowing good seed in his field, and, while men are sleeping, his enemy came and sowed weeds in the midst of the wheat, and went away, and when the herb sprang up and yielded fruit, then appeared also the weeds."*
*"The meaning of the parable is: He who is sowing the good seed is the Son of Man, and the field is the world, and the good seed, these are the sons of the Kingdom, and the weeds are the sons of the evil one, and the enemy who sowed them is the devil, and the harvest is a full end of the age, and the reapers are angels. As, then, the weeds are gathered up, and burned with fire, so shall it be in the full end of this age, the Son of Man shall send forth his angels, and they shall gather up out of his kingdom all the stumbling-blocks, and those doing the unlawlessness, and shall cast them into the furnace of fire; there shall be the weeping and the gnashing of the teeth. Then shall the righteous shine forth as the sun in the Kingdom of their Father. He who is having ears to hear -- let him hear."*

## Chapter 7. (March 6AD)
## Jesus' Bar Mitzvah

A woman arrayed with the sun, the moon under her feet

*On the platform constructed next to the Queen's house, Jesus was standing next to his Mother Mary. She looked like a true David Queen wearing a band containing twelve jewels for the twelve tribes of Israel. She was the thirtieth member of the council of thirty that represented the Moon and, having the blessing of the presiding council, she was the Sun.*

*As Jesus looked up at her face, he could see that she was troubled as she looked over to Joazar Boethus, being like a dragon having been the head of the seven spiritual leaders, based on the seven days of the week, and in charge of the ten provinces of the Diaspora and still determined to exclude the uncircumcised, who were as numerous as the stars.*

*She looked over to the Sadducee Ananus, the new High Priest for assurance and then to Joseph, who was staring into the distance. With both hands, she nudged Jesus gently forward to the audience. Then she left having just enough time to return to Mird by nightfall.*

Jesus begins, "I have chosen to explain the parable of the Sower and the Weeds. "The kingdom of heaven was likened to a man sowing good seed in his field..."

*The First Seven Years of the Mission 6-12AD (First Angel - Ananus)*
*Rev 8:7 The first (not an angel) did sound, and there came hail and fire, mingled with blood (refers to the 1st & 7th plague of Moses against Pharaoh - system of plagues against Rome), and it was cast to the land, and the third of the trees was burnt up (Archelaus & Joazar deposed), and all the green grass was burnt up.(Gentiles excluded)*

*Luke 02:08-14 And there were shepherds in the same region, lodging in the field, and keeping the night-watches over their flock, and lo, an angel of the Lord stood over them, and the glory of the Lord shone around them, and they feared a great fear. And the angel said to them, "Fear not, for lo, I bring you tidings of great joy, that shall be to all the people -- because there was born to you to-day a Saviour -- who is Christ the Lord -- in the city of David, and this is to you the sign: You shall find a babe wrapped up, lying in the manger." And suddenly there came with the angel a multitude of the heavenly host, praising God, and saying, "Glory in the highest to God, and upon earth peace, among men -- good will."*

*Acts 5:37 "After this one rose up, Judas the Galilean, in the days of the enrollment, and drew away many people after him, and that one perished, and all, as many as were obeying him, were scattered;"*
*Antiq 18.1.1 "Yet was there one Judas the Galilean, who, taking with him Sadduc (Theudus-Barabbas), a Pharisee, became zealous to draw them to a revolt, who both said that this taxation was no better than an introduction to slavery, and exhorted the nation to assert their liberty;"*

*Acts 5:36 "for before these days rose up Theudas, saying, that himself was someone, to whom a number of men did join themselves, as it were four hundred, who was slain, and all, as many as were obeying him, were scattered, and came to naught."*
*Antiq 20.5.1a "A certain magician, whose name was Theudas, persuaded a great part of the people to follow him to the river Jordan. He had told them he was a prophet like Moses, and that he would, by his own command, divide the river, and afford them an easy passage over it. Fadus sent a troop of horsemen out against them; who, falling upon them unexpectedly, slew many of them, and took many of them alive. They also took Theudas alive, and cut off his head, and carried it to Jerusalem." (46AD (6AD+40))*

## Chapter 8. (March 7BC<--)
## Therapeuts are Shepherds

The High Priest Ananus, acting as an Essene angel says, "Theudas, I know that you are influential with Therapeuts from Egypt, who live in the wilderness of Mird herding sheep, calling this place Egypt, the place where Joseph and Mary found refuge from King Herod. As Nicodemus, I hope that you will respect the peace that I have negotiated."

Theudas answers, "As the Joshua of this tribe and I am prepared to use my skills in warfare until that foretold day when we can cross over the Jordan River into the Promised Land, but for now, I will embrace peace." *(putting his arm around Jesus)* "Being Joseph's brother, I welcome you, my nephew and god-son. Mother Mary, as our Miriam, participates in our religious reenactments opening the floodgates of the wadi (crossing Jordan). Congratulations, Jesus, a Joshua, on becoming a man. I pledge my fealty to you as our anointed prince."

Jesus says, "I am honored by your faith in me and I look forward to attending your services to reenact the allegories of Exodus, that are such an important connection with the Creator."

"Come on a festival day, where we devote ourselves wholly to meditation and virtue from morning through the whole night, with choruses of men and women singing psalms and hymns to God that are composed in every kind of meter and melody imaginable, almost surely putting the participant into a mystic state without alcohol."

Jesus exclaims, "These traditions are truly the model for churches of the future, but I am going to enter the monastic life now."

*Luke 02:40-45 And the child grew and was strengthened in spirit, being filled with wisdom, and the grace of God was upon him. And his parents were going yearly to Jerusalem, at the feast of the Passover, and when he became twelve years old. (Jesus' Bar Mitzvah 6AD + 12 (inclusive counting) 17AD.) They having gone up to Jerusalem, according to the custom of the feast, and having finished the days, in their returning the child Jesus remained behind in Jerusalem, and Joseph and his mother did not know, and, having supposed him to be in the company, they went a day's journey, and were seeking him among the kindred and among the acquaintances, and not having found him, they turned back to Jerusalem seeking him.*

### Membership at Qumran

- One year outside with loincloth and a mattock for burying excrement (after proof of his temperance is given the purer kind of holy water)
- 1QSa 1:8 - At the age of 20 years he shall be enrolled, performing duties so as to be joined to the holy congregation, having remained celibate. (Lower novice and novice) two years more to test his character, and only then, if found worthy, is he enrolled in the society.
- (member) becomes a proselyte after swearing oaths of piety towards the Deity, justice towards men, fight for the just, never abuse his authority nor, either in dress or by other outward marks of superiority, outshine his subjects, be forever a lover of truth and to expose liars, keep from stealing and his soul pure from unholy gain, conceal nothing from the members of the sect, and to preserve the books of the sect and the names of the angels. angels. Such are the oaths by which they secure their proselytes.
- (deacon, presbyter, bishop, archbishop/cardinal) four grades to advance to according to the duration of their discipline.

### Essene Daily Schedule

- Rise at dawn and say a prayer
- Work at assigned crafts
- 5th hour (11 AM) bathe in cold water, dress in linen, go to refectory, for breakfast
- loaves are served in order and one plate of food, the priest says grace before eating
- Priest says grace following the meal, and they change out of the linen clothes
- Work until evening and attend supper with guests as before

# Chapter 9. (March 17AD)
## At age 23 Jesus is accepted into Qumran.

*It is Passover. Joseph and Mary find Jesus in the temple in the Essene Quarter of Jerusalem*

Joseph is frustrated, saying, "Jesus, you are now 23 years old. You have been hiding in this religious cocoon too long. As my first born, it is time you take over the political details of our struggle against Rome."

Jesus answers, "My studies with Eleazar ended three years ago and I began the preliminary steps to enter the monastery, remaining outside for one year with a small hatchet and a loincloth and white surplus that they gave to me. After two more years probation, I was allowed to share the purer kind of holy water, but not yet received into the meetings of the community. Today, I hope to be judged eligible to be enrolled as an Essene!"

"Are you serious! Is this the way of a king! Spending three years burying your excrement with your own silver hatchet. I expect you to come back with me to Ein Feshkha. Dangerous events are brewing."

"It would be disrespectful to the council to not appear at my acceptance hearing."

Joseph stands up, "Mary and I will head back home and wait at Emmaus for you to join us."

*Jesus did not arrive, and they walk back only to find Jesus dressed in the white robe of the Essenes. Joseph glares at him, then turns, and marches off.*

Mary hesitates, then smiles, saying, "Be at peace, my son."

*Luke 13:1-5* And there were present certain at that time, telling him about the Galileans, whose blood Pilate did mingle with their sacrifices; and Jesus answering said to them, "Think you that these Galileans became sinners beyond all the Galileans because they have suffered such things? No -- I say to you, but, if you may not reform, all you even so shall perish."
"Or those eighteen, on whom the tower in Siloam fell, and killed them; think you that these became debtors beyond all men who are dwelling in Jerusalem? (In Greek text ten & eight (18) is an adjective with no noun, therefore is an assumed year, thus the 18th year of the age of Wrath with year 1 gives 18 + 5= 23AD.) No -- I say to you, but, if you may not reform, all you in like manner shall perish."
*War 2.9.4* After this, he raised another disturbance, by expending that sacred treasure which is called Corban (Church money) upon aqueducts, whereby he brought water from the distance of four hundred furlongs. At this the multitude had indignation; and when Pilate came to Jerusalem, they came about his tribunal, and made a clamor at it. Now when he was apprized aforehand of this disturbance, he mixed his own soldiers in their armor with the multitude, and ordered them to conceal themselves under the habits of private men, and not indeed to use their swords, but with their staves to beat those that made the clamor. He then gave the signal from his tribunal to do as he had bidden them. Now the Jews were so badly beaten, that many of them perished by the stripes they received, and many of them perished as trodden to death by themselves;

*Luke 13:10-17* And he was teaching in one of the synagogues on the Sabbath, and lo, there was a woman having a spirit of infirmity eighteen years, and she was bowed together, and not able to bend back at all, and Jesus having seen her, did call [her] near, and said to her, "Woman, you have been loosed from your infirmity;" and he laid his hands on her, and presently she sat upright, glorifying God.
This one, being a daughter of Abraham, whom the Satan bound, 18 years, should she not be loosed from this bond on the Sabbath-day?
And he saying these things, all who were opposed to him were being ashamed, and all the multitude were rejoicing over all the glorious things that are being done by him.
(The "for 18 years" means the same as above: "at the eighteenth year of the Age of Wrath". "With a spirit of infirmity" is not old and decrepit, but rather Jesus confirms that Mother Mary is now a member of the esteemed widow class because her husband is dead.")

## Chapter 10. (23AD)
## Joseph is killed by Pilate leaving Mary a widow

*It was not long since Jesus saw Mary again when he attended his father's funeral, having died at age 66.*

Uncle Theudas goes up to Jesus, "I am so sorry about your father. I was there too, but it was chaos with Pilate having hidden soldiers in regular clothes. It was right for us to protest his use of Church funds to build the aqueduct. Spiritual thirst is greater than water."

Jesus walking over to console his mother, "He died doing what he believed in. At last, you will get some needed calm and respect as a widow."

"But I am not a widow! Being only 48, having been espoused to Joseph at the age of 18, I need two more years for widowhood. Who will care for me?"

Jesus turns saying, "Father Jonathan, why should widowhood be based on law alone? May I tell you a parable of the Widow's Mite:

> *The prophet, having sat down across from the treasury, was beholding how the multitude did put brass into the treasury, and many rich were putting in much Then having come, a poor widow did put in two mites. The prophet, having called near his disciples, said to them, 'Verily I say to you, that this poor widow has put in more than all those putting into the treasury; for all, out of their abundance, put in, but she, out of her want, all that she had put in was all her living'."*

Jonathan smiling, "Jesus speaks truly. I grant Mother Mary the two years."
*(At the funeral were Jesus' brothers: James (22), Joses (15) Jude (8) and Simon (1).)*

*Rev 8:10,11 And the third angel (John the Baptist) 20-26AD did sound, and there fell out of the heaven a great star (Joseph), burning as a lamp, and it did fall upon the third of the rivers, and upon the fountains of waters, and the name of the star is called Wormwood (Simon Magus - the mastermind in the poisoning of Agrippa I), and the third of the waters (initiates on Tiber Island) does become wormwood, and many of the men did die of the waters, because they were made bitter.*

*"And in the Age of Wrath (6AD)... they perceived their iniquity and recognized that they were guilty men, yet for twenty years (Cairo-Damascus Document CD 1:9-11) (6AD + 20 = 26AD) they were like blind men groping for the way. And God observed their deeds, that they sought Him with a whole heart, and raised for them a Teacher of Righteousness (John the Baptist Pope 27AD) to guide them in the way of His Heart." (CD 1.5-16) Pontius Pilate prefect 26AD.*

*Matt 3:4-6 And this John had his clothing of camel's hair, and a girdle of skin around his loins, and his nourishment was locusts and honey of the field. Many were going forth unto him into Jerusalem (Qumran), and all Judea, and all the region round about the Jordan, and they were baptized in the Jordan by him, confessing their sins.*

*R.2.7 (Simon Magus: His History and Doctrine) Simon's father was Antonius[1]; his mother Rachel. By nation a Samaritan, from a village of the Gettones; by profession a magician yet exceedingly well trained in the Greek literature; desirous of glory, and boasting above all the human race, so that he wishes himself to be believed to be an exalted power, which is above God the Creator, and to be called the Standing One. H.2.22,2.32 He rejects Jerusalem and substitutes Mount Gerizim for it. Instead of our Christ, he proclaims himself. (Simon's Magic) He makes statues walk; rolls himself on fire and is not burnt; sometimes he flies; he makes loaves of stones; he becomes a serpent; he transforms himself into a goat; he becomes two-faced; he changes himself into gold; he opens lockfast gates; he melts iron; at banquets he produces images of all manner of forms; he makes dishes be seen as borne of themselves to wait upon him, no bearers being seen.*

(1) The gens Antonia was a Roman family of great antiquity being of Mark Antony, the triumvirate with Octavian, therefore his father must be related. Jullus Antonius, a son of Antony, had a son Lucius Antonius (20BC-25AD) who was banished to Marseilles after his father's affair with Julia, the daughter of Augustus, resulting in his forced suicide. It is assumed that Lucius had an affair at age 16 with Rachel, Simon born in 3BC would then be a nephew of James and John!

## Chapter 11. (September 26AD)
## John the Baptist becomes Pope at age 33

Herod Antipas having called John the Baptist to appear before him at Tiberius on the Sea of Galilee says, "I hear that you have established a council of 30 for the moon's cycle. That was an ingenious move to have a female *(worth half a man)* to represent the lunar month which is as I am told 29 1/2 days. I am concerned that this is trying to usurp my authority as the head of the Church, bequeved to me by my father Herod the Great."

"Please understand my purpose to open the Church to the common people that by being baptized and taking Nazarite vows, as in the days of Samson, that they will have a chance at salvation. My church is the wilderness of Mird."

"You mean there are others like you who wish to dress in 'camel's hair, with a leather girdle about their loins'; neither eating nor drinking; surviving on 'locusts and wild honey' in the wilderness?"

"I introduced baptism and wilderness retreats as an alternative to the Essenes to allow people to continue to live regular lives. This is not a threat to the Herodian Church as no tithes will be lost."

"All right then, you can be Pope to the riffraff, but you must stop declaring my marriage to Herodias as immoral. It may be true that her first husband is still alive, but this brother-in-law of mine, Thomas, the disinherited son of Herod, is of the type that prefers male companionship, so he does not care. He is merely the father of my step-daughter, Salome."

*Rev 13:11-18 And I saw another beast coming up out of the land, and it had two horns, like a lamb, and it was speaking as a dragon, and all the authority of the first beast does it do before it, and it makes the land and those dwelling in it that they shall bow before the first beast, whose deadly stroke was healed (Lazarus raised from the dead), and it does great signs, that fire also it may make to come down from the heaven to the earth before men, and it leads astray those dwelling on the land, because of the signs that were given it to do before the beast, saying to those dwelling upon the land to make an image to the beast that has the stroke of the sword (Horseman #4 wielding the sword of excommunication: death) and did live, and there was given to it to give a spirit to the image of the beast, that also the image of the beast may speak (making statues to talk by magic), and that it may cause as many as shall not bow before the image of the beast, that they may be killed. And it makes all, the small, and the great, and the rich, and the poor, and the freemen, and the servants, that it may give to them a mark upon their right hand or upon their foreheads, and that no one may be able to buy, or to sell (Ananias-Simon Magus excommunicated by Peter), except he who is having the mark, or the name of the beast, or the number of his name. Here is the wisdom! He who is having the understanding, let him count the number of the beast, for the number of a man it is, and its number is **666**.*

*H.2.23 (Simon Magus a Disciple of the Baptist takes over as Pope) There was one John, a day-baptist, who was also, according to the method of combination, the forerunner of our Lord Jesus; and as the Lord had twelve apostles, bearing the number of the twelve months of the sun, so also he, John, had thirty chief men, fulfilling the monthly reckoning of the moon, in which number was a certain woman called Helena (Luna), that not even this might be without a dispensational significance. For a woman, being half a man, made up the imperfect number of the triacontad; as also in the case of the moon, whose revolution does not make the complete course of the month. But of these thirty, the first and the most esteemed by John was Simon.*

*R.2.11 Meantime, at the outset, as soon as he (Simon Magus) was reckoned among the thirty disciples of Dositheus (Jonathan Ananus who took over for John the Baptist), he began to depreciate Dositheus himself, saying that he did not teach purely or perfectly, and that this was the result not of ill intention, but. of ignorance. But Dositheus, when he perceived that Simon was depreciating him, moved with rage, when they met as usual at the school, seized a rod, and began to beat Simon; but suddenly the rod seemed to pass through his body, as if it had been smoke. On which Dositheus, being astonished and perceiving that he himself was not the Standing One, fell down and worshipped him, and gave up his own place as chief to Simon, ordering all the rank of thirty men to obey him; himself taking the inferior place which Simon formerly occupied. Not long after, he died: (excommunicated).*

# Chapter 12. (March 27AD)
## The Rise of the Beast 666

Disciple of Jesus:
Simon the Canaanite/Zealot
Acts 8:9 And a certain man, by name Simon, was using magic and amazing the nation of Samaria

*There is no more controversial person in the New Testament than Simon Magus. The writers of the Gospels try to hide his influence in the Gospels with names like Zebedee, Cyrene, Lazarus, and 'leper'; but they could not disguise the fact that he is actually one of the twelve disciples named as Simon the Canaanite in Matthew and Mark and Simon the Zealot in Luke. Who was this disciple? All they can say from his description in the disciple list is that he was "zealous for the faith". Throughout history, he has been treated as the personification of evil, yet he was Jesus' superior, his friend, and as Magdalene's adoptive father, his father-in-law. His intellectual prowess allowed him to surpass Jonathan Ananus and be declared Pope in John the Baptist's place.*

*He is finally revealed in Acts 8:9 as Simon the magician! He gets in trouble with Peter under the name of Ananias and is 'killed' by Peter over money (yet shows up alive as the cardinal whom Jesus sends Paul to after his blinding!) and in Revelation he is described as an enemy, being called the beast 666, over doctrinal differences.*

*In the Clementines, when he is up against Peter in a series of debates, Peter was no match for him, although the author, Pope Clement I, pretends that he is. He was also an accomplished magician, a master of 'smoke and mirrors', which caused him to attract huge crowds. His most amazing feat was to appear to fly through the air. It was a malfunction of this apparatus that caused him to meet his death in Rome in the time of Nero as Peter prayed to God.*

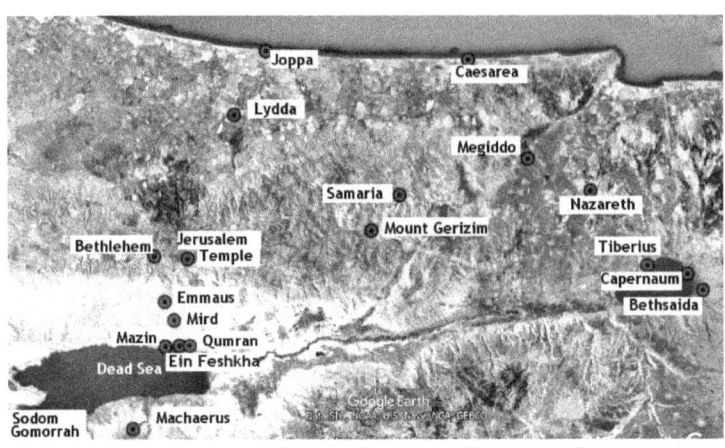

## Qumran as the mirror of Jerusalem

## SECTION 2 (March 29AD (Jesus' 35th birthday) to Sept 30AD)

*"In the beginning was the Word" (John 1:1)*

***Jesus leaves the monastery of Qumran in March for Marriage to fulfill his requirement to continue the David Line and becomes embroiled in Simon's plot to depose John the Baptist, thus assembling the Twelve Disciples***

*THE QUMRAN PESHER ON HABAKKUK (1QpHab) (extracts only; translated by B.T.)*
*1:12-13*
*[For the wicked one surrounds] the righteous one (Habakkuk 1:4)*
*[Its pesher, the wicked one is the Wicked Priest (Jesus), and the righteous one] is the Teacher of Righteousness... (John the Baptist)*

*John 1:14 And the Word became flesh and did tabernacle among us, and we (John Mark, the scribe, using 'we' to indicate that Jesus is present as he does in Acts) beheld his glory, glory as of an only begotten of a father, full of grace and truth.*

*Luke 03:23 And Jesus himself was beginning to be about thirty years of age, (Jesus is not thirty years old, thus the 'about', but rather this is the 30th year beginning at year at 1AD thus 35th. The year 1AD is ironically the birth date of James, the younger brother of Jesus. Dionysius botched the calendar by using an orthodox one that declared James as the true savior because of Jesus' illegitimacy had excluded him.)*

*A Great Jubilee cycle (50\*12)=600 from Ezekiel (29AD).*
*Luke 4:21 He (Jesus) began to tell them, "Today, this scripture has been fulfilled in your hearing."*

*John 1:28-31 These things came to pass in Bethabara, beyond the Jordan, where John was baptizing, on the morrow John sees Jesus coming unto him, and said, "Lo, the Lamb of God, who is taking away the sin of the world (the 'Lamb of God' thus 'The Suffering Servant' of Isaiah 53 and therefore not of high rank because he is disqualified by his illegitimate status); this is he concerning whom I said, After me (my subordinate) does come a man (Jesus), who has come before me (just standing in front of him), because he was before me (proposed to me): and I knew him not (I do not recognize him), but, that he might be manifested to Israel (be the representative of Israel with his father's title of the Holy Spirit as third under him), because of this I came with the water baptizing (ironic statement: you are just wasting my time).*

*Matt 3:13-15 Then comes Jesus from Galilee upon the Jordan, unto John to be baptized by him, but John was forbidding him, saying, "I have need by you to be baptized -- and you do come unto me!" (an ironic statement) But Jesus answering said to him, "Permit now (let your second in command, Jonathan Ananus, perform the baptism), for thus it is becoming to us to fulfill all righteousness," then he does permit him.*

*John 01:40-43,45 Andrew, the brother of Simon Peter, was one of the two who heard from John, and followed him; this one does first find his own brother Simon, and said to him, "We have found the Messiah", and he brought him unto Jesus: and having looked upon him, Jesus said, "You are Simon, the son of Jonas, you shall be called Cephas (Aramaic for Peter)". On the morrow, he goes forth to Galilee, finds Philip, and says to him, "Be following me." Philip finds Nathanael (Jonathan). (Philip's superior is John Mark, the head of the monastery of the tribe of Dan. When John Mark left with Mary Magdalene (Acts 13:13) in 45AD, Philip went with him. When John Mark returned as Eutychus (Acts 20:7-12) in 58AD with Philip, it is shown in Acts 21:8.9, as taking care of Magdalene, she being daughter of level 4.)*

## Chapter 13. (March 29AD)
## John refuses to baptize Jesus

*Jesus waits at the River Jordan to be baptized. Philip and Andrew are observing.*

Baptist sneering, "Jesus, the suffering servant of Isaiah, why do you come to be baptized by me, is it not I, that should be baptized by you?"

"Dearest Pope John, I come here in reverence."

"I have been sent to bring the repentant Jews of the Diaspora back to the fold, but not to one who flouts the laws of the Essenes and claims to be one of them."

"Your mother Elizabeth accepted my mother Mary and the High Priest Caiaphas is married to the daughter of Ananus, who accepts me as legitimate."

Jonathan intercedes, "Honorable Pope, this is meant to be a reconciliation, not a confrontation."

I will not dirty my hands with the son of a Zealot and a rapist. Jonathan, as my second, you do it!"

Jonathan dunks Jesus and says, "I baptize you in the name of the Holy Spirit."

Philip whispers, "Andrew, do you see the dove, flying! I believe that God has chosen him over John."

Andrew says, "Philip, I see it too! Even Jonathan, the son of Ananus, the tax collector, appears to choose him! He may be the hope of the Gentiles."

*Andrew returns to Ein Feshkha and tells his brother Peter. Peter, Andrew, and Philip go to Jesus to ask if they can follow him and he accepts.*

*Rev 08:12 And the fourth angel (Jonathan Ananus) 27-33AD did sound: smitten was the third of the sun - that darkened (John the Baptist imprisoned in January 30 by Herod Antipas) and a third of the moon - the day may not shine (Luna's deception), and the third of the stars - the night in like manner (David star: Jesus baptizing at night).*

*DDS: The Community Rule 1QS VIII In the Council of the Community there shall be twelve men and three Priests. DDS: War Scroll VIII They shall write on all the shields of the towers: on the first Michael, on the second Gabriel, and on the third Sariel and on the fourth Raphael. (2 Chron 29:4 "priests and levites on left side" implies Michael and Gabriel on the left and Sariel and Raphael on the right.)*

*John 01:45-51 Philip finds Nathanael, and said to him, "Him of whom Moses wrote in the Law, and the prophets, we have found, Jesus the son of Joseph, who is from Nazareth (Nazara: Mird-Hyrcania);" and Nathanael said to him, "Out of Nazareth is any good thing able to be?" Philip said to him, "Come and see." Jesus saw Nathanael coming unto him, and he said concerning him, "Lo, truly an Israelite, in whom guile is not;" Nathanael said to him, "From where do you know me?" Jesus answered and said to him, "Before Philip's calling you, being under the fig-tree (the Zealot party), I saw you." Nathanael answered and said to him, "Rabbi, you are the Son of God, you are the king of Israel." Jesus answered and said to him,"Because I said to you, I saw you under the fig-tree, you do believe; greater things than these you shall see: "Truly, I say to you, henceforth you shall see the heaven opened, and the angels of God going up and coming down upon the Son of Man."*

*Antiq 19.6.4 (Showing Jonathan's character In 43AD, the now king Agrippa took the high priesthood away from Simon Cantheras, and put Jonathan, the son of Ananus, into it again, saying that he was more worthy of that dignity than the other. But this was not a thing acceptable to him, to recover his former dignity. (Having been excommunicated as Stephen in 37AD) So he refused it, and said, "O king! I rejoice in the honor that thou hast for me, and take it kindly that thou would give me such a dignity, although God (the council) hath judged that I am not at all worthy of the high priesthood. I am satisfied with having once put on the sacred garments; for I then put them on after a more holy manner than I should now receive them again. But if you desire a person more worthy than myself for this honorable employment, give me leave to name such a one. I have a brother that is pure from all sin against God, and of all offenses against yourself; I recommend him to you, as one that is fit for this dignity." So the king was pleased with these words of his, and passed by Jonathan, and, according to his brother's desire, bestowed the high priesthood upon Matthias (Matthew)*

# Chapter 14. (May 29AD)
## Jonathan Ananus aligns with Jesus

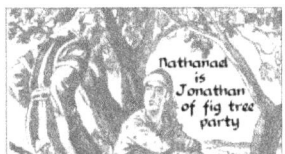

*Philip is with Jonathan Ananus as Jesus arrives.*

Jesus says, "Nathaniel, or should I say Jonathan, I am glad you are a man of your word. Do you know what that was all about?"

Jonathan answers, "I cannot fathom his sudden antagonism to you. I had introduced him to Simon Magus a while ago and he seemed to have had an immediate dislike for him. Maybe he thinks you are conspiring with Simon to take over."

"At least, you tried your best as a Good Samaritan to get him to align with our group, 'The Way', as you have done, and not to stay with his 'Fig Tree' group that is actually ready to depose him."

Jonathan says, "I have heard that Herod Antipas is concerned that John's Restoration date of 30AD will cause riots and is considering arresting him."

"He is also foolishly still angering Antipas and Herodias in condemning their illegitimate marriage."

Philip says, "Does the dove that I saw coming down from Heaven when you were baptized mean you are the 'Son of God'?"

Jesus says, "Did a special dove greet me! It would represent the Holy Spirit, which was my father Joseph's position. Technically, I am not 'Son of God', but 'Son of Man'. 'Man' is the 'Gabriel' as the image and likeness of God in Man. It was our hope that John would be the 'Michael' as Pope, and Father Jonathan would be the 'Gabriel' as his second and that I would be the 'Sariel-Raphael' as the Holy Spirit."

*Matt 8:1-4 And when he came down from the mount, great multitudes did follow him, and lo, a leper (forward reference to Matt 26:6 Simon the leper) having come, was bowing to him, saying, "Sir, if you are willing, you are able to cleanse me;" and having stretched forth the hand, Jesus touched him, saying, "I will; be you cleansed," and immediately his leprosy was cleansed. And Jesus said to him, "See, you may tell no one, but go, yourself show to the priest (Father Jonathan), and bring the gift that Moses (third position: Jesus) commanded for a testimony to them."*

*Mark 03:22 and the scribes who are from Jerusalem (Qumran) having come down, said -- "He (Jesus) has Beelzebub," and -- "By the ruler of the demons (Simon Magus) he does cast out the demons."*

*Acts 8:9-11 "And a certain man, by name Simon, was before in the city using magic, and amazing the nation of Samaria, saying himself to be a certain great one, to whom they were all giving heed, from small unto great, saying, 'This one is the great power of God;' and they were giving heed to him, because of his having for a long time amazed them with deeds of magic."*

*Simon Magus and Helena R.2.9 But not long after he fell in love with that woman whom they call Luna; and he confided all things to us as his friends: how he was a magician, and how he loved Luna, and how, being desirous of glory, he was unwilling to enjoy her ingloriously, but that he was waiting patiently till he could enjoy her honorably; yet so if we also would conspire with him towards the accomplishment of his desires.*

*H.2.25 Simon is going about in company with Helena. And he says that he has brought down this Helena from the highest heavens to the world; being queen, as the all-bearing being, and wisdom, for whose sake, says he, the Greeks and barbarians fought, having before their eyes but an image of truth (Sophia).*

**Names of Simon Magus (the magician) Acts 8:9, The Clementine Books**
*Simon, the Canaanite ( Matt 10:4, Mark 3:18)\* Simon, the Zealot ( Luke 6:15, Acts 1:13)\* Zebedee ( Matthew 4:21, Mark 1:19-20, Luke 5:8-10)\* Simon of Cyrene ( Matthew 27:32, Mark15:21, Luke 23:26)\* Lazarus ( John 11:1-44, John 12:1-10, Luke 16:20-23)\* Simon the leper ( Matt 18 1-4, Matt 26:6, Mark 14:3)\* young man naked man (Mark 14:51)\* Simon the tanner ( Acts 9:43, Acts 10:6)\* Ananias ( Acts 5:1-5, Acts 9:10-17, Antiq 20, 34-47)\* "the great power of God" ( Acts 8:10, Acts of Peter, Eccl Hist 2.1.11)\* Demetrius, the silversmith (Acts 19:24)\* Beast 666 (Revelation 13:18)*

## Chapter 15. (June 29AD)
## Aligning with Simon Magus

Jesus is walking to Qumran from Ein Feshkha, when Simon Magus overtakes him, saying, "Please Sir, can you cleanse me. The Jews have shunned me; I am a leper now."

Jesus touches his shoulder smiling "Be cleansed, Simon; but tell me how do I get the devil off my back as they are saying I teach from Beelzebub?"

"I would heal you also, but can the devil heal the devil? Alas, that is just another name they have given me like Canaanite and Zealot. It is more fitting to name Judas the Sicarii after that garbage fly."

Jesus says, "I have already swatted him away from Magdalene."

"My consort Helena also has many names like the Syrophoenician and, since she was a priestess in the Temple of Artemis, they also call her a prostitute because many of these professionals work the temples illegally. She will always be Helena to me for her beauty that can launch a 1000 ships. I believe that the more names and personas that one can master, the more influence one has."

"Yes, A magician must always be a master of disguises."

"Jesus, it was good to see you, but I must hurry along to meet Herod Antipas in Hyrcania about John the Baptist. Helena can tell you more."

*John 4:05-26* He comes, therefore, to a city of Samaria, called Sychar, near to the place that Jacob gave to Joseph his son; and there was there a well of Jacob. Jesus, therefore having been weary from the journeying, was sitting thus on the well; it was as it were the sixth hour; there comes a woman out of Samaria to draw water. Jesus said to her, "Give me to drink;" for his disciples were gone away to the city, that they may buy victuals; the Samaritan woman, therefore said to him, "How do you, being a Jew, ask drink from me, being a Samaritan woman?" for Jews have no dealings with Samaritans.
*Jesus answered and said to her, "If you had known the gift of God, and who it is who is saying to you, Give me to drink, you would have asked him, and he would have given you living water."*
*The woman said to him, "Sir, you have not even a vessel to draw with, and the well is deep; whence, then, have you the living water? Are you greater than our father Jacob, who did give us the well and himself out of it did drink, and his sons, and his cattle?"*
*Jesus answered and said to her, "Everyone who is drinking of this water shall thirst again; but whoever may drink of the water that I will give him, may not thirst -- to the age; and the water that I will give him shall become in him a well of water, springing up to life age-during."*
*The woman said unto him, "Sir, give me this water, that I may not thirst, nor come hither to draw."*
*Jesus said to her, "Go, call your husband, and come hither;" the woman answered and said, "I have not a husband." Jesus said to her, "Well did you say -- A husband I have not; for five husbands you have had, and, now, he whom you have is not your husband; this have you said truly."*
*The woman said to him, "Sir, I perceive that you are a prophet; Your fathers in this mountain did worship, and you say that Jerusalem (Qumran) is the place where it behooves to worship."*
*Jesus said to her, "Woman, believe me, that there does come an hour, when neither in this mountain, nor in Jerusalem(Qumran), shall you worship the Father; you worship what you have not known; we worship what we have known, because the salvation is of the Jews; but, there comes an hour, and it now is, when the true worshippers will worship the Father in spirit and truth, for the Father also does seek such to worship him; God is Spirit, and those worshipping Him, in spirit and truth it does behove to worship."*
*The woman said to him, "I have known that Messiah does come, who is called Christ, when that one may come, he will tell us all things;" Jesus said to her, "I am he who am speaking to you."*

# Chapter 16. (September 29AD)
## A Secret Meeting with Helena by the Well

*Helena finds Jesus at Jacob's well.*

Jesus asks, "The disciples have gone away; Helena, would you give me a drink?"

Helena pretends to be affronted, "How do you, being a Jew, ask a drink from me, being a Samaritan woman? Jews have no dealings with Samaritans!"

"Would you not give me a drop of water in exchange for 'living water'?"

Helena replies, "Is this well of your ancestor Jacob deep enough to sustain you? Is this 'living water' more powerful than the waters of the Jordan River?"

"I suspect it is your husband who asks."

"I am merely the consort of Simon Magus. I can ask for myself and my question is, 'Will the anointed one come soon'?"

Jesus replies, "I do believe, as in Isaiah (61:1), that 'the Holy Spirit is upon me because the Lord has anointed me to bring the gospel to the afflicted'. One day I will establish a new Jerusalem to supersede Mount Gerizim and Mount Zion."

Helena says, "That day will be sooner than you think. We rejoice that you will accept that role with us."
*She runs off leaving her water jar.*

*Mark 06:21-25 An opportune day having come, when Herod on his birthday was making a supper to his great men, and to the chiefs of thousands, and to the first men of Galilee, and the daughter of (subordinate of) Herodias (Helena) having come in, and having danced, and having pleased Herod and those dining with him, the king said to the damsel, He swears to her -- "Whatever you may ask me, I will give to you -- unto the half of my kingdom." (Real daughter is Salome - Antiq 18.5.4) And (coached by her mother Herodias) she said, upon a plate, the head of John the Baptist."*

Helena's Dance

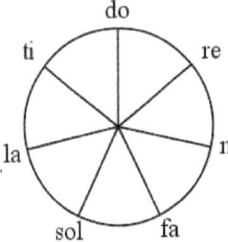

Blessed are the meek, for they shall inherit the earth* Blessed are the peacemakers, for they shall be called the children of god* Blessed are the merciful, for they shall obtain mercy* Blessed are the pure of heart, for they shall see god* "Blessed are they who are persecuted for righteousness' sake for theirs is the kingdom of heaven* Blessed are they who hunger and thirst after righteousness, for they shall be filed* Blessed are they who mourn, for they shall be comforted* "Blessed are the poor in spirit for theirs is the kingdom of heaven"

*Antiq 18.5.2 Now some of the Jews thought that the destruction of Herod's army came from God, and that very justly, as a punishment of what he did against John, that was called the Baptist: for Herod slew him, who was a good man, and commanded the Jews to exercise virtue, both as to righteousness towards one another, and piety towards God, and so to come to baptism; for that the washing with water would be acceptable to him, if they made use of it, not in order to the putting away of some sins, but for the purification of the body; supposing still that the soul was thoroughly purified beforehand by righteousness. Accordingly, he was sent a prisoner, out of Herod's suspicious temper, to Macherus, the castle I before mentioned, and was there put to death. Now the Jews had an opinion that the destruction of this army was sent as a punishment upon Herod and a mark of God's displeasure to him.*

# Chapter 17. (March 30AD)
## The Overthrow John the Baptist by Simon Magus and Helena

Bernardino Luini (1512-1532)

*Beginning of March 30AD (Passover #1) John 2:13 "And the Jewish Passover was at hand."*

There the is a great hall with spectators which includes Antipas Herod, Herodias, and Salome (age 12) on thrones watching Simon Magus (age 32) performing a magic act. He stands inside a circle of flame that is lit with saltpeter. The smoke fills the air and obscures him.

When the smoke clears, and they see him standing rigidly like a pillar, shouting, "I am Moses. I am the Standing One. I am the Pillar of Fire. I remain unharmed! Now, may I present the dancer from the Temple of Artemis who is Luna, the 30th person of John the Baptist's council and the teacher of Salome."

*The spectators are cheering as Helena (age 42), still the most beautiful dancer of the temple of Artemis, starts to dance to music played by oud and a flute. Her dance moves from point to point on a circle of seven equal divisions clockwise starting at 12 o'clock, and within each point on the circle, she twirls around saying a phrase from the Beatitudes.*

**The dance is over.** Antipas Herod announces, "My daughter Salome is becoming a woman today. I have promised her whatever she wants if her teacher's dance pleases me." Salome answers, having been coached by her mother, "The head of John the Baptist on a platter." *The audience gasps.*

*Mark 01:14 And after the delivering up of John, Jesus came to Galilee, proclaiming the good news of the kingdom of heaven,*
*Matt 04:18-20 And Jesus, walking by the sea of Galilee, saw two brothers, Simon named Peter and Andrew his brother, casting a drag into the sea -- for they were fishers -- and he said to them, "Come you after me, and I will make you fishers of men," and they, immediately, having left the nets, did follow him.*

*Luke 5:3-6,10 and having entered into one of the boats, that was Simon's, he asked him to put back a little from the land, and having sat down, was teaching the multitudes out of the boat. And when he left off speaking, he said unto Simon, "Put back to the deep, and let down your nets for a draught;" and Simon answering said to him, "Master, through the whole night, having labored, we have taken nothing, but at your saying I will let down the net." And having done this, they enclosed a great multitude of fishes (Titus-Marsyas), and their net was breaking, ... "Fear not, henceforth you shall be catching men;"*

*Peter's First Epistle to Pontus, Galatia, Cappadocia, Asia, and Bithynia 1Peter 3:20b-21a "When God's patience waited in the days of Noah, during the building of the ark, in which a few, that is, eight persons, were saved through water. Baptism, which corresponds to this, now saves you, not as a removal of dirt from the body but as an appeal to God for a clear conscience..."*

*Antiq 18.6.1 So Marsyas (Titus) desired of Protos (Peter), who was the freedman of Bernice, Agrippa's mother, and by the right of her testament was bequeathed to Antonia, to lend so much upon Agrippa's own bond and security; but he accused Agrippa of having defrauded him of certain sums of money;*

*Peter's brother, Andrew, like Peter was a freedman. Andrew had served the household of the King of Cappadocia, the father of Glaphyra, the mother-in-law of Peter. While her husband Alexander was still alive Peter and Andrew served together in Herod's court. In Qumran, they were once again reunited at Mird and Ein Feshkha.*

## Chapter 18. (March 30AD)
## Peter and Andrew, Fishers of Men, and Philip

*Jesus appears at Mazin ('Capernaum') on the Dead Sea (6 hr from Qumran-shorter by boat). Peter and Andrew are baptizing Gentiles in the salt water by lifting them up onto the boats with a net."*

Jesus says, "My father brought me up to build churches, so I am a carpenter, other missionaries who travel are tentmakers, but you are true 'fishers of men'."

Andrew says, "As freedmen and kinsmen, I from the household of the King of Cappadocia and Peter from the mother of Agrippa, we feel that it is our duty to reach out to Gentile believers."

Jesus reminiscing, "When I was a child in Rome on Tiber Island, my grandfather Heli would tell me tales of how he established this method there as a reenactment of Noah saving the Gentiles from the sea, having pulled them up into his ark."

Peter adds, "Still I think Gentiles should be allowed baptism in clear water later after proper teaching, so that I, Andrew, and Philip can take an active part in your inner circle."

Jesus says, "A good idea. I plan to fix that soon."

Peter says, "You are our Teacher."

"Peter you indicated that your mother-in-law Glaphyra is wanting Confession. Shall we leave for Mird in the morning with your wife to absolve our Mother Superior from sin?"
"Thank you, she is in distress."

*Matt 8:14,15 And Jesus having come into the house of Peter, saw his mother-in-law laid, and fevered, and he touched her hand, and the fever left her, and she arose, and was ministering to them.*

*Antiq 17.1.2 ("Alexander had two sons by Glaphyra") & 17.13.1 ("Alexander had three children by her). Antiq 17.8.4 The like accident befell Glaphyra his wife, who was the daughter of King Archelaus (of Cappadocia), who, as I said before, was married (18BC), while she was a virgin, to Alexander, the son of Herod, and brother of Archelaus; but since it fell out so that Alexander was slain by his father, she was married to Juba, the king of Libya; and when he was dead, and she lived in widowhood in Cappadocia with her father (King of Cappadocia). Archelaus (ethnarch of Judea recalled by Caesar) divorced his former wife Mariamne, and married her, so great was his affection for this Glaphyra; (Her grandmother, also Glaphyra, was a well-known courtesan with Mark Antony, being the subject of vulgar poem from Octavian (Augustus) Caesar, so marriage is unlikely.)*

*Antiq 17.13.4 In a dream Glaphyra thought she saw Alexander standing by her, at which she rejoiced, and embraced him with great affection; but that he complained to her, and said, O Glaphyra! thou provest that saying to be true, which assures us that women are not to be trusted. Did you not pledge your faith to me? and were you not married to me when you were a virgin? and had we not children between us? Yet have you forgotten the affection I bear to you, out of a desire of a second husband. Nor have you been satisfied with that injury you did to me, but you have been so bold as to procure yourself a third husband to lie by you, and in an indecent and imprudent manner has entered into my house, and has been married to Archelaus, your husband and my brother. However, I will not forget your former kind affection for me, but will set you free from every such reproachful action, and cause you to be mine again, as you once were. When she had related this to her female companions, in a few days' time she departed this life. (Metaphoric death: she became the head of the Asher convent).*

*(The Mother Superior of the Asher convent had a history of using seduction as a method of advancement starting with Glaphyra with ethnarch Archelaus, Helena with Simon Magus, and Bernice with Titus.)*

*Clement of Alexandria in Stromata, Book 3, 52 says "Peter and Philip had children." Although he mistakenly took the daughters of Philip" as children instead of as nuns, it shows that Peter had at least one child. In the Acts of Peter: Peter's daughter, a virgin (metaphorically 'crippled') is called Petronilla.*

# Chapter 19. (April 30AD)
## Absolution of Peter's mother-in-law

Peter's is mother-in-law is Glaphyra, Mother Superior

*Peter and his wife meet Jesus at Ein Feshkha to begin the 8-hour walk to Mird where the convent is located.*

Jesus asks, "Peter, I would like to know how you met your wife and how you became part of my grandfather's mission to the Diaspora."

Peter replies, "Having been made a freedman of Agrippa's mother Bernice, I managed some of her funds at the Herodian court to care for Glaphyra's daughter, who was conceived when Herod's son Alexander was still alive. Her father's kingdom is located in Cappadocia where my brother Andrew was also a freedman. Both Andrew and I were recruited by your grandfather Heli."

Peter's wife says, "We had a lavish wedding attended by my grandfather Archelaus the King of Cappadocia. Mark Antony gave him the kingship through the wiles of my great-grandmother, Glaphyra, and he was a good friend of Herod the Great."

They arrive and Jesus says, "Glaphyra are you ready to confess your sins before God?"

Glaphyra says, "I confess my sins of having many affairs with such men as Juba and Archelaus, the deposed ruler of Judea. From my vanity, I fell into the ways of my grandmother, but since then I have served faithfully as the headmistress of the Asher convent."

Jesus says, "Your good works have absolved you. You are free to turn over the leadership to Helena, who will be the new Martha."

Matt 04:21 *And having advanced from there, he saw other two brothers, James of Zebedee, and John his brother, in the boat with Zebedee their father (Simon Magus-stepfather), refitting their nets, and he called them, and they, immediately, having left the boat and their father, did follow him.*

H.12.8 (Family History) Then Peter inquired, "Are you really, then, alone in your family?" Then I (Clement) answered, "There are indeed many and great men, being of the kindred of Caesar. Wherefore Caesar himself gave a wife of his own family to my father, who was his foster-brother; and of her three sons of us were born, two before me, who were twins and very like each other, as my father told me. But I scarcely know either them or our mother, but bear about with me an obscure image of them, as through dreams. My mother's name was Mattidia, and my father's, Faustus; and of my brothers one was called Faustinus (Niceta: James), and the other Faustinianus (Aquila: John). Then after I, their third son (Clement), was born, my mother saw a vision -- so my father told me -- which told her, that unless she immediately took away her twin sons, and left the city of Rome for exile for twelve years, she and they must die by an all-destructive fate."

R.7.32 (He Brings Them To Their Desired Haven) Then Niceta (James) began to say: "On that night, O mother, when the ship was broken up, and we were being tossed upon the sea, supported on a fragment of the wreck, certain men, whose business it was to rob by sea, found us, and placed us in their boat, and overcoming the power of the waves by rowing, by various stretches brought us to Caesarea Stratonis. There they starved us, and beat us, and terrified us, that we might not disclose the truth; and having changed our names, they sold us to a certain widow, a very honorable woman, named Justa (Helena). She, having bought us, treated us as sons, so that she carefully educated us in Greek literature and liberal arts."

H.13.8 (Niceta is Deceived by Simon Magus) "We were brought up along with one Simon, a magician; and in consequence of our friendly intercourse with him, we were in danger of being led astray. But when we were going to be led astray by Simon, a friend of our lord Peter, by name Zacchaeus (Ananus, the youngest son of the High Priest Ananas), came to us and warned us not to be led astray by the magician; and when Peter came, he brought us to him that he might give us full information, and convince us in regard to those matters that related to piety."

## Chapter 20. (May 30AD)
## The twins James and John of Royal Lineage

*At Ein Feshkha Jesus meets with James and John.* He says "Father Jonathan told me you have forsaken Simon Magus, your step-father and nephew, and are influenced by Jonathan Ananus' younger brother Zacchaeus-Ananus. Have you changed then from 'Sons of Lightning' to 'Sons of Thunder'?"

Niceta answers, "Sons of Father Jonathan perhaps, but wishing to be 'Sons of the Messiah'!"

"That prophecy is yet to be tested, but meanwhile I am honored to welcome the 'Sons of Caesar' as disciples. I hear tell you have an amazing story of how you got here?"

Niceta answers,"We were born as illegitimate twin sons, thus banished from Rome by sea, but were shipwrecked and captured by pirates. Our real parents are Julia, the daughter of Augustus and Jullus Antonius, son of Mark Antony and Fulvia. Our real names were Faustus and Faustinianus, but the pirates named us Niceta and Aquila. Julia had been exiled to the island of Pandateria and Jullus was convicted of treason and had to commit suicide."

Aquila adds, "It was good fortune that Julia was able to alert our step-mother Helena so that she could purchase us at the slave market. When Simon rescued her from prostitution at the Temple of Artemis, he also adopted us, being related to us as the son of our father's older legitimate son, Lucius Antonius."

Jesus says, "Yes, an amazing story! One could say you were bound by fate and blood, Philip can instruct you on your preparation for baptism as James and John."

*Antiq 18.6.2 The future king Agrippa had thoughts of suicide; but his wife Cypros perceived his intentions, and tried all sorts of methods to divert him from his taking such a course; so she sent a letter to his sister Herodias, who was now the wife of Antipas Herod, and let her know Agrippa's present design, and what necessity it was which drove him thereto, and desired her, as a kinswoman of his, to give him her help, and to engage her husband to do the same. So they sent for him, appointed him some income of money for his maintenance, and made him a **magistrate of that city of Tiberias**, to honor him.*

*Luke 7:1-10 At Capernaum; A certain centurion (Herod Agrippa above) said that his servant (Eutychus) was ill, about to die, who was much valued by him, and having heard about Jesus, he sent unto him elders of the Jews, beseeching him, that having come he might thoroughly save his servant. And they, having come near unto Jesus, were calling upon him earnestly, saying "He is worthy to whom you shall do this, for he does love our nation, and the synagogue he did build to us." And Jesus was going on with them, and now when he is not far distant from the house the centurion sent unto him friends, saying to him, "Sir, be not troubled, for I am not worthy that under my roof you may enter; wherefore not even myself thought I worthy to come unto you, but say the word, and my lad shall be healed; for I also am a man placed under authority, having under myself soldiers, and I say to this one, "Go, and he goes; and to another, come, and he comes; and to my servant, do this, and he does it." And having heard these things Jesus wondered at him, and having turned to the multitude following him, he said, "I say to you, not even in Israel so much faith did I find;" and those sent, having turned back to the house, found the ailing servant in health.*

*Antiq 18.6.5,6 Now Eutychus, was Agrippa's freedman (Eutychus is John Mark's name before he was baptized in the Church as seen in Acts 20:7-12 with Paul in March 58AD) , and drove his chariot, heard these words: Agrippa said to Nero, 'Oh that the day would once come when this old fellow Tiberius would die and name you for emperor of the habitable earth! Thus his grandson would have no hindrance and that earth would be happy, and I happy also.' (For this Tiberius had Agrippa put in chains; Caligula released him with a golden chain when he became emperor.) Here is where John Mark is introduced.*

*Acts 12:12 When Peter realized this, he went to the house of Mary, the mother of **John whose other name was Mark***

*Before that he was the merely called the disciple that Jesus loved (John 13:23;20:01) and later (Acts.20:9) A young man named Eutychus was sitting in the window.*

# Chapter 21. (June 30AD)
## The Centurion's Servant (John Mark - Bartholomew is recruited)

Agrippa, the grandson Herod the Great, who executed his father Aristobulus, calls out, "Hello, Jesus."

Jesus answers, "Greetings Agrippa. Are you enjoying your position as magistrate of Tiberias that your uncle Herod Antipas and his wife Herodias gave to you?"

"No, it is boring. I miss my time when I was friends with Drusus, the emperor Tiberius's son. My mother Bernice had a friendship with Antonia, the wife of Drusus the Great and encouraged me to advance myself, but I incurred huge debts from my time in Rome. I have sought you out because you asked if my charioteer, Eutychus, could be made a freedman to assist you as a scribe for the journal you are keeping."

"I appreciate that. I have been realizing that many of my followers are freedmen. I am already indebted to your late mother Bernice for making Peter a freedman."

Agrippa says, "Interesting that a nobleman-centurion like me, can make a man to be free under Roman law, in the same way that you, the servant of God, can make a man free from sin under God's law."
"Imagine, when you are king, you could convert many. I intend to baptize him as John Mark."

"First, I must get back to Rome. I need a loan from Peter of my mother's inheritance and also Eutychus as my charioteer until my return."

"Peter was saying you defrauded him previously."
"He would say that; I will speak to Titus."

*Luke 08:26-39 And they sailed down to the region of the Gadarenes, that is across from Galilee, and Jesus, having disembarked, met him a certain man, outside of the city, who had demons (Zealots) for a long time, unclothed, and not abiding in a house, but tombs (the basement of the Church), and having seen Jesus, cried out and fell before him, and with a loud voice, said, "Why have you, Jesus, Son of God Most High, come to afflict me!" And Jesus questioned him, saying, "What is your name?" and he said, "Legion," (because many demons had entered into him) and they were calling on him not to command them to go into the abyss, and there was there a herd of many swine (Romans) feeding in the mountain calling on him. Jesus said let those demons go forth from the man and they did enter into the swine, and the herd rushed down the steep cliff to the lake and were choked. And those feeding them (associating with Romans), came forth to see what had come to pass, and they came unto Jesus, and found the man sitting, out of whom the demons had gone forth, clothed, and right-minded, at the feet of Jesus, and they were afraid; and those also having seen it, told them how the demoniac was saved. And the man from whom the demons had gone forth was beseeching of him to be with him, and Jesus sent him away, saying, "Turn back to your house (Church), and preach the great things God did to you;"*

*John 3:1-12 And there was a man of the Pharisees, Nicodemus (Theudas, having the honorary title of "Conquering One") his name, a ruler of the Jews, this one came unto him by night, and said to him, "Rabbi, we have known that from God you have come as a teacher, for no one would be able to do that you do, if God were not with him." Jesus answered and said to him, "Verily, verily, I say to you, If anyone may not be born from above, he is not able to see the kingdom of heaven;" Nicodemus said unto him, "How is a man able to be born, being old? Is he able into the womb of his mother a second time to enter, and to be born?" Jesus answered, "Verily, verily, I say to you, If anyone may not be born of water, and the Spirit, he is not able to enter into the kingdom of heaven; that which has been born of the flesh is flesh, and that which has been born of the Spirit is spirit." Jesus answered, "Thou art the teacher of Israel and these things you do not know?" "Verily, verily, I say to you, What we know; we speak, and what we see; we testify but our testimony you do not receive. If the earthly things I have said to you, and you do not believe, how will you believe if I shall say to you the heavenly things?*

# Chapter 22. (June 30AD)
## Gadarenes demonic and the swine
## (Theudas is recruited)

*Jesus crosses the Dead Sea from Capernaum (Mazin) to Gadara (Macherus) by boat.*

Jesus says, "Theudas, Nicodemus, the Conquering One! I hear that you are considering reverting to the time when you were the Prodigal Son, befriending the Roman women. Beware of this or you will join this graveyard of heroes like John the Baptist."

Theudas says, "The ineffectiveness of the Zealot struggle discourages me. The people here have become complacent. They might as well be pork-eaters as they have accepted Roman rules. If the people forget the laws of God, He will not let us cross the river Jordan."

"Perhaps it is time to put aside your sword and be baptized with the Holy Spirit."

"Why would that make a difference? Spirit is invisible."

Jesus answers, "I understand that you want change, but change does not come from the earthly plane, but from the Spiritual plane. Baptism allows you to be born again from Spirit."

"Does this Spirit have a womb?"

"Perhaps all military leaders like you are pragmatic. I can only tell you, dear Uncle, 'What is born of flesh is flesh, what is born of Spirit is Spirit'."

*Romans 16:13 Paul:* "Greet Rufus (Thomas: Esau had red hair), eminent in the Lord, also his mother (Mariamne II) and mine (Herodias, step-mother)."
*Resurrection: John 20:24* Now Thomas, one of the twelve, called the Twin, was not with them when Jesus came.
*(The name Didymus, given to a Thomas in the gospel period, means "twin". The biblical Jacob had had a twin brother, Esau, who lost his birthright (Genesis 27) like Thomas lost his inheritance with Herod the Great.)*
*War 1.30.7* When Herod inquired about Pheroras's death, a discovery was made that Antipater had prepared a poisonous draught for him. Herod casts Doris and her accomplices, as also Mariamne, out of the palace and blots her son Herod (Thomas) out of his Testament. When she had said this, she brought the box, which had a small quantity of this potion in it: but the king let her alone, and transferred the tortures to Antiphilus's mother and brother; who both confessed that Antiphilus brought the box out of Egypt, and that they had received the potion from a brother of his, who was a physician at Alexandria. Then did the ghosts of Alexander and Aristobulus go round all the palace, and became the inquisitors and discoverers of what could not otherwise have been found out and brought such as were the freest from suspicion to be examined; whereby it was discovered that Mariamne II, the high priest (Boethus') daughter, was conscious of this plot; and her very brothers, when they were tortured, declared it so to be. Whereupon the king avenged this insolent attempt of the mother upon her son, and blotted Herod, whom he had by her, out of his testament, who had been before named therein as successor to Antipater.

*Antiq 18.5.4* But Herodias, their sister, was married to Herod (Thomas), the son of Herod the Great, who was born of Mariamne, the daughter of Simon the high priest, who had a daughter, Salome; after whose birth Herodias took upon her to confound the laws of our country, and divorced herself from her husband while he was alive, and was married to Herod (Antipas), her husband's brother by the father's side, he was tetrarch of Galilee; but her daughter Salome was married to Philip, the son of Herod, and tetrarch of Trachonitis; and as he died childless, Aristobulus, the son of Herod, the brother of Agrippa, married her; they had three sons, Herod, Agrippa, and Aristobulus (Timothy, Tychicus, and Trophimus).

# Chapter 23. (September 30AD)
## Thomas the Twin, the disinherited Esau

*Jesus had walked from Ein Feshkha to Mird to meet with Judas.* When he arrived he saw Thomas and says, "Good afternoon, red-haired Thomas Didymus. I was thinking how everything would have been different if you had inherited Judea instead of your half-brother Archelaus. You would have been a kind and fair-minded Herod. If Marriamme, your mother, had not been aware of the poison plot to kill Herod the Great, then you would not have been cheated of your birthright like Esau by Jacob."

Thomas replies, "I do not think of that anymore. It is fulfilling to occupy the king position of the Eastern wing of the Church. There I can visit Persia and India and discover the tools of the spiritual kingdom, such as the 'Hymn of the Pearl'. Let me recite some of it to you." "Yes gladly." *They sit down on the grass.*

> "The hymn tells the story of a boy, 'the son of the king of kings', who is sent to Egypt to retrieve a pearl from a serpent. During the quest, he is seduced by Egyptians and forgets his origin and his family. But, a letter is sent to remind him of his purpose: 'From Us – King of Kings, your Father, and your Mother, Queen of the Dawn-land, And from Our Second, your Brother – To you, Son, down in Egypt, Our Greeting! Up and arise from your sleep, Give ear to the words of Our Letter! 'Remember that thou art a King's son; See whom thou hast served in your slavedom. Think to yourself of the Pearl, for which thou didst journey to Egypt. Remember your Glorious Robe, your Splendid Mantle, remember, to put on and wear as adornment, when your Name may be read in the Book of the Heroes, and with Our Successor, your Brother, thou mayest be Heir in Our Kingdom'."

*Luke 4:33-36 And in the synagogue was a man, having a spirit of an unclean demon, and he cried out with a great voice, saying, "Away, what -- to us and to you, Jesus, O Nazarene? you did come to destroy us; I have known you who you are -- the Holy One of God." And Jesus did rebuke him, saying, "Be silenced, and come forth out of him;" and the demon having cast him into the midst, came forth from him, having hurt him naught;*

**Judas offering Jesus positions under him:**

**Moses 3rd in the hierarchy** *Luke 4:1-13 And Jesus, full of the Holy Spirit, turned back from the Jordan, and was brought in the Spirit to the wilderness, forty days being tempted by Satan, and he did not eat anything in those days, and they having been ended, he afterward hungered, and Satan said to him, "If Son you are of God, speak to this stone that it may become bread." And Jesus says, "It has been written, that, not on bread only shall man live, but on every saying of God."*

**Levite 2nd in the hierarchy** *And he brought him to Jerusalem, and set him on the pinnacle of the temple, and said to him, "If the Son you are of God, cast yourself down hence, for it has been written 'to His angels He will give charge concerning you, to guard over you,' and on hands they shall bear you up, lest at any time you may dash against a stone your foot." And Jesus says, "It has been said, You shall not tempt the Lord your God."*

**David King third in the hierarchy** *And Satan having brought him up to a high mountain, showed to him all the kingdoms of the world in a moment of time, and Satan said to him, "To you I will give all this authority, and their glory, because to me it has been delivered, and to whomsoever I will, I do give it; you, then, if you may bow before me, all shall be yours." Jesus says, "Get you behind me, Satan, for it has been written, You shall bow before the Lord your God, and Him only you shall serve."*

*Luke 8:2 and certain women, who were healed of evil spirits and infirmities, Mary who is called Magdalene, from whom seven demons (Judas at position 7) had gone forth,*

*Antiq 20.8.10 And then it was that the <u>Sicarii</u>, as they were called, who were robbers, grew numerous. They made use of small swords, not much different in length from the Persian acinacae, but somewhat crooked, and like the Roman sicae (sickles), as they were called; and from these weapons, these robbers got their denomination, and with these weapons, they slew a great many;*

## Chapter 24. (September 30AD)
## Judas Sicarii (Iscariot) the Tester

Jesus is at Mird and says to Judas, "I am here to fulfill my Nazarite vow to prepare for marriage."

Judas says, "It is my job to make sure that the Essene rules are followed and, as Satan, I will test you for your fitness for marriage."

Judas begins his instruction, "I trust that you will not make the error of your father of mistaking betrothal for marriage. Are you clear about it?"

"Yes, but what I am not clear about is whether I am allowed to kiss Magdalene on the mouth in public."

"Sounds like your mind is already in the gutter. It is not be done in public."

"I see that as unreasonable, as I kiss the disciples in that manner, but as you wish."

"Are you prepared to spend the marriage requirement of forty days in the wilderness without bread to sustain you, medicines to heal you, and others to minister unto you?"

"I will live on manna as Moses did, and, if necessary, apply the healing potions of the Therapeuts, and entrust my life to God."

"You will do well then. I would be glad to have you with me when I am the Pope."

"Sorry, but I have already made my vows to my superiors."

*The five sons and daughter of Ananus (Ananus) High Priest (ruling 6–15AD) (Antiq 18.2.1)*

daughter married to Caiaphas (18-36): John 18:13 And they led him (Jesus) away to Ananas first, for he was the father-in-law of Caiaphas, who was chief priest of that year,

**1.** *Eleazar Ananus (16-17AD) (Antiq 18.2.2)*
**2.** *Jonathan Ananus (36-37AD) (Antiq 18.4.3; 19.6.4; 20.8.5; War 2.13.3) (James son of Alphaeus, disciple of Jesus; "Father" that Jesus spoke to in the Garden of Gethsemane; "Stephen" from Greek "stephanos" meaning crown: excommunicated-not martyred in 37AD (Acts 6:1-8, 7:54 to 8:2); As "Sceva" murdered in 57AD by procurator Felix (Acts 19:14-16).*

Mark 2:14 "And as he passed by, he saw Levi the son of Alphaeus sitting at the receipt of custom*, and said unto him, "Follow me". And he arose and followed him."
Luke 5:27,29 "And after these things he went forth, and saw a publican, named Levi, sitting at the receipt of custom*: and he said unto him, Follow me." And Levi made him a great feast in his own house: and there was a great company of publicans and of others that sat down with them.

**3.** *Theophilus Ananus (37- 41AD) (Antiq 18.5.3; 19.6.2)* **(Gospel of Luke and Acts** *are dedicated to him)*
*-- (Matthias, the son of Theophilus Ananus (65-66AD) (War 20.9.7))*
**4.** *Matthias Ananus (43) (Antiq 19.6.4; 19.8.1) (Matthew, disciple of Jesus and author of the* **Gospel of Matthew**)

Matthew 9:9 "And as Jesus passed forth from thence, he saw a man, named Matthew, sitting at the receipt of custom*: and he said unto him, Follow me. And he arose, and followed him."

**5.** *Ananus Ananus (62AD) (Antiq 20.6.2; 20.9.1; War 4.5.2 )*
*("Demas" (2Timothy 4:10) - Paul's associate;) Killed at the Temple of Jerusalem by the Zealots in 68AD*

Luke 19:1-8 And having entered, he was passing through Jericho, and lo, a man, by name called Zacchaeus, and he was a chief tax-gatherer*, and he was rich, ... in stature he was small ... went up on a sycamore ... Zacchaeus having stood, said unto the Lord, "Lo, the half of my goods, sir, I give to the poor, and if of anyone anything I did take by false accusation, I give back fourfold."

\* *"receipt of custom/tax-gatherer" is a joke for Sadducee priests who collect church tithes.*

# Chapter 25. (October 30AD)
## The Tax Collectors complete the Twelve

Seeing Jesus outside of Qumran where the money changers set up shop, Father Jonathan calls to Jesus, "Wait, let me speak with you."

He takes Jesus aside, "The money changers are asking me to intervene with you about your desire to overturn their tables. (Matt 21:12) They would like me to explain to you that they are merely allowing pilgrims to exchange their currencies, such as Tyrian shekels to Roman shekels for the upkeep of Qumran and the Temple in Jerusalem."

Jesus answers, "This whole concept of paying money for a Temple from which my followers are excluded enrages me. I once sarcastically suggested that Peter catch a fish that had a four-drachma coin in its mouth that would be enough to pay the temple tax for two, (Matt 17:27) but my initiate fishes are not that rich."

"I understand where you are coming from as I myself and my younger brothers Matthew and Zacchaeus are derided as 'tax-collectors' just because we collect the tithes. You have said rightly, 'Render to Caesar the things that are Caesar's, and to God, the things that are God's.' (Mark 12:17) It is a necessary evil."

"All right, I promise to control my rage."

"Let me invite you to share the sacrament with us sinners: tax collectors and publicans. In discussion, we can explain to you why us Sadducees do not believe in the after-life. I and Matthew are at your service."

**Six disciples under Jesus (two groups of three)**
(1-1) Peter, brother of Andrew, freedman of Agrippa's mother, Bernice, married to Glaphyra's daughter, wrote the Gospel of Peter scribed and edited by Mark

(1-2,3) James Niceta and John Aquila, illegitimate twins of Augustus Caesar's daughter, Julia the Elder with Mark Anthony's son Jullus Antonius, who were adopted by Helena, consort of Simon Magus (Zebedee).
(John and Priscilla' son is John the Presbyter)

(2-1) Bartholomew, John Mark, freedman Eutychus of Agrippa, the disciple that Jesus loved, scribed the Gospel of John written by Jesus and Simon Magus. (Luke-Cornelius substituted for him during his absence, scribing the Gospel of Luke for Jesus)

(2-2) Philip, freedman, (head of the daughters of Philip: Mary Magdalene), wrote the Gospel of Philip

(2-3) Andrew, brother of Peter, freedman of King of Cappadocia

**Six associates of Jesus (two groups of three)**
(3-1) Simon Canaanite/Zealot, Simon Magus (magician), Zebedee, Lazarus, Simon: the leper/tanner, Simon of Cyrene, Ananias, Demetrius the silversmith, Beast 666

(3-2) Judas Iscariot, Zealot, Satan (Tester) 7
(replaced by Jesus' second brother, Joses-Bar(n -->s)abas, Mathias)

(3-3) Thaddaeus, Theudas, Bar-(s)abbas, Leader of Therapeuts, Nicodemus, "Judas of James" (brother of Joseph thus Jesus' uncle Cleopas)

(4-1) James son of "Alphaeus" (son of Ananus), Sadducee ("tax collector"), Jonathan Ananus, Nathaniel, Stephen, Sceva

(4-2) Matthew (Ananus), Sadducee ("tax collector"), younger brother of Jonathan, wrote the Gospel of Matthew, presided over the canonizing of the Gospels

(4-3) Thomas, dispossessed son of Herod the Great (Rufus: the Twin as Esau/Jacob), natural father of Salome, wrote the Gospel of Thomas (dismissed as "doubting")

## Chapter 26. (October 30AD)
## The Twelve Disciples

At Mird, Jesus designates the twelve disciples saying, "In the tradition of the Hebrew-Essene faith and after much deliberation, we have identified twelve trusted members of our Church that is called 'The Way'. These twelve are divided into two groups of six and within the six, two groups of three which follow the Essene principle of 'Michael', 'Gabriel', 'Sariel'. I have been given the leadership of one of the groups of six which is made up of the Diaspora and the Gentiles, who have traditionally reported to my grandfather Heli. My two leaders are Peter and John Mark.
The other group of six are Pharisees and Sadducees under the direction of the High Priest and King or Tetrarch. Their two leaders are Simon Magus and Jonathan Ananus as 'Michael' and 'Gabriel' who are superior to me as 'Sariel/Raphael'. May God sanctify this union and lead us to a peaceful Restoration."

"To my group of six, I charge you: Do not get any gold or silver or copper to take with you in your belts: no bag for the journey or extra shirt or sandals or a staff, for the worker is worth his keep. Whatever town or village you enter, search there for some worthy person and stay at their house until you leave. As you enter the home, give it your greeting. If the home is deserving, let your peace rest on it; if it is not, let your peace return to you. If anyone will not welcome you or listen to your words, leave that home or town and shake the dust off your feet."
"I am sending you out like sheep among wolves. Therefore be as shrewd as snakes and as innocent as doves. Be on your guard; you will be handed over to the local councils and be flogged in the synagogues. On my account, you will be brought before governors and kings as witnesses to them and to the Gentiles. But when they arrest you, do not worry about what to say or how to say it. At that time you will be given what to say, for it will not be you speaking, but the Spirit of your Father speaking through you." (Matt 10:9-20)

# SECTION 3 (29AD to 30AD)
## The Marriage of Jesus and Mary Magdalene

'Giotto Voyage to Marseilles' of Mary Magdalene 1320s

*H.2.19 (Justa, a Proselyte) There is amongst us one Justa (feminine of Justus meaning of high rank - implied to be Helena and thus Luna), a Syro-Phoenician, by race a Canaanite, whose daughter was oppressed with a grievous disease. And she came to our Lord, crying out, and entreating that He would heal her daughter. But He, being asked also by us, said, "It is not lawful to heal the Gentiles, who are like to dogs on account of their using various meats and practices, while the table in the kingdom has been given to the sons of Israel." But she, hearing this, and begging to partake like a dog of the crumbs that fall from this table, having changed what she was, by living like the sons of the kingdom, she obtained healing of her daughter, as she asked.*

*Matt 10:5,6 These twelve Jesus sent out, charging them, "Go nowhere among the Gentiles, and enter no town of the Samaritans, but go rather to the lost sheep of the house of Israel."*

*Matt 15:21,22,26-28 And Jesus having come forth from there, withdrew to the parts of Tyre and Sidon, and lo, a woman, a Canaanite, from those borders having come forth, did call to him, saying, "Deal kindly with me, Sir, Son of David; my daughter is miserably demonized." (Luke 8:2 and certain women, who were healed of evil spirits and infirmities, Mary who is called Magdalene, from whom seven demons had gone forth) Jesus says, "It is not good to take the children's bread, and to cast to the dogs." And she said, "Yes, sir, for even the dogs do eat of the crumbs that are falling from their lord's table;" then Jesus said to her, "O woman, great is your faith, let it be to you as you will." Her daughter was healed that hour.*

*H.2.20 (Divorced for the Faith) She, therefore, having taken up a manner of life according to the law, was, with the daughter who had been healed, driven out from her home by her husband (temple priest), whose sentiments were opposed to ours. But she, being faithful to her engagements, and being in affluent circumstances, remained a widow herself, but **gave her daughter (Mary Magdalene) in marriage to a certain man who was attached to the true faith (Jesus!!), and who was poor (member of the Essene monastery known as 'the poor')**. "And, abstaining from marriage for the sake of her daughter, she bought two boys [Niceta (James) & Aquila (John)] and educated them, and had them in place of sons. And they being educated from their boyhood with Simon Magus, have learned all things concerning him. For such was their friendship, that they were associated with him in all things in which he wished to unite with them.*

# Chapter 27. (June 29AD)
## The Mother of Mary Magdalene makes a request of Jesus

*Jesus visits the convent at Mird where Magdalene is cloistered. Her mother Helena touches his garment.*

Jesus says, "Who is touching my garment?"

Helena says, "Yes, it is I because I am very worried. I was shocked, when you sent out your six disciples and you told them to avoid the Samaritans, for, as you know, Magdalene, my natural daughter, is a Samaritan."

"Mother Superior, you know that some accept the Samaritans as Jews and some do not. I was just trying to limit the scope of the mission."

"Yes, but when you divide the loaves at the holy table and distribute them to the Jewish elders and pilgrims, even the dogs get to eat the crumbs that fall from the table."

"You are astute as always Helena. You are making me aware of the impending scorn of Pharisees and Scribes who will say, 'It is a marriage of illegitimates.' I have been meaning to expand the mission of Peter and Andrew to the Gentiles and I must do so without delay."

"Thank you, my future son-in-law, You are truly a man of compassion and a progressive leader of the Essene poor."

*Luke 8:41,42 Lo, there came a man, whose name is Jairus (Judas), and he was a chief of the synagogue, and having fallen at the feet of Jesus, was calling on him to come to his house; because he had an only daughter about twelve years old, and she was dying.*

*Note how this story is inserted inside the story of the twelve-year-old girl to show that menstruation is to the Essenes like a fatal disease!*

*Luke 8:43-48 And a woman, having an issue of blood for twelve years, who, having spent on physicians all her living, was not able to be healed by any, having come near behind, touched the fringe of his garment, and presently the issue of her blood stood. And Jesus said, "Who is it that touched me?" and all denying, And Jesus said, "someone did touch me, for I knew power having gone forth from me." And the woman, having seen that she was not hidden, trembling, came, and having fallen before him, for what cause she touched him declared to him before all the people, and how she was healed presently; and he said to her, "Take courage, daughter, your faith has saved you, be going on to peace."*

*Luke 8:49-56 While he is yet speaking, there does come a certain one from the chief of the synagogue's house, saying to him -- "Your daughter has died, harass not the Teacher;" and Jesus having heard, answered him, saying, "Be not afraid, only believe, and she shall be saved." And having come to the house, he suffered no one to go in, except Peter, and James, and John, and the father of the child, and the mother; and they were all weeping, and beating themselves for her, and he said, "Weep not, she did not die, but does sleep; and they were deriding him, knowing that she did die;*
*And Jesus having put all forth without, and having taken hold of her hand, called, saying, "Child, arise;" and her spirit came back, and she arose presently, and he directed that there be given to her to eat; and her parents were amazed, but he charged them to say to no one what was come to pass. (A dangerous precedent to give females equal status.)*

*Judas objects to Jesus & Mary Magdalene's marriage*
*John 12:4 Therefore said one of his disciples -- Judas Iscariot under Simon (Magus),"Therefore was not this ointment sold for three hundred denaries, and given to the poor?" and he said this, not because he was caring for the poor, but because he was a thief, and had the bag, and in charge of the money.*
*Mark 16:9 He appeared first to Mary Magdalene, out of whom he had cast seven devils."*

## Chapter 28. (August 29AD)
## The Bat Mitzvah of Mary Magdalene

Outside of the convent, Jesus says, "Judas, where is Magdalene? She has not come out."

Judas says, "Did Helena defile you just now. You know she had an issue of blood for over twelve years. At twelve Magdalene should have had her Bat Mitzvah and she is too old now to be blessed, so by Essene standards she is infertile for motherhood."

Jesus replies, "As I have said before, 'get you behind me Satan'. It is laughable that you consider a woman as being defiled just because she is capable of menstruating, for such is a nun and a virgin. You can be assured that she is not on her period today or she would have been forbidden to touch me. After her betrothal, Magdalene will be free of your meddling."

*Jesus goes inside the convent with Peter, James, and John; Magdalene is sobbing.* "Judas says I am too old and, not a Jew, and I might as well be dead."

Jesus says to Magdalene, "Young maiden, although you are now age 26, next week shall be your Bat Mitzvah. Before my disciples, I will declare your entry from girl to woman as a true member of the Tribe of Asher. It will not be a sorrowful day, but a celebration of the life-giving force that was granted to Eve. In March we will be betrothed."

Drying her tears and blushing, "You have made me young again. I pray that our marriage will be fruitful."

*The betrothal of Jesus and Mary Magdalene is in March and the disciples have been invited. By Essene rules: betrothal would occur in March and the couple would have to wait until after October to have sexual relations. (This can be determined from the date that Zechariah was not allowed to be in the temple followed by the birth of John the Baptist in September and Jesus' illegitimate conception in June shown by her visiting the pregnant Elizabeth in Mird.)*

*John 2:5-11 And the third day (symbolic of the three-year requirement for full initiation into the Community. After a ritual washing the three year process of entry into the Community results in full membership and thus being to sit at the holy table and be offered new wine) a marriage happened in Cana of Galilee, and the mother of Jesus was there, and also Jesus was called, and his disciples, to the marriage; and wine having failed, the mother of Jesus said unto him, "Wine they have not;" Jesus said to her, "What -- to me and to you, woman? not yet is mine hour come." His mother said to the ministrants, "Whatever he may say to you -- do." And there were there six water-jugs of stone, placed according to the purifying of the Jews, holding each two or three measures. (The size of the water jugs carved out of limestone is immense: possibly 20-30 gallons each! They are also described as for the use of purification. These two facts show that they are really designed for ritual bathing or baptisms. Jesus has them filled to the top and therefore after the miracle, there will be 180 gallons of wine! This concept of exaggeration is used in John to emphasize a point as when Theudas (Nicodemus) brings a hundred pounds of myrrh and aloes to bury Jesus - John 19:39.) Jesus said to them, "Fill the water-jugs with water;" and they filled them -- unto the brim; and he said to them, "Draw out, now, and bear to the director of the apartment;" and they bear. And as the director of the apartment tasted the water become wine, and knew not whence it is, (but the ministrants knew, who have drawn the water,) the director of the feast does call the bridegroom, and said to him, "Every man, at first, the good wine does set forth; and when they may have drunk freely, then the inferior; you did keep the good wine till now." This is the beginning of the signs did Jesus in Cana of Galilee, and manifested his glory, and his disciples believed in him;*

*Seating at the Wedding:*
*The Common Table has six seats on each side like the Last Supper: Jesus and Pope Magus are at the north center, to the right of Jesus is Mother Mary and Magdalene's mother Helena, to the Pope's left is Father Jonathan and Mary Magdalene. Her two step-brothers James and John are south center with Andrew, Peter, John Mark, Philip: left and right.*

## Chapter 29. (March 30AD)
## First Miracle of Water into Wine: Betrothal of Jesus & Mary Magdalene

*It is March 30AD. All are seated at the Common Table. Joses, son three, begins pouring from a large jug into his mother's silver wine goblet.*

Mother Mary exclaims, "This is just water! This is a terrible mistake, have we forgotten to order the wine?"

"Joses, continue pouring," Jesus says, "Wait until they are all filled ... Now before you are goblets containing fresh water from the huge limestone jugs that are normally used for baptism ... no one drinks until we say a prayer to God ... bow your heads and close your eyes." As Father Jonathan gives a long prayer ending with "May God find this day acceptable to Him", Simon switches the goblets.

*They open their eyes astonished to see that the water has turned to wine.*

Peter shouts, "A miracle! Let us toast the bride!"

Helena, tasting it, says, "But the bad wine is usually served last." *They laugh.*

Jesus says, "From today all baptized Gentiles and women will be welcomed at the Common Table."

Father Jonathan joins the hands of Jesus and Magdalene together, says "Jesus and Mary, you are now betrothed."

*Dead Sea Scrolls: Community Rule QS 1.6* **Every man born of Israel**, *who freely pledges himself to join the Council of the Community shall be examined by the Guardian at the head of the Congregation concerning his understanding and his deeds. If he is fitted to the discipline, he shall admit him into the Covenant that he may be converted to the truth and depart from all injustice; and he shall instruct him in all the rules of the Community. And later, when he comes to stand before the Congregation, they shall all deliberate his case, and according to the decision of the Council of the Congregation, he shall enter or depart. After he has entered the Council of the community he shall not touch the pure Meal of the Congregation until one full year is completed ...*
*He shall not touch the Drink of the Congregation until he has completed the second year among the men of the Community.*

*John 8:2-11 The scribes and the Pharisees bring unto him a woman having been taken in adultery, and having set her in the midst, they say to him, "Teacher, this woman was taken in the very crime of adultery, and in the law, Moses did command us that such be stoned; you, therefore, what do you say?" and this they said, trying him, that they might have to accuse him. And Jesus, having stooped down, with the finger he was writing on the ground, and when they continued asking him, having bent himself back, he said unto them, "The sinless of you, let him first cast the stone at her;" and again having stooped down, he was writing on the ground, and they having heard, and by the conscience being convicted, were going forth one by one, having begun from the elders, unto the last; and Jesus was left alone, and the woman standing in the midst.*
*And Jesus having bent himself back, and having seen no one but the woman, said to her, "Woman, where are those -- your accusers? did no one pass sentence upon you?" and she said, "No one, Sir;" and Jesus said to her, "Neither do I pass sentence on you; go and sin no more."*

**Names of Helena (Clementine Books)**
*Justa (H.2.19)\* Luna (H.2.23, R.2.12 )\* "daughter" of Herodias (Mark 6:21-29)\* Syrophoenician woman (Mark 7:26, H.2.19)\* woman of Samaria (John 4:4-42)\* adulterous woman (John 08:1-11)\* mother of the sons of Zebedee (Matt 20:20, Matt 27:56, H.2.20)\* sister of Mother Mary (John 19:25)\* the other Mary (Matt 28:01)\* Martha (John 11:1, John 12:2, Luke 10:38)\* Joanna (Luke 8:3), Luke 24:10, Luna (H.2.23, R.2.12 ) )\* Salome (Mark 15:40, Mark 16:1)\* Sapphira (Acts 5:1)\**

# Chapter 30. (October 30AD) The Sins of the Mother

*Jesus had returned tired and hungry from spending forty days and nights in the wilderness of Mird to prepare for his marriage bed.*

Certain Pharisees are pointing to Helena, saying "We denounce you as a prostitute." *They pick up stones.*

Helena says, "You accuse me wrongly. I served as a virgin at the Temple of Artemis. Although the ignorant believe these temples to be brothels, they are respected by the Emperor. If you have an issue with me you should speak to him."

"Well said!" Jesus helps her up, "This woman has been baptized and cleared of all sin. Who of you would like to give me a written accusation against her that I can forward to Tiberius?"

One of the Pharisees shouts as he leaves, "Her daughter, Mary Magdalene, is also a whore like her."

Jesus answers, "The sins of the fathers and the mothers are not passed to the child. Our Church baptizes and forgives all sin."

Jesus comforting Helena who is shaken, "It seems that people are so fast to see the bad and never the good."

*Luke 7:36-48 And a certain one of the Pharisees (Simon Magus) was asking him (Jesus) that he might eat with him, and, having gone into the house of the Pharisee, he dined, and lo, a woman in the city, who was a sinner, having known that he (Jesus) dines in the house of the Pharisee, having provided an alabaster box of ointment, and having stood behind, beside his feet, weeping, she began to wet his feet with the tears, and with the hairs of her head she was wiping, and was kissing his feet, and was anointing with the ointment. And the Pharisee who did call him, having seen, speaks within himself, saying, "This one, if he were a prophet, would have known who and of what kind is the woman who does touch him, that she is a sinner." And Jesus answering said unto him, "Simon (Magus), I have something to say to you;" and he said, "Teacher, say on."*

*Luke 07:41-43 'Two debtors were to a certain creditor; the one was owing 500 denaries, and the other 50; and they not having wherewith to give back, he forgave both; which then of them, say you, will love him more?' And Simon answering said, 'I suppose that to whom he forgave the more;' and he said to him, 'Rightly you did judge.'*

*And having turned unto the woman, he said to Simon, "See you this woman? I entered into your house; water for my feet you did not give, but this woman with tears did wet my feet, and with the hairs of her head did wipe; a kiss to me you did not give, but this woman, from what time I came in, did not cease kissing my feet; with oil my head you did not anoint, but this woman with ointment did anoint my feet; therefore I say to you, her many sins have been forgiven, because she did love much; but to whom little is forgiven, little he does love." And he said to her, "Your sins have been forgiven;" and those dining with him began to say within themselves, "Who is this, who also does forgive sins?" and he said unto the woman, "Your faith has saved you, be going on to peace."*

*Magdalene's Trip to Marseilles legend has a connection with Lucius Antonius' (20BC-25AD), banishment to Marseilles after his father Jullus Antonius' affair with Julia, the daughter of Augustus, resulting in his forced suicide. Simon Magus (Lazarus) was his son and since James and John were illegitimate sons of from the above affair, Simon was their nephew, but also their step-father and Magdalene's, since her natural mother was Helena, the consort of Simon. Simon and the Jews were ejected from Rome in 19AD by Tiberius, obviously not after the Ascension:*

"It is an ancient popular tradition of the inhabitants of Provence, in France, that St. Mary Magdalene, or perhaps Mary, the sister of Lazarus, St. Martha, and St. Lazarus, with some other disciples of our Lord, after his ascension, being expelled by the Jews, put to sea, and landed safe at Marseilles, of which church they were the founders, St. Lazarus being made the first bishop of that city." (The Lives of the Saints 1866. Butler (1711–73) Volume VII: July 22)

# Chapter 31. (October 30AD)
## The Marriage - Song of Solomon

*Pope Magus is seated at the table and is joined by Jesus. Magdalene knells and washes Jesus' feet and takes out the myrrh ointment from an alabaster box and rubs it on his feet with her head scarf as her tears fall on his feet also.*

Gently pulling her up, Jesus says, "Mary, do not cry. Those people, who were going to stone your mother and called you a whore are just self-righteous sinners. You and your mother are without sin." *He kisses her on the lips.*

Pope Simon says, "What are we to do about her dowry? Being a daughter of the Asher convent, she has retained her money when she joined."

*Jesus answers, "Two debtors were to a certain creditor; the one was owing 500 denaries, and the other 50; and they not having wherewith to give back, he forgave both; which then of them, say you, will love him more?' As a sinner does she not deserve to be forgiven more?"*

"Skillful use of sin! There you are using those parables again. It seems that the only sin here is the wasting of the expensive myrrh on you."

Jesus says, "That sounds like something that Judas would say. I am glad he is not here."

Simon begins the ceremony, "Arise and be joined together in marriage. Jesus, you have already kissed the bride; now depart with her to the Garden of Solomon."

# SECTION 4 (September 30AD to December 32AD)
## Miracles are Metaphors

Ancient Christian Sarcophagus (magic wand)
Miracle at Cana, Healing the paralytic, Raising Lazarus - Vatican Inv. 31556

*Mark 2:1-12 And again he entered into Capernaum (Mazin), after some days, and it was heard that he is in the house, and immediately many were gathered together, so that there was no more room, not even at the door, and he was speaking to them the word. And they come unto him, bringing a paralytic, borne by four (being part of the hierarchy of four: Michael, Gabriel, Sariel, Raphael), and not being able to come near to him because of the multitude, they uncovered the roof where he was, and, having broken it up (slid it open), they let down the couch on which the paralytic was lying, (fancy pulley system that lower him to the upper floor) and Jesus having seen their faith, said to the paralytic, "Child, your sins have been forgiven you."*
*And there were certain of the scribes there sitting, and reasoning in their hearts, "Why does this one thus speak evil words? who is able to forgive sins except one -- God?"*
*And immediately Jesus, having known in his spirit that they thus reason in themselves, said to them, "Why these things reason you in your hearts? Which is easier, to say to the paralytic, The sins have been forgiven to you? or to say, Rise, and take up your couch, and walk? and, that you may know that the Son of Man has authority on the earth to forgive sins*
*(he said to the paralytic) I say to you, Rise, and take up your couch, and go away to your house;" and he rose immediately, and having taken up the couch, he went forth before all, so that all were astonished, and do glorify God, saying -- "Never thus did we see."*

*Parable of The Great Banquet (Matt 22:1-14; Luke 14:12-33) shows the levels of the Church*
*And Jesus answering, again spoke to them in parables, saying, "The kingdom of heaven was likened to a man, a king, who made marriage-feasts for his son, and he sent forth his servants to call those having been called to the marriage-feasts, and they were not willing to come..."*
*"And they began with one consent all to excuse themselves: The first said to him, A field I bought, and I have need to go forth and see it; I beg of you, have me excused. and another said, Five yoke of oxen I bought, and I go on to prove them; I beg of you, have me excused: and another said, A wife I married, and because of this I am not able to come. And that servant having come, told to his lord these things, then the master of the house, having been angry, said to his servant, Go forth quickly to the broad places and lanes of the city, and bring in hither the poor, and maimed, and lame, and blind. And the servant said, Sir, it has been done as you did command, and still there is room."*

*The Church in Ein Feshkha was built with an upper floor, which was half the size of the lower floor. When the noon service begins, the roof is slid open to the sky to let the light shine on the priest, blinding the congregation. The priest then is lowered down by pulleys to the upper floor.*

## Chapter 32. (September 30AD)
## Father Ananus, a paralytic, let down through the roof of the Church

*The service begins and the roof is slid open to the sky. Jesus is on the raised floor (stage right) explaining the parable of the Great Banquet, as a pulley system lowers Father Jonathan to the center of the stage in his palanquin.*

*"In this Parable of the Banquet of King Herod, those who refused were the three classes of the Church: the first is the Father, who was too busy expanding the church than attending to the flock; the second is the Son of the Father, who represents the bishops being too busy with mundane affairs, and the third are the priests conflicted with the temptations of marriage. These chosen ones wasted their chance of being at heavenly banquet."*

(Jesus, helping Jonathan, whispers "Take up your bed and walk." *Jonathan gives him a scolding look.*)

Jesus explains, "Since those that were called first did not show up, the King invited all seekers of the truth:

1. The 'poor', being the members of the Essenes order,
2. the 'maimed', being the uncircumcised, like females, in the sense of being bereft of the sacred cutting,
3. the 'lame', being a common term for the Nazarite when fasting on retreat,
4. the 'blind', being the initiates, having not yet learned the true path
5. and, the last group, being pilgrims, like you, who bring offerings for the table in exchange for teaching."

Jonathan says praises to God and ends with "Amen"

*Matt 8:23-27 And when he entered into the boat his disciples did follow him, and lo, a great tempest arose in the sea, so that the boat was being covered by the waves, but he was sleeping, and his disciples having come to him, awoke him, saying, "Sir, save us; we are perishing." And he said to them, "Why are you fearful, O you of little faith?" Then having risen, he rebuked the winds and the sea, and there was a great calm; and the men wondered, saying, "What kind -- is this, that even the wind and the sea do obey him?"*

*Matt 14:22-33 And immediately Jesus constrained his disciples to go into the boat, and to go before him to the other side, till he might let away the multitudes; and having let away the multitudes, he went up to the mountain by himself to pray, and evening having come, he was there alone, and the boat was now in the midst of the sea, distressed by the waves, for the wind was contrary. And in the fourth watch of the night Jesus went away to them, walking upon the sea, and the disciples having seen him walking upon the sea, were troubled saying -- "It is an apparition," and from the fear they cried out; and immediately Jesus spoke to them, saying, "Be of good courage, I am he, be not afraid."*
*And Peter answering him said, "Sir, if it is you, bid me come to you upon the waters;" and he said, "Come;" and having gone down from the boat, Peter walked upon the waters to come unto Jesus, but seeing the wind vehement, he was afraid, and having begun to sink, he cried out, saying, "Sir, save me." And immediately Jesus, having stretched forth the hand, laid hold of him, and said to him, "Little faith! For what did you waver?" And they having gone to the boat as the wind lulled, and those in the boat having come, did bow to him, saying, "Truly -- God's Son are you."*

*After the Resurrection (153 Fish)*
*John 21:7 That disciple, therefore, whom Jesus was loving (John Mark) said to Peter, "The Lord it is!" Simon Peter, therefore, having heard that it is the Lord, did gird on the outer coat, (for he was naked,) and did cast himself into the sea;*

*Baptism the Gentiles:*
*Peter and Andrew arrive at the dock in the early morning and greet the pre-initiates who are waiting to be baptized in the salt sea. (They are not allowed fresh water yet.) Using oil lamps, Peter and Andrew (in loincloths) direct them to enter the boat and row out past the jetty which is 45 meters long. They instruct the pre-initiates to jump into the water. Then they fish each person out onto the boat using a strong net. Father Jonathan in a white robe, having walked out on the jetty, blesses them as they disembark.*

## Chapter 33. (March 31AD)
## Jesus Commands the Sea and Walks on Water

*Beginning of March 31AD (Passover #2) John 5:1 "After that there was a feast of the Jews."*

Before dawn Jesus goes with Peter and Andrew by boat from Ein Feshkha to Mazin (6 kilometers south of Qumran on the Dead Sea), where Peter and Andrew are the 'fishers of men'. A storm comes up.

Peter says, "The prophecy of John the Baptist has failed. We will all die!"

Jesus answers, "Our Restoration is in 33AD, 30AD is long past. Trust me, this is just the weather."

*It is early morning and a great fog arises as they disembark to prepare for the Baptism of the Gentiles. Jesus says goodbye. They row out and start fishing out the Gentiles, expecting Father Jonathan who would walk out on the jetty to bless them. Meanwhile, Jesus has changed into a white robe and walks out on the jetty.*

Andrew says, "Look, I see a figure, white as a ghost, walking towards us on the water. Jesus is that you?"

Jesus replies, "Yes, it is I. I am coming to bless the initiates. Peter, would you like to do the honors?"

Peter says, "You are supposed to be Jonathan." *Flustered he falls into the sea.*

Jesus laughs, "Priesthood is not based on heredity. If you had faith, you could walk on water."

*Luke 7:11-15 And it came to pass, on the morrow, he was going on to a city called Nain, and there were going with him many of his disciples, and a great multitude, and as he came near to the gate of the city, then, lo, one dead was being carried forth, an only son of his mother, and she a widow, and a great multitude of the city was with her. And the Lord having seen her, was moved with compassion towards her, and said to her, "Be not weeping;" and having come near, he touched the bier, and those bearing it stood still, and he said, "Young man, to you I say, Arise;" and the dead sat up, and began to speak, and he gave him to his mother; (This person is James, the brother of Jesus as is the next healing below. The purpose of this healing is to show how James is still conspiring against Jesus with his mother.)*

*John 5:1-14 After these things there was a feast of the Jews, and Jesus went up to Jerusalem(Qumran),and there is in Jerusalem(Qumran) by the sheep-[gate] a pool that is called in Hebrew Bethesda, having five porches, in these were lying a great multitude of the ailing, blind, lame, withered, waiting for the moving of the water, for a angel at a set time was going down in the pool, and was troubling the water, the first then having gone in after the troubling of the water, became whole of whatever sickness he was held.*

*And there was a certain man there being in ailment thirty and eight years (31AD - 8BC, John the Baptist's birthday). Jesus having seen him lying, and having known that he is already a long time, he said to him, "Do you wish to become whole?"*

*The ailing man answered him, "Sir, I have no man, that, when the water may be troubled, he may put me into the pool, and while I am coming, another does go down before me."*

*Jesus said to him, "Rise, take up your couch, and be walking;" and immediately the man became whole, and he took up his couch, and was walking, and it was a Sabbath on that day,*

*After these things, Jesus finds him in the temple, and said to him, "Lo, you have become whole; sin no more, lest something worse may happen to you."*

# Chapter 34. (March 31AD)
## Impotent Man *(James brother of Jesus)* at the Pool of Bethesda

Jesus says, "James, my brother, why are you sitting in a palanquin next to the pool of Bethesda?"

James replies, "I must keep my body holy by using my palanquin, as Father Jonathan does, to keep me from contamination of the Gentiles. It is 38 years since John the Baptist's birthday in 8BC and the Restoration is still imminent."

Jesus says "When I was in Nain you pretended that you were the only son of our mother. Your dogmatic belief that you are the only legitimate son, prevented you from joining me, even though you could have life in the Church. Now with John the Baptist gone last year, his failed predictions leave you literally with no leg to stand on. How long will straddle the space between John's ghost and me? I bid you to accept a lesser role as my crown prince and be healed. Arise take up your bed and walk!"

"It is the Sabbath, I am not allowed to lift it."

"Your stubbornness has made you impotent."

*Rev 9:4 and it was said to them that they may not injure "the Grass of the earth, nor any Green thing"*

*The Parable of the Sower was the spreading of the Word of God to the Diaspora ("the Green Grass") to gain proselytes and collect tithes and offerings for the Church. This great wealth is described in the Copper Scroll (Dead Sea Scrolls). In Rome alone, there were more than 8,000 Jewish residents, many living mostly in Trastevere on the west bank of the Tiber, with its base being on Tiber Island ("the Sea") accessible by bridge to Rome. The Sowers included Jesus' father Joseph (Brother of the Prodigal Son Theudas) and grandfather Heli ("the Jacob" Matt 01:16) working primarily in Rome. In 1AD Joseph and Mary, with the newborn James and the seven year old Jesus ("the Word"), were there. Matt 13:3-9 Jesus spoke to them many things in parables, saying: "Lo, the sower went forth to sow, and in his sowing, some indeed fell by the way, and the fowls did come and devour them, and others fell upon the rocky places, where they had not much earth, and immediately they sprang forth, through not having depth of earth, and the sun having risen they were scorched, and through not having root, they withered, and others fell upon the thorns, and the thorns did come up and choke them, and others fell upon the good ground, and were giving fruit, some indeed a hundredfold, and some sixty, and some thirty. He who is having ears to hear -- let him hear."*

Matt 13:4-8 Some indeed fell by the way, and the **fowls** did come and devour them, (Initially the Way was the Essene path and their leaders called angels would not recognize uncircumcised Gentiles.) and others fell upon the **rocky places**, where they had not much earth, and immediately they sprang forth, through not having depth of earth, and the sun having risen they were scorched, and through not having root, they withered, (John the Baptist, being the solar Zadokite priest, took an elitist position of criticizing Herod Antipas on his marriage, balked at baptizing Jesus because of his illegitimate birth, and excluded the Gentiles in the Diaspora. He placed his whole power on his prediction of the timing of the coming Restoration. When it did not come, John was put to death.) and others fell upon the **thorns**, and the thorns did come up and choke them, (The thorns were the Sadducees who wore a crown with a thorn in front, described by Josephus as haughty and judgmental and we learn that they are associated with thorns as Paul describes his trouble with Jonathan Annas, a Sadducee, 2Corinthians12:07) and others fell upon the good ground, and were giving fruit, some indeed a hundredfold, and some sixty, and some thirty. (Refers to the opening up of schools for the Gentiles in ten provinces having studies of ten year (100), 6 year (60), and 3 year (30) sessions.)

# Chapter 35a (21BC<– to March 32AD)
## The Mission: Parable of the Sower

*Beginning of March 32AD (Passover #3) John 6:4 "And the passover, a feast of the Jews, was nigh."*

Jesus speaks to his followers who are reclining in the green grass, "Lo, the sower went forth to sow ... He who has ears to hear, let him hear ...
You are all part of the Way that was inspired by the Essenes and now includes Jews and Gentiles. I myself traveled to Rome when I was a boy of seven years in the misassigned Year One of our Lord with Mary and Joseph and my younger brother James. Many of you will be called to be sowers to the Diaspora, but first, you must learn the history of the Word which is the Seed and the three impediments to its growth:

1. The Essene angels showed us the true Way and warned us of the Age of Wrath that would proceed the Restoration, but they excluded the Diaspora and 'devoured the Word';
2. John the Baptist, who made the Word accessible to many by baptism, sadly was too elitist with his Zadok heredity, ignoring the Gentiles and angering many. 'The Word withered at his death';
3. "The Sadducee priests, whom you despise as tax collectors, and the Pharisees who teach merely the literal Jewish customs and regulations of Moses, 'choked the Word'."

"Yet, I now teach you to know of pure 'agapé' love, that will open your hearts to the 'Word' and show you the way to the Kingdom of God. If you still hunger for the 'Word', enroll with my disciples James and John."

*Five Thousand*
*Mark 6:35-44 And now the hour being advanced, his disciples having come near to him, say, -- "The place is desolate, and the hour is now advanced, let them away, that, having gone away to the surrounding fields and villages, they may buy to themselves loaves, for what they may eat they have not." And he answering said to them, "Give you them to eat," and they say to him, "Having gone away, may we buy **two hundred denaries** worth of loaves, and give to them to eat?" And he said to them, "How many loaves have you? go and see;" and having known, they say, **"Five, and two fishes."** And he commanded them to make all recline in companies upon the green grass, and they sat down in squares, by hundreds, and by fifties. And having taken the five loaves and the two fishes, having looked up to the heaven, he blessed, and brake the loaves, and was giving to his disciples, that they may set before them, and the 2 fishes divided he to all, and they did all eat, and were filled, and they took up of broken pieces **12 hand-baskets** full, and of the fishes, and those eating of the loaves were about **5000**.*

*Four Thousand*
*Mark 8:1-9; 17-21 In those days the multitude being very great, and not having what they may eat, Jesus having called near his disciples, said to them, "I have compassion on the multitude, because now three days they do continue with me, and they have not what they may eat; and if I shall let them away fasting to their home, they will faint in the way, for certain of them are come from far." And his disciples answered him, "Whence shall anyone be able these here to feed with bread in a wilderness?" And he was questioning them, "How many loaves have you?" and they said, "7." And he commanded the multitude to sit down upon the ground, and having taken the **7** loaves, having given thanks, he brakes them, and was giving to his disciples that they may set before them; and they did set before the multitude. And they had **a few small fishes**, and having blessed, he said to set them also before them; and they did eat and were filled, and they took up that which was over of broken pieces -- seven baskets; and those eating were about **4000**. And he let them away, And Jesus having known, said to them, "Why do you (disciples) reason, because you have no loaves? do you not yet perceive, nor understand, yet have you your heart hardened? Having eyes, do you not see? and having ears, do you not hear? and do you not remember? When the 5 loaves I did brake to the **5000**, how many hand-baskets full of broken pieces took you up?" they say to him, **"12"** and when the 7 to the **4000**, how many hand-baskets full of broken pieces took you up?" and they said, **"7."** "Do you understand!"*

# Chapter 35b. (March 32AD)
## The Mission: Feeding of the Five and Four Thousand

A huge crowd rushes towards James and John, as Andrew calls out, "Married men and women go to John who will distribute the five barley loaves."

Peter calls out, "The unmarried go to James who will distribute the four barley loaves."

Philip calls out to Titus, "So glad you have come. Jesus has promoted you as Fish 2 as the head of Ham representing the Ethiopians and Egyptians." The other two sons of Noah are me as Shem representing the Arabians and John Mark, as Japheth representing the Greeks and Romans."

After crowds are gone, Peter asks Jesus, "Why are there 4,000 for James and 5,000 for John?"

> "We are using the sacred Pythagorean triangle of 3,4,5 with each side multiplied by 1,000. The formulas are five loaves feed 5000, leaving 12 baskets and four loaves feed 4000, leaving 7 baskets. The baskets represent the number of meetings thus the 5000 meet monthly and the 4000 meet weekly, as they are the more dedicated unmarried ones. Since 5000 divided by 200 denaries can feed 25 people, it shows that 25 people converted by the mission can generate one denary."

John says, "My wife, Priscilla will help me to head this larger group, once a month."

James says, "My group of celibates seem dedicated."

Jesus says, "An exciting day for the Diaspora!"

*Pesher on Habakkuk (1QpHab 11:2-8 ) (translated by B.T.)* "Woe to him who gives drink to his neighbors, pouring it from the wineskin till they are drunk, so that he can gaze on their naked bodies!"(Habakkuk 2:15) Its pesher refers to the Wicked Priest who pursued after the Teacher of Righteousness to his house of exile to swallow him up in his furious anger. At the period of a feast, at the rest time of the Day of Atonement, he appeared to them to swallow them up and to cause them to stumble on the day of fasting, the sabbath of their rest.

*Luke 9:28-36* And it came to pass, after these words, as it were eight days, that having taken Peter, and John, and James, he went up to the mountain to pray, and it came to pass, in his praying, the appearance of his face became altered, and his garment white -- sparkling.

*John 07:37-39* And in the last, the great day of the feast, Jesus stood and cried, saying, "If anyone does thirst, let him come unto me and drink; he who is believing in me, according as the Writing said, Rivers out of his belly shall flow of living water;" and this he said of the Spirit, which those believing in him were about to receive; for not yet was the Holy Spirit, because Jesus was not yet glorified.

And lo, two men were speaking together with him, who were Moses and Elijah, who having appeared in glory, speaks of his leaving that he was about to fulfill in Jerusalem, but Peter and those with him were heavy with sleep, and having waked, they saw his glory, and the two men standing with him.

And it came to pass, in their parting from him, Peter said unto Jesus, "Master, it is good to us to be here; and we may make three booths, one for you, and one for Moses, and one for Elijah,"not knowing what he said.

*John 7:43-45,51* And certain of them were willing to seize him, but no one laid hands on him; the officers came, therefore, unto the chief priests and Pharisees, and they said to them, "Therefore did you not bring him?" Nicodemus said unto them (he who came by night unto him) being one of them, "Does our law judge the man, if it may not hear from him first, and know what he does?"

And as he was speaking these things, there came a cloud and overshadowed them, and they feared in their entering into the cloud, and a voice came out of the cloud saying, "This is My Son -- the Beloved; hear you him;" and when the voice was past, Jesus was found alone; and they were silent, and declared to no one in those days anything of what they have seen.

## Chapter 36. (October 32AD)
## Transfiguration of Jesus

*September 32AD John 7:2 "It would soon be the Jewish Feast of the Tabernacles."*
*(Actually: Atonement - September 10;*
*later the Feast of the Tabernacles - September 15)*

On the Day of Atonement, Peter, James, and John are seated in the village pews. Father Jonathan and Theudas are on the top floor wondering why Jesus is not there. Suddenly, the roof opens, blinding the congregation as Jesus is lowered onto the stage. The congregation gasps when they see Jesus in the white vestments of the High Priest.

Jesus speaks in a loud voice, "Today is the Day of Atonement, if anyone does thirst, let him come unto me and drink; he who is believing in me, according to Zechariah (14:8.9), can receive the 'living water of the One God.' David (Psalm 110) says 'The Lord shall send forth from Zion my mighty scepter and I shall rule as a priest forever in the order of Melchizedek'."

The congregation shocked and confused, "This is blasphemy. What gives Jesus the right to represent 'The Glory' and usurp Father Jonathan? Jesus is merely the Christ, representing 'the Kingdom'."

Theudas trying to calm them, "'The Glory' does not have to be a priest; when I act as Moses, I can be 'the Glory'."

Peter comes up to the raised floor saying, "Let us set up three booths for the Moses, Elijah, and Christ."

Father Jonathan correcting him, "Peter get back to your studies. it is not Tabernacles!"
Jonathan begins to spread a cloud of incense telling the congregation, "Quiet down. This is the House of God. Jesus is my son; forgive his transgression."

*Deaf and Dumb man: Joses replaces James as Jesus' crown prince*
*Mark 7:31-37 And again, having gone forth from the coasts of Tyre and Sidon, he came unto the sea of Galilee, through the midst of the coasts of Decapolis, and they bring to him a deaf, stuttering man, and they call on him that he may put the hand on him. And having taken him away from the multitude by himself, he put his fingers to his ears, and having spit, he touched his tongue, and having looked to the heaven, he sighed, and said to him, "Ephphasa,"that is, "Be you opened;" and immediately were his ears opened, and the string of his tongue was loosed, and he was speaking plain. And he charged them that they may tell no one, but the more he was charging them, the more abundantly they were proclaiming it, and he sent him away to his house, saying, "Neither to the village may you go, nor tell it to any in the village."*

*Blind man of Bethsaida: Joses is promoted*
*Mark 8:22-26 And he comes to Bethsaida, and they bring to him a blind man, and call upon him that he may touch him, and having taken the hand of the blind man, he led him forth without the village, and having spit on his eyes, having put his hands on him, he was questioning him if he does behold anything: and he, having looked up, said, "I behold men, as I see trees, walking." Afterwards again he put his hands on his eyes, and made him look up, and he was restored and discerned all things clearly, and he sent him away to his house, saying, "Neither to the village may you go, nor tell it to any in the village."*

*Epileptic: Zacchaeus is Ananus the Younger, the youngest son of the former High Priest Ananus*
*Luke 9:38-42 Lo, a man from the multitude cried out, saying, "Teacher, I beseech you, look upon my son, because he is my only begotten; and lo, a spirit does take him, and suddenly he does cry out, and it tears him, with foaming, and it hardly departs from him, bruising him, and I besought your disciples that they might cast it out, and they were not able." Jesus says, "Bring hither your son;" and as he is yet coming near, the demon rent him, and tore him sore, and he rebuked the unclean spirit, and healed the youth, and gave him back to his father.*
*Luke 17:5,6 And the apostles said to the Lord, "How do we increase faith?" and the Lord said, "If you had faith as a grain of mustard, you would have said to this Sycamore fig, Be uprooted, and be planted in the Sea, and it would have obeyed you."*

## Chapter 37. (November 32AD)
## Healing the Dumb and Deaf man, Blind man, and an Epileptic

Jesus' brother, Joses, says to Jesus, "Your brother, James, is confusing our followers by insisting that Gentiles must be circumcised. He is colluding with the High Priest Caiaphas and claiming that his word is superior to yours because he was born legitimate."

Jesus says, "James has tried my patience too long. I need to replace him as my crown prince. You are the next in line after James. Would you be my ear to speak for me as my crown prince?"

"How can you make a deaf man like me to hear or a dumb man like me to speak?"

"I could spit on my hands, touch your tongue and ears and say the magic word, 'Ephphasa', if you would like." Joses laughs, "No, that is fine; I accept."

"You are now age 24, being born in 8AD, and thus eligible to be a pre-initiate in the Essene Monastery and technically of the class defined as 'blind'. Your blindness will be cured by entering the monastery and washing in the cistern."

*Just then, Zacchaeus falls out of a sycamore tree and gets up staggering like an epileptic.* Jesus helping to steady him, "Are you all right?" "I am fine. I have been meaning to ask you if would be my teacher?"

Jesus says, "Of course you can, Ananas, youngest son of High Priest Ananus." Then, while helping him to brush the dirt off his robe, Jesus adds, "You are after all already a priest of the people."

*A leper, 10 lepers, Lazarus; all are Simon Magus*
*Luke 14:1-4b And it came to pass, on his going into the house of a certain one of the chiefs of the **Pharisees**, on a Sabbath, to eat bread, that they were watching him, and lo, there was a certain dropsied man (leper) before him; and having taken hold of him, he healed him, and let him go; (This leper is Simon Magus - see below)*
*In first anointing of Jesus by Mary Magdalene (unnamed) in "the house of the Pharisee (Simon) with an alabaster box.*
*In third anointing of Jesus by Mary (Magdalene) in "the house of Simon the leper" with an alabaster box.*
*With leper being associated with an outcaste status and the fact that a dead person would have a pallor like leprosy and given these connections above: Simon Magus is a Pharisee and the leper Lazarus, having been raised from excommunication.*

*Luke 17:11-18 And it came to pass, in his going on to Jerusalem, that he passed through the midst of Samaria and Galilee, and he entering into a certain village, there met him ten leprous men, who stood afar off, and they lifted up the voice, saying, "Jesus, master, deal kindly with us;" and having seen them, he said to them, "Having gone on, show yourselves to the priests;" and it came to pass, in their going, they were cleansed, and one of them having seen that he was healed did turn back, with a loud voice glorifying God, and he fell upon his face at his feet, giving thanks to him, and he was a Samaritan.*
*And Jesus answering said, "Were not the ten cleansed, and the nine are where? There were not found who did turn back to give glory to God, except this stranger;" and he said to him, "Having risen, be going on, your faith has saved you."*
*Another clue to connect Simon Magus (Lazarus) to a leper, although clearly an in-joke since Simon's excommunication took him to exclusion; but, after Jesus raised him, he moved up to level 10. The reason why 9 lepers did not turn back to thank Jesus was that there were not any in the first place!*

## Chapter 38a. (December 32AD)
## The Excommunication of Simon as Lazarus

*November 32AD (Feast of the Dedication) John 10:22 "It was the the Dedications at Jerusalem (Qumran). It was winter."*

Magdalene and Jesus are in their nuptials in bed at Ein Feshkha. Mary is rubbing myrrh over Jesus' naked body.

Helena is shouting from outside, "You must save Simon right now, he is as good as dead." *Jesus quickly puts on his robe and comes to the door.*

*Helena, Simon Magus' consort, being 'Martha' in charge of the 'Marys', is in tears as she stands there.* "I saw them roll the round stone, closing the priest's cave (#4), south of the monastery. True it is just an excommunication, but he could suffocate."

Magdalene appears and joins them at the door looking at Jesus lovingly, "What will you do, we all love him?"

"I am sorry Helena, my hands are tied, I do not have a high enough level to remove his excommunication; I must wait to see if Father Jonathan acts. This is a delicate situation. Caiaphas is out for blood, but I promise you I will not let him die."

"Thank you, Jesus, I apologize for the interruption."

*John 11:1-5,18,19,21-23,28,29,33-35,38-40,43,44 And there was a certain one ailing, Lazarus, from Bethany, of the village of Mary and Martha her sister (and it was Mary who did anoint the Lord with ointment, and did wipe his feet with her hair, whose brother Lazarus was ailing) therefore sent the sisters unto him, saying, "Sir, lo, he whom you do love is ailing;" and Jesus having heard, said, "This ailment is not unto death, but for the glory of God, that the Son of God may be glorified through it." And Jesus was loving Martha, and her sister, and Lazarus.*

*Bethany (Ain Feshkha) was near to Jerusalem(Qumran), about fifteen furlongs off (3 hours walk), and many of the Jews had come unto Martha and Mary, that they might comfort them concerning their brother; Martha, therefore, said unto Jesus, "Sir, if you had been here, my brother had not died; but even now, I have known that whatever you may ask of God, God will give to you;" Jesus said to her, "Your brother shall rise again." And these things having said, she went away, and called Mary her sister privately, saying, "The Teacher is present, and does call you;" she, when she heard, rises up quickly, and does come to him; ...Jesus, therefore, when he saw her weeping, and the Jews who came with her weeping, did groan in the spirit, and troubled himself, and he said, "Where have you laid him? "They say to him, "Sir, come and see;" (SM 2.26a Jesus went with her to the garden where the tomb was.) Jesus wept. Jesus, therefore, again groaning in himself, comes to the tomb, and it was a cave, and a stone was lying upon it,*

*(SM 2.26, SM 3.1,2 **immediately a great sound was heard from the tomb**,) Jesus said, "Take you away the stone;" The sister of him who has died -- Martha -- said to him, "Sir, already he stinks, for he is four days dead;" Jesus said to her, "did I not tell you, that if you may believe, you shall see the glory of God?" and Jesus, going toward it rolled away the stone from the entrance to the tomb.) And these things saying, with a loud voice he cried out, "Lazarus, come forth;" and he who died came forth, being bound feet and hands with grave-clothes, and his visage with a napkin was bound about; Jesus said to them, "Loose him, and suffer to go."*

*(SM 3.04-10 Then, the man looked at him and loved him and he began to call him to his side, that he might be with him. And going from the tomb, they went to the house of the young man. For he was rich. And after six days, Jesus instructed him. And when it was late, the young man went to him. He had put a linen around his naked body (loincloth), and he remained with him through that night. For Jesus taught him the mystery of the kingdom of God.)*

# Chapter 38b. December 32AD
## Removing the Excommunication of Simon as Lazarus

On the morning of the fourth day, Mary jumps out of bed saying to Jesus, "If you won't do anything. I am going to the Cave to roll away the stone myself."

Jesus replies, "Mary, you do you want my head to be delivered to you on a platter? I am going today."

Mary kneels down at the edge of the bed crying, "I am sorry, my Teacher. I could not live without you."

*Below the cave crowds have gathered.* One asks, "How can a body that has been dead for four days be raised?" Another says, "They say he brought back his brother to life at Nain and Jarius' daughter, but they were only dead for less than a day."

Jesus approaches the cave, a voice inside in a muffled groan says, "Jesus, you're late!" *The people look around wondering who said this.*

With tears in his eyes, Jesus rolls the stone back, saying in a loud voice, "Arise, my dear friend, you are raised from excommunication. I had hoped that Jonathan would release you, and now I will be a dead man, too."
*Simon appears looking like a corpse.*

Martha kisses Simon, saying, "Thank God you are alive, but you stink to the high heaven."

*The crowds cheer as he is helped down the hill.*

# SECTION 5 (March 33AD)
## Month before the Last Supper

Mattias Stom (1600-1652)

*Matt 16:13-15 And Jesus, having come to the parts of Caesarea Philippi, was asking his disciples, saying, "Who do men say me to be -- the Son of Man?" Matt 16:14 And they said, "Some, John the Baptist, and others, Elijah, and others, Jeremiah, or one of the prophets." Matt 16:15 He said to them, " and you -- who do you say me to be?"*

*John 6:69 Simon Peter, therefore, answered him, "you are the Holy One of God." (ἅγιος θεοῦ)*
*Mark 8:29 Peter answering said to him, "You are the Christ." (χριστός)*
*Luke 9:20 Peter answering said, "The Christ of God." (χριστὸν θεοῦ*
*Matt 16:16 And Simon Peter answering said, "You are the Christ, the Son of the living God." (χριστὸς υἱὸς θεοῦ ζῶντος)*

*DSS Messianic Rule 2.19 "And when they shall gather for the common table to eat and to drink new wine ... let no man extend his hand over the firstfruits of bread and wine before the Priest (the Messiah of Aaron), for it is he who shall bless the wine and bread. Thereafter the Messiah of Israel shall extend his hand over the bread..."*

*Matt 20:20,21 Then came near to him the mother of the sons of Zebedee, with her sons, bowing and asking something from him, and he said to her, "What will you?" She said to him, "Say, that they may sit -- these my two sons -- one on your right hand, and one on the left, in your Kingdom."*

*Matt 7:24-26 "Therefore, everyone who does hear of me these words, and does do them, I will liken him to a wise man who built his house upon the rock; and the rain did descend, and the streams came, and the winds blew, and they beat on that house, and it fell not, for it had been founded on the rock. And everyone who is hearing of me these words, and is not doing them, shall be likened to a foolish man who built his house upon the sand;*

*John 15:20 "Remember the word that I said to you, A servant is not greater than his lord;*

*Matt 22:41,42 And the Pharisees having been gathered together, Jesus did question them saying, "What do you think concerning the Christ? Of whom is he son?" They say to him, "Of David."*

*Psalm 110:1 The LORD says to David: "Sit at my right hand till I make your enemies your footstool."*

# Chapter 39. (February 33AD)
## Upon the rock of Peter; James and John in Glory

Jesus asks the disciples, "Who do you think I am?"

Peter says, "You are the Christ, the anointed one of David, the Son of the Living God thus the Messiah of Israel under the Father, the Messiah of Aaron."

Jesus says, "Rightly spoken. You are Petros, and upon this 'petra'; I will build my Church."

*The disciples begin to argue among themselves, being envious of Peter.*

Helena asks, "Since you have promoted Peter, can my step-sons James and John sit on your right hand and left hand, to sit in your glory?"

Jesus says, "You are all confused. I only used a 'Janus Parallelism':

> For instance (Solomon's Song 2:12) 'Blossoms appear on the earth; the time of **ezmir** has arrived; The voice of the turtledove is heard in the land.' *('ezmir' has two meanings: that of 'pruning' belongs to the first phrase and that of 'singing' applies to the last)*
> And thus: 'You are Πέτρος *(Peter: Firstborn)* and upon this '**petra**', I will build my Church'."

"I also used the double meaning of 'petra'. My meaning is that my Church would be built on a firm foundation. It is not to be one person, for all my disciples share equally in it."

Peter says, "So I am your rock then!"

Jesus is frustrated, "So be it."

*Matt 26:3-5 Then were gathered together the chief priests, and the scribes, and the elders of the people, to the court of the chief priest who was called Caiaphas; and they consulted together that they might take Jesus by guile, and kill him, and they said, "Not in the feast, that there may not be a tumult among the people."*
*John 11:48 if we may let him alone thus, all will believe in him; and the Romans will come, and will take away both our place and nation."*
*John 11:53-57 From that day, therefore, they took counsel together that they may kill him; Jesus, therefore, was no more freely walking among the Jews, but went away thence to the region near the wilderness, to a city called Ephraim, and there he tarried with his disciples. And the Passover of the Jews was near, and many went up to Jerusalem(Qumran) out of the country before the Passover, that they might purify themselves; they were seeking, therefore, Jesus, and said one with another, standing in the temple, "What does appear to you -- that he may not come to the feast?" And both the chief priests and the Pharisees had given a command, that if anyone may know where he is, he may show it, so that they may seize him.*
*John 12:9-11 A great multitude, therefore, of the Jews knew that he is there, and they came, not because of Jesus only, but that Lazarus also they may see, whom he raised out of the dead; and the chief priests took counsel, that also Lazarus they may kill, because on account of him many of the Jews were going away, and were believing in Jesus.*

*Luke 22:3 And the Satan entered into Judas,*
*Matt 26:14-16 Then one of the twelve, who is called Judas Iscariot, having gone unto the chief priests, said, "What are you willing to give me, and I will deliver him up to you?" and they weighed out to him thirty pieces of silver, and from that time he was seeking a convenient season to deliver him up."*

*H.2.23 There was one John, a day-baptist, who was also, according to the method of combination, the forerunner of our Lord Jesus; and as the Lord had twelve apostles, bearing the number of the twelve months of the sun, so also he, John, had thirty chief men, fulfilling the monthly reckoning of the moon's cycle (triacontad), in which number was a woman, being half a man, made up the imperfect of 29 and one-half days ... was a certain woman called Helena.*

# Chapter 40. (March 33AD)
## Judas and the 30 pieces of silver

At the Sanhedrin, Caiaphas speaks, "Clearly Jesus has convicted himself by aiding Simon Magus. Now we have two that would be better off dead. Maybe we can get Pilate to crucify them as enemies of Rome."

Nicodemus stands up to leave, "Pilate will never come to Qumran. It is absurd!" and turning, "Joseph of Arimathea are you following me?" *James stays.*

Judas Iscariot enters and speaks, "On Thursday, Jesus and Simon will be at Qumran, the purer Jerusalem-in-exile for the Sacred Supper. It is a day early for Passover because Jesus intends to go to monastery on the next day and also less risk of being found out. I can leave the Sacred Super early and alert the temple guards and lead them to Jesus and Simon. At midnight they will be in the Garden of Gethsemane where they can be arrested and tried by your Council before dawn on the day of Passover, ready to be tried by Pilate."

Caiaphas says, "Yes, we could entice Pilate by offering him Simon and pretend to offer Nicodemus (who is really Theudas Barabbas) who are wanted by Pilate having been responsible for the recent riot that resulted in Roman deaths. Then we could trade Jesus for Barabbas. If Pilate leaves at morning light by horseback, he can be at Qumran by morning."

Judas says, "I do not ask for a reward of treasure, just to have John the Baptist's position as the silver moon's cycle of 30 members."
"It is yours."

*1Kings 01:28-34* 28 Then king David answered, "Call to me Bathsheba." She came into the king's presence and stood before the king. The king swore, and said, "As Yahweh lives, who has redeemed my soul out of all adversity, most certainly as I swore to you by Yahweh, the God of Israel, saying, -Assuredly Solomon your son shall reign after me, and he shall sit on my throne in my place;- most certainly so will I do this day." Then Bathsheba bowed with her face to the earth, and did obeisance to the king, and said, "Let my lord king David live forever!" King David said, "Call to me Zadok the priest, Nathan the prophet, and Benaiah the son of Jehoiada." They came before the king. The king said to them, "Take with you the servants of your lord, and cause Solomon, my son, to ride on my own mule, and bring him down to Gihon. Let Zadok the priest and Nathan the prophet anoint him there king over Israel. Blow the trumpet, and say, -Long live king Solomon!
*2Kings 09:13* And they haste and take each his garment, and put it under him at the top of the stairs, and blow with a trumpet, and say, `Reigned hath Jehu!'
*Matt 21:1,2;6-9* And when they came near to Jerusalem(Qumran), and came to Bethphage, unto the mount of the Olives, then Jesus sent two disciples, saying to them, "Go on to the village opposite you, and immediately you shall find an ass bound, and a colt with her.
*John 12:14* and Jesus having found a young ass did sit upon it, according as it is written,
And the disciples having gone and having done as Jesus commanded them, brought the ass and the colt, and did put on them their garments, and set upon them; and the very great multitude spread their own garments in the way, and others were cutting branches from the trees, and were strewing in the way, and the multitudes who were going before, and who were following, were crying, saying, "Hosanna to the Son of David, blessed is he who is coming in the name of the Lord; Hosanna in the highest."

## Chapter 41. (March 33AD)
## Jesus rides a donkey into Jerusalem

Agrippa stopping Jesus at the Queen's house, says, "As you know I intend to be King over the kingdom of Herod the Great. I have been advised that in 1st & 2nd Kings, David had his son Solomon ride on a donkey up to Jerusalem. I want to reenact that pageant in hopes to further my goal. It is the Qumran followers that I need to impress."

Jesus says, "I have no desire to be a king such as David, my subjects are of the Spirit, not the earth."

"You can have their Spirits, but it is their adulation that I seek. You should be glad that I am willing to share it with you, I have procured a young donkey colt for you to ride with me."

"I am sorry, but I must refuse."

Agrippa says, "You need to take this as a command or perhaps you should ask John the Baptist's head about the power of my command."

"So you were responsible for his death!"

*Agrippa mounts the donkey and Jesus the colt. As they ride, the people throw palm leaves and cloaks in their path. When they dismount, Jesus disappears into the crowd.*

*(No conception winter of 30AD; second try November 31AD)*
*Luke 10:38-42 And it came to pass, in their going on, that he entered into a certain village, and a certain woman, by name Martha (Helena), did receive him into her house, and she had also a sister, called Mary, who also, having seated herself beside the feet of Jesus, was hearing the word, and Martha was distracted about much serving, and having stood by him, she said, "Sir, do you not care that my sister left me alone to serve? say then to her, that she may partake along with me." And Jesus answering said to her, "Martha, Martha, you are anxious and disquieted about many things, but of one thing there is need of, and Mary the good part did choose, that shall not be taken away from her."*

*(March 33AD Mary announces that she is three months pregnant)*
*John 12:1-8 Jesus, therefore, six days before the Passover, came to Bethany, where was Lazarus, who had died, whom he raised out of the dead; they made, therefore, to him a supper there, and Martha (Helena) was ministering, and Lazarus was one of those reclining together (at dinner) with him;*
*Mark 14:3 And he, being in Bethany, in the house of **Simon the leper**, at his reclining (at dinner), there came a woman having an alabaster box of ointment, of spikenard, very precious, and having broken the alabaster box, did pour on his head*

*SM 3.14-16 And the sister (Magdalene) of the young man whom Jesus loved (Lazarus) was there, as well as his mother and Salome (Helena).*

*Mary, therefore, having taken a pound of ointment of spikenard, of great price, anointed the feet of Jesus and did wipe with her hair (head scarf) his feet, and the house was filled with the fragrance of the ointment.*
*Therefore said one of his disciples -- Judas Iscariot, of Simon, who is about to deliver him up -- "Therefore was not this ointment sold for three hundred denaries, and given to the poor?" and he said this, not because he was caring for the poor, but because he was a thief, and had the bag, and what things were put in he was carrying. (In charge of the convent funds.) Jesus, therefore, said, "Suffer her; for the day of my embalming (returning to monastery) she has kept it, for the poor you have always with yourselves, and me you have not always."*

# Chapter 42. (March 33AD)
## Mary Magdalene announces their child

*At the house of Simon (Lazarus), Helena (Martha), and Jesus are seated.* Magdalene stands in front of Jesus, saying "Remember the second time we tried for a child in November 31AD when Helena said that I should be helping out rather than sulking and now it is three months from last December and this was the last time that it will be allowed."

*Magdalene kneels at Jesus' feet and begins to wash his feet and anoint them with spikenard from an alabaster jar using her head scarf.*

Then after a time, she looks up to Jesus, saying, "Are you surprised yet?"

Jesus says, "Oh Holy God, you are carrying our child, aren't you!"

"Yes, my Teacher." She stands exposing her belly and Jesus kisses her belly, saying, "Hello, my little Jesus."

Judas mutters, "What a waste of precious ointment."

# SECTION 6 (8AM to 10PM Thursday, April 2, 33AD)
## The Last Supper (Sacrament 8PM to 9PM)

*(Last Passover #4)*
*Matt 26:2 "You have known that after two days the Passover takes place, and the Son of Man is delivered up to be crucified."*
*Mark 14:1 And the Passover and the unleavened food were after two days*
*Luke 22:1 And the feast of the unleavened food was coming near, that is called Passover*
*John 11:55 "And the Jewish Passover was near."*

Ducio (1308-1311)

*The imagined Heavenly Man on the vestry floor*

| | | | | | |
|---|---|---|---|---|---|
| | | | | | 5 |
| | | Mind Soul | | | 6 |
| Guest Pillar | Eyes | Nose Ears Mouth | | Guest Pillar | 7 |
| | | Neck | | | 8 |
| | | | | | 9 |
| | | Chest Heart Strength Bosom | | | 10 |
| | | | | | 11 |
| | | Loins Belly | | | 12 |
| Dais | | Testicles Earth | | Dais | |
| Step | | | | Step | 13 |
| | | | | | 14 |
| | | | | | 15 |
| | | | | | 16 |
| | | | | | 17 |
| | | Sea | | | 18 |

The upper room of the Last Supper (101) at Qumran was in the north area of the vestry, it was raised from the lower section (102) at the step at row 13. Laid out on the floor was an imagined Heavenly Man/Woman complete with eyes, ears, breast/chest, with belly (womb) and stones (testicles). It was numbered in rows starting at the bottom of row 18 called the Sea where there was a door then up to row 13 where there was a step called the Earth up to a raised area. Each square is a cubit (the length of an arm: 1.5 ft). The Table was assembled in two rows 8 and 9. There were six seats on each side: the lower side (Row 10); the upper side (row 7; row 6: the two leaders: Simon & Jonathan; row 5: (Herod King if present, supposedly like God): Herod the Great; the tetrarchs: Archelaus, Antipas, & Philip; Herod Agrippa I&II.) The upper floor, held up by two pillars would be where leaders would stand on row 7 & 6 & 5, but for purposes of the Holy Supper, they used the lower floor.

Mark 14:13-15 *And he sends forth two of his disciples, and said to them, "Go to the city; there meet you a man bearing a pitcher of water; he will show you a large upper room, furnished, prepared."*

# Chapter 43a (Thursday, April 2, 33AD)
## Finding the location

*The raised north floor area of the vestry (101) is the what was used for the Last Supper.*

Jesus says to twins James and John, "This being our last Passover together before I enter the monastery, we should all spend it together. We need to do it in secret because Caiaphas will be looking to arrest Simon and me and, obviously, we cannot invite Herod Antipas to be in the King position or it will be John the Baptist all over again."

John Aquila asks, "Will Simon be there?"
"Yes, he told me he would meet us in disguise as the man with a water jar (Aquarius: position 11 in the disciples list). Since Simon is only an initiate having been excommunicated as Lazarus, I will be taking his position and Joses will take my position as crown prince. Ever since the Pool of Bethesda, I have distrusted my unjust brother James."

James Niceta says, "I will check, but the vestry area at Qumran should be available on our Passover since it will be the day before the Pharisees."
*The 13 are welcomed in by the man with a water jar.*

*Normal Holy Table seating (pillars cause guest to move to arrow positions. Guests: Joses, Jesus' crown prince & Thomas, honorary King)*

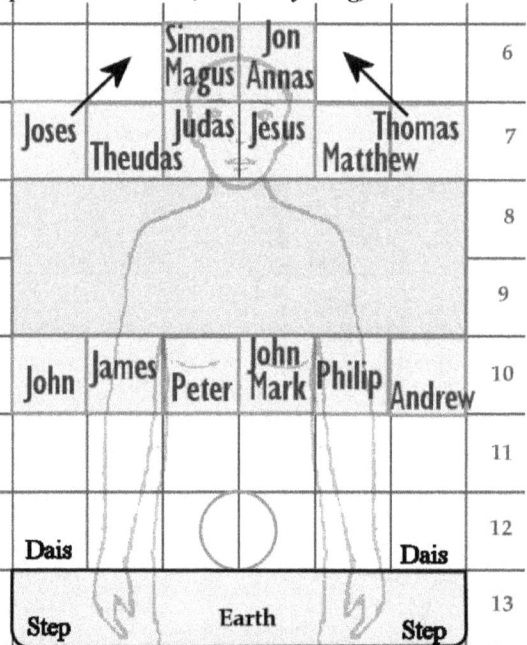

Dead Sea Scrolls:1Q28a/1QSa "This is the rule for all the congregation of Israel in the last days ... The Priest-Messiah shall come ... and the Messiah of Israel shall come ... And when they shall gather for the common table, to eat and to drink new wine, when the common table shall be set for eating and the new wine poured for drinking, let no man extend his hand over the firstfruits of bread and wine before the Priest; for it is he who shall bless the firstfruits of bread and wine, and shall be the first to extend his hand over the bread. Thereafter, the Messiah of Israel shall extend his hand over the bread, and all the congregation of the Community shall utter a blessing, each man in the other of his dignity. It is according to this statute that they shall proceed at every meal at which at least ten men are gathered together."

John 13:1,3-6,8 And before the feast of the Passover, Jesus, knowing that his hour has come, that he may remove out of this world unto the Father *(returning to monastery)*, having loved his own who are in the world; knowing that all things the Father *(Jonathan)* has given to him into his hands, and that from God *(in the monastery)* he came forth, and unto God he goes, does rise from the supper, and does lay down his garments, and having taken a towel, girded himself. Afterwards, he puts water into the basin, and began to wash the feet of his disciples and to wipe with the towel with which he was girded. Coming to Peter, who says, "You may not wash my feet until the age *(Restoration)*." Jesus answered him, "If I may not wash you, you have no part with me"

## Chapter 43b. (Thursday, April 2, 33AD 6PM)
## Washing the feet of the disciples

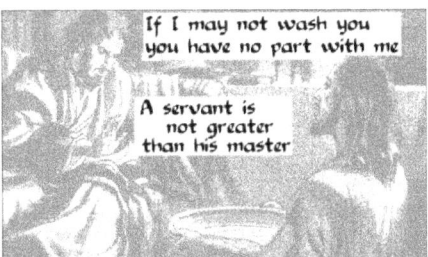

*The Holy Table has been prepared. Jesus and the disciples are sitting in the raised section of the vestry.*

Jesus says, "In preparing for the promised Restoration, I will act as Moses who spoke to the 'I am', Yahweh, in the burning bush. I affirm to you my disciples, the sent ones, that you also have received this promise from 'I am' through me."

*Jesus takes off his robe, and in his loincloth, he takes a towel and a basin of water and begins to wash the disciple's feet.*

Peter says, "It is I who should be washing your feet."

Jesus says, "You are misunderstanding my lesson that by washing your feet, I am demonstrating that in this new world to come, there will be no servants or masters because all will be equal."

Peter says, "Then wash also my hands and head."

*The other disciples move their chairs closer to be washed.*

*Holy Table seating due to the excommunication of Simon Magus; Jesus takes Simon's place; Simon is to his right as a guest; Joses, crown prince, takes Jesus' seat (Jesus is son of Jonathan)*

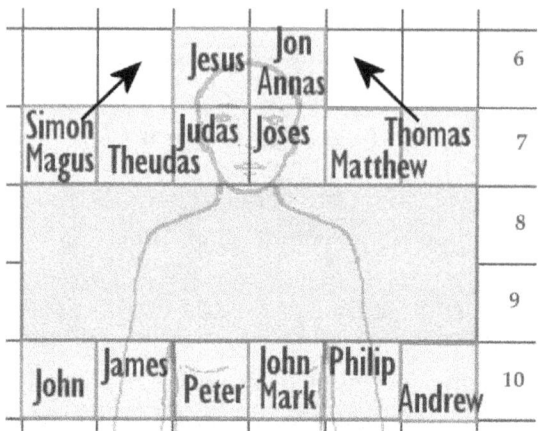

*John 13:21,26b,27* These things having said, Jesus was troubled in the spirit (sad that it was his last time with the disciples before returning to monastery), and did testify, and said, "Verily, verily, I say to you, that one of you will 'beside-give for me' (translators, knowing that Judas betrayed Jesus, used 'betrayed' ('paradōsei'), but the roots of the word are 'para' meaning 'beside' and 'didōmi' meaning to beside-give, thus in religious terms to act beside me as my servant thus announcing that Judas will not get Simon's seat as might be expected and will remain in his usual place as 'son of Simon'. (Simon's rank is now only initiate, having been excommunicated as Lazarus, and is only eligible to be a guest with Jesus filling in for him, next to Jonathan.) Thus Jesus having dipped the morsel from half the loaf, gives it to Judas (Iscariot). Clearly by the tone, the disciples resented that Judas would be Jesus' second, but Jesus' crown prince Joses (James having been passed over previously) has the honor of taking Jesus' normal place as 'son of Jonathan'.
And after having received the morsel, then the Satan ("Satan the tester" and "having the bag" in charge of the money are already his nicknames used to embellish), that one immediately went forth, and it was night.
(Theudas moves over to Judas' place as "son of" Jesus thus at discussion time: *John 14:22* "Judas (not Iscariot) said to him, ...";
The rest of the morsels are distributed, but next is the reseating discussion where the "Is it I" questions apply. (The transposition in time editing was to prove that Jesus had foreknowledge, but he did not.)
"What you do; do quickly." (applies to the reseating, not to Judas)

# Chapter 43c. (Thursday, April 2, 33AD 8PM)
## The Sacrament; Judas leaves

*Thursday (Day before Good Friday, the Day of Preparation) April 2, 33AD 8 PM. Having taken their seats, Jesus said to them:*

*"I am the bread of the life; he who is coming unto me may not hunger, and he who is believing in me may not thirst -- at any time; but I said to you, that you also have seen me, and you believe not; all that the Father does give to me will come unto me; and him who is coming unto me, I may in no wise cast without, because I have come down from the heaven, not that do my will, but the will of Him who sent me"*

*"Verily, verily, I say to you, If you may not eat the flesh of the Son of Man, and may not drink his blood, you have no life in you; He who is eating my flesh, and is drinking my blood, has eternal life, and I will raise him up at the last day; for my flesh truly is food, and my blood truly is drink; he who is eating my flesh, and is drinking my blood, does remain in me, and I in him." (John 6:35-38, 53-55)*

*And I say to you, "That henceforth from this day, we shall not be drinking this produce of the vine, until that day when we may drink it with you new in God's Kingdom in the Restoration." (Matt 26:29)*

Jesus and Father Jonathan each break off 1/6 of his half loaf as Jesus says, "I am the bread of the life so that he who is coming unto me may not hunger and my blood in the wine is so you will not thirst and to have eternal life in the Resurrection and now I beside-give the rest of the loaf to Judas and my cup to distribute to the right of him." *Judas takes his 1/6, dips it in the cup, and passes it to Theudas, then abruptly leaves. All are astonished.*

Jesus says, "Let us bring this ceremony to a conclusion with all haste." *Theudas, who has temporarily moved over to Judas' seat as Jesus' assistant, reaches across to Peter who gives to James and John, who walks around to Simon. Father Jonathan completes his side, to Joses, who gives to Matthew, who reaches across to John Mark, who gives to Philip and Andrew, then around to Thomas. And they sing a hymn. (Mark 14:26)*

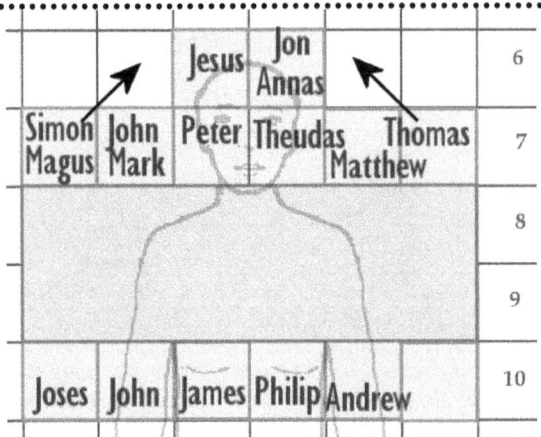

*John 14:22 Judas said to him, (not the Iscariot) ... (This defines Theudas during discussion time who was briefly sitting in Judas' place below Jesus after he left, but was moved over to the seat below Jonathan during discussion time.)*

*Matt 26:22b And began every one of them to say, 'is it I, Lord"*
*Luke 22:22-26,36b,38 And indeed the Son of Man (Judas' position) does go according to what has been determined, but Woe to that man through whom he acts beside as a servant." And they began to reason among themselves, who then of them it may be, who is about to do this thing. And there happened also a strife among them -- who of them is accounted to be greater. And he said to them, "The kings of the nations do exercise lordship over them, and those exercising authority upon them are called benefactors; but you are not so. He who is greater among you: let him be as the younger; and he who is leading, as he who is ministering; ... and he who is not having (scrip), let him sell his garment, and buy a sword ... And they said, "Sir, lo, here are two swords; (Peter and John Mark)" and he said to them, "It is sufficient." (meaning "that is enough - be quiet") Matt 26:25 And -- Theudas who is in Judas Iscariot beside-give position answering said, "Is it I, Rabbi?" He said to him, "You have said. (meaning "your opinion is noted")*

*John 13:23-25,36b,38 And there was one of his disciples (John Mark) reclining (at dinner) in the bosom of Jesus (at the square of the Heavenly Man representing "bosom"), whom Jesus was loving; Simon Peter, then, does beckon to this one, to inquire who he may be concerning whom he speaks, and that one having leant back on the breast of Jesus, responds to him, "Sir, who is it?" Peter and John Mark fighting over #1 as in the 153 fish section (John 21:1-11).*

# Chapter 43d. (Thursday, April 2, 33AD 9PM)
## Musical Chairs at Discussion Time

Thomas says, "Since Judas is in charge of the Church money did he go out to get supplies for the poor outside?"

Simon says, 'There is treachery here. Leaving is forbidden; not even for the Salt latrine."

*The disciples start to squabble amongst themselves as to where they are to be reseated.*

Theudas says, "Since Judas gave me the loaf, can I stay in Judas' seat?"
Jesus disagrees, "No, that should be one of my two swords of the Garden of Eden, either Peter or John Mark."

John Mark says, "Should it be me as the stand-in for Magdalene at the female bosom square?"
Peter says, "Should it be me at the male breast square, who declared you to be the Christ?"

Jesus says, "Jonathan, can Theudas take my usual position?" He nods.
Jesus says "Here is my final seating plan:

*Theudas will move over below Jonathan, Peter will sit in Judas' seat below me with John Mark to his right. James Niceta and John Aquila will move to their right opening up a seat for Joses. James is then opposite Peter. Philip and Andrew will move to their left with Philip opposite Theudas. I, Jesus, represents the 'Kingdom'; Jonathan represents the 'Power'; Peter and Theudas share in the 'Glory'.*

Let us quiet down and be reseated for my sermon on 'Loving Your Enemies'."

*Loving Your Enemies Matt 5:43-48 "You heard that it was said: You should love your neighbor, and hate your enemy; but I say to you, Love your enemies, bless those who curse you, do good to those who hate you, and pray for those who accuse and persecute you falsely that you may be sons of your heavenly Father. In this world there is evil and good; people are righteous and unrighteous. If you love those who love you, what reward have you? Do not the priests also do the same? And if you greet only your brothers and sisters, what is exceptional about that? Do not the pagans also do the same? Rather, you should strive for perfection because your Father in heaven is perfect."*

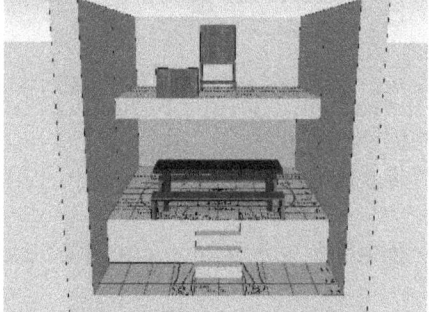

*The vestry showing the upper level floor where the leaders would stand during the service. The two pillar seats hold up its south edge.*

At midnight Jesus' Essene day loses 3 hours to adjust to the Jewish Calendar; this does not happen until noon for Caiaphas' day

**Correct statement 2 cock crows - 3 denies (missing hours)**

Matt 26:34 "ere the cock crow thrice you will be renouncing me."

wrong: 3 crock crowswrong: 1 deny

Mark 14:30 "before a cock shall crow twice, three times you shall deny me."

right: 2 cock crowsright: 3 denies

Luke 22:34 "a cock shall not crow to-day, before thrice you may disown knowing me."

almost right: 1 cock crow afterright: 3 denies

John 13:38 "a cock will not crow till you may deny me thrice."

almost right: 1 cock crow afterright: 3 denies

# Chapter 43e. (Thurs, April 2, 33AD 9:45 PM)
## The cock will crow twice, three hours denied (12 midnight=3AM)

Jesus says, "It is now time for discussion. As you know, I have conceived a child and will be returning to monastery. Since you will not be able to see me very often, I want to expand on the first commandment that I gave to you:

> *I bid you love one another as I love you. This love is more than 'phileo' love that seeks to have love returned, but rather it is 'agapé' love that is given freely from the heart. When we greet each other with a kiss on the mouth, we share the breath of the Word which fills the heart." (John 21)*

Philip says, "We wish that we could kiss you always in the marriage of Christ." Peter says, "Let me follow you even to monastery." Jesus replies, "Not while you are married. And Peter; let me tell you before the cock crows twice, you will deny me thrice."

Peter says, "I catch your humor, Master. It is not my fault that, as the cock crow-er for three in the morning, when midnight is called, I will immediately call the hour of three, stealing three hours."

> *Matthew asks, "It is three cock crows for one hour?" John Mark says, "No I think the cock will not crow at all until three hours?"*
> *Thomas says, "This is boggling my mind."*
> *Simon explains, "This is an attempt to synchronize the Essene clock with the luna clock of the Baptist. What is important here is that we will adjust at midnight, but Pharisees will wait until noon."*

## SECTION 7 (10PM, Thursday to 8:15AM, Friday, April 3, 33AD) Counter-plot, Arrest, and Trial

William_Hole (1846–1917)

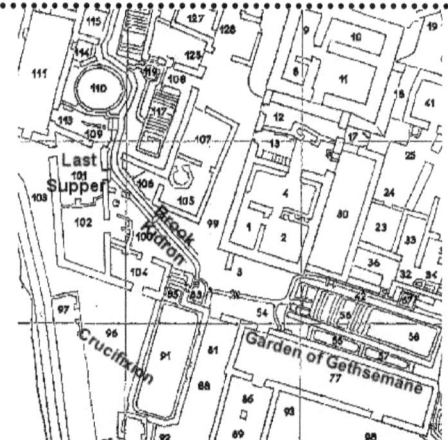

*Matt 26:30,36,37* They went forth to the mount of the Olives (beyond the brook of Kedron *John 18:1*). Then does Jesus, having taken Peter, and the two sons of Zebedee, come with to a place called Gethsemane, and he said to the disciples, "Sit you here, till having gone away, I shall pray yonder." He began to be sorrowful, and to be very heavy;

*Luke 22:43,44* And there appeared to him an angel from heaven strengthening him; and having been in agony, he was more earnestly praying, and his sweat became, as it were, great drops of blood falling upon the ground.

*Matt 26:38-42,45,46* Then said he to them, "Exceedingly sorrowful is my soul -- unto death; abide you here, and watch with me." And having gone forward a little, he fell on his face, praying, and saying, "My Father, if it be possible, **let this cup pass from me**; nevertheless, not my will but yours."

And he comes unto the disciples, and finds them sleeping (in meditation), and he said to Peter, "So! You were not able one hour to (keep) watch with me! Watch, and pray, that you may not enter into temptation: the spirit indeed is forward, but the flesh weak. Again, a second time, having gone away, he prayed, saying, "My Father, if this cup cannot pass away from me except I drink it, Your will be done;" then comes he unto his disciples, and said to them, "Sleep on and rest!

Lo, the hour has come near, and the Son of Man is delivered up to the hands of sinners. Rise, let us go; lo, he has come near who is delivering me up." (Judas who was my assistant at the Holy Supper.)

# Chapter 44. (Thursday, April 2, 33AD 10PM)
## Garden of Gethsemane

*The service was over at 10 pm. Jesus leaves with the disciples going over the aqueduct to the olive garden Gethsemane. The plot of Judas is revealed to them and that Pilate is coming in the morning.*

As they walk to the garden, Simon says, "Pilate has already made it known that he wants Simon Magus and Theudas for sedition. He will certainly crucify both of us."

Theudas says, "I have a poison that simulates death. By taking it on the cross, Pilate might take us down before we die."

Simon says, "The three-hour time advance would shorten the time. Let us draw up a plan."
*He leaves with the others.*

*Jesus, Peter, James, John, and Jonathan are in the garden.* Father Jonathan calls Jesus aside, "I am afraid that your uncle Theudas is too old to survive crucifixion. Would you consider taking his place?"

Jesus looks faint, "Father, do not ask me to do this. The spirit is willing but the flesh is weak. Cannot this cup pass from me? But if it is your will."

Returning to the disciples, Jesus says, "The soldiers are coming to arrest me for trial."

The disciples say, "But why would they take you?"
Jesus says, "Remain in your slumbers! Caiaphas wants me dead."

*Mark 14:43-46,48,49 And immediately -- while he is yet speaking -- comes near Judas, one of the twelve, and with him a great multitude, with swords and sticks, from the chief priests, and the scribes, and the elders; and he, who is delivering him up, had given a token to them, saying, "Whomsoever I shall kiss, he it is; lay hold on him, and lead him away safely," and having come, immediately, having gone near him, he said, "Rabbi, Rabbi," and kissed him. And they laid on him their hands, and kept hold on him; And Jesus answering said to them, "As against a robber you came out, with swords and sticks, to take me! daily I was with you in the temple teaching, and you did not lay hold on me -- but that the Writings may be fulfilled (using the code line for poison in Psalm 22)."*

*John 18:10,11 Simon Peter, therefore, having a sword, drew it, and struck the chief priest's servant, and cut off his right ear (symbol for spokesman having replaced Jesus on the right side) -- and the name of the servant was Malchus ('Melek' meaning king - thus it is Jesus' young brother James) -- Jesus, therefore, said to Peter, "Put the sword into the sheath; the cup that the Father has given to me, may I not drink it? (It is my fate.)"*

*Mark 14:50-52 And having left him they all fled; and a certain young man (same as young man in tomb: Lazarus, Simon Magus - SM 3.04-10; 3.14-16) was following him, having put a linen cloth about his naked body, and the young men lay hold on him, and he, having left the linen cloth, did flee from them naked.*

*John 18:12 The band, therefore, and the captain, and the officers of the Jews, took hold on Jesus, and bound him.*

# Chapter 45. (Friday, April 3, 33AD midnight)
## (Passover)
## The Arrest

The group of soldiers from Caiaphas arrive with Judas saying, "Teacher" and kissing Jesus on the mouth.

Jesus says, "How is it now that you act as my disciple when clearly you had issues with me. Why did you not speak of them?"

Peter seeing James (the brother of Jesus) says to him, "I challenge your ability to act in my position as 'ear' and spokesman. It is I, who is the ear and the sword of Jesus."

James laughs, "Better trade your sword for a fish net."

Peter scowls, "Not likely, you will be on your knees praying to be rescued again when I cut off your ear."

Jesus says, "Let it go, I must follow my destiny, whatever it may be."

Simon, seeing that no one is paying attention to him, starts to run away. James, pointing to Simon, shouts, "Soldiers, Arrest that imposter. He thinks himself the Pope but, as excommunicated, he is naked."

*The soldier grabs his linen smock as he struggles to get free. It comes off exposing his loincloth.*

*They bind Jesus and Simon and take them away.*

*The court at Qumran was held in the area north of north wall of the vestry (101) near the fireplace.*

*John 18:13,14,19-23 And they led him away to Ananus first, for he was the father-in-law of Caiaphas, who was chief priest of that year, and Caiaphas was he who gave counsel to the Jews, that it is good for one man to perish for the people. The chief priest, therefore, questioned Jesus concerning his disciples, and concerning his teaching; Jesus answered him, "I speak freely to the world, I did always teach in a synagogue, and in the temple, where the Jews do always come together; and in secret I speak nothing; why me do you question? question those having heard what I speak to them; lo, these have known what I said."*

*And he having said these things, one of the officers standing by did give Jesus a slap, saying, "Thus do you answer the chief priest?" Jesus answered him, "If I speak ill, testify concerning the ill; and if well, why do you smite me?"*

*John 18:24 Ananus then sent him bound to Caiaphas the chief priest. Matt 26:59-62 And the chief priests, and the elders, and all the council, were seeking false witness against Jesus, that they might put him to death, and they did not find; and many false witnesses having come near, they did not find; and at last two false witnesses having come near, said, "This one said, I am able to throw down the sanctuary of God, and after three days to build it." And the chief priest having stood up, said to him, "Nothing you do answer! What do these witness against you?*

*Mark 14:61-65 and he was keeping silent, and did not answer anything. Again the chief priest was questioning him, and said to him, "Are you the Christ -- the Son of the Blessed?"*

*And Jesus said, "I am (the Christ); and hereafter you shall see the Son of Man sitting on the right hand of the power (Psalms 110:01), and coming upon the clouds of heaven (Daniel 07:13)."*

*And the chief priest, having rent his garments, said, "What need have we yet of witnesses? You heard the evil speaking, what appears to you?" and they all condemned him to be worthy of death, and certain ones began to spit on him, and to cover his face, and to buffet him, and to say to him, "Prophesy;" and the officers were striking him with their palms.*

*John 18:28 "They led, therefore, Jesus from Caiaphas to the Praetorium (the praetorium is southeast of the wall of the vestry (102)) ...*

# Chapter 46. (Friday, April 3, 33AD 6AM)
## Trial of Jesus before Ananus and Caiaphas

*The soldiers bring Jesus to court area north of the vestry.*

Jesus says, "I request to speak to Ananus first?"

Ananus arrives and Jesus says, "Your grace, why am I being treated like an enemy of Rome? Your son Jonathan is my Holy Father and I follow his will."

Ananus replies, "Not when you raised Simon Magus from excommunication!"

"Caiaphas enters, "You have become as dangerous as the Baptist. You need to be tried by Pilate for the sake of all our good people. The Sanhedrin has heard witnesses that show that you are guilty of blasphemy and that you will throw down the sanctuary and build it up in three days."

Jesus says, "Since when is blasphemy a capital offense?"

Caiaphas says, "And what do you call claiming that you are the Christ, the Son of the Living God and King of Israel?"

Jesus replies, "David's Psalm (110) declares that my position as the descendent of David is at the right hand of the power of God in the position next to his Glory" and Daniel (7:13) prophesies "the Son of Man will come with the clouds of Heaven"

"This prophecy applies to your brother James, the legitimate David king, not to you. Send him to Pilate at the Praetorium quarter."

*The parable of The Faithful Servant (Mark 13:35 "Watch you, therefore, for you have not known when the lord of the house does come, at even, or at midnight, or at cock-crowing, or at the morning") shows three defined times in the night: midnight, cock-crowing, and morning and since morning is 6 AM, cock-crowing can be assumed to be 3 AM.*

*John 18:15-18,25-27 And following Jesus was Simon Peter, and the other disciple, and that disciple was known to the chief priest, and he entered with Jesus into the hall of the chief priest, John and Peter was standing at the door without, therefore went forth the other disciple who was known to the chief priest (Father Jonathan, brother-in-law, being son of Ananus whose daughter was married to Caiaphas), and he speaks to the female keeping the door (Mary Magdalene being pregnant thus clean of menstruation), and he brought in Peter. (Three denials by Peter are added here due to the literal confusion of the crow-crowing where denials were a metaphor for hours.) Then said the maid keeping the door to Peter, "Are you also of the disciples of this man?" he said, "I am not;" (denial 1) And the servants and the officers were standing, having made a fire of coals, because it was cold, and they were warming themselves, and Peter was standing with them, and warming himself. And Simon Peter was standing and warming himself, they said then to him, "Are you also of his disciples?" he denied, and said, "I am not."(denial 2). One of the servants of the chief priest, being a kinsman of him whose ear Peter cut off (Joses, brother of James), said, "Did not I see you in the garden with him?" John again, therefore, Peter denied, and immediately a cock crew.(denial 3).*

*Matt 26:75 and Peter remembered the saying of Jesus, he having said to him -- "Before cock-crowing, thrice you will deny me;" and having gone without, he did weep bitterly.*

## Chapter 47. (Friday, April 3, 33AD 6:30AM)
## Peter Weeps

*Previously, Peter and Father Jonathan had followed Jesus into the area north of the vestry where the trial was being held.* The doorkeeper Mary Magdalene whispers, "Announce yourselves".

"We are two who you know."

Magdalene says, "Oh, Peter, I thought they arrested you, too?"
Peter says, " Please be quiet, they might be looking for me."
Magdalene asks Peter, "What transpired in the Garden earlier?"
Peter replies, "James has usurped me!" Magdalene says, "That does not bode well for Jesus. It is like my dream."

*Peter walks to the fire pit.*
Standing there is Zacchaeus, the youngest son of Ananus says, "Jesus is certainly innocent under Roman Law? I think I will try to see if Jewish law can save them all."

Peter says to Zacchaeus, "Wasn't that so strange: you announcing the midnight call, while I, at the same second, did the cock-crowing for 3AM?"
Joses says, "Now I understand what Jesus said. You did steal the three hours!"

Peter says, "This night is so unsettling, I could weep, but I will just go and relieve myself at the Salt."

As Jesus is being brought out of the door, Magdalene whispers to him, "It was my dream that your brother James would betray you."

*John 18:28-31* They led, therefore, Jesus from Caiaphas to the Praetorium, and it was early, and they themselves did not enter into the Praetorium, that they might not be defiled, but that they might eat the Passover; Pilate, therefore, went forth unto them, and said, "What accusation do you bring against this man?" they answered and said to him, "If he were not an evil-doer, we had not delivered him to you." Pilate, therefore, said to them, "Take you him and according to your law judge him;" the Jews, therefore, said to him, "It is not lawful to us to put anyone to death;"

*Matt 27:18,19* For Jesus had known that because of envy they had delivered him up. And as Jesus is sitting on the tribunal, his wife (Jesus' wife Mary Magdalene) sent unto him, saying, "Have nothing to do with that righteous one (James the Just), for many things did I suffer today in a dream because of him."

*Luke 23:1,2* And having risen, the whole multitude of them did lead him to Pilate, and began to accuse him, saying, "This one we found perverting the nation and forbidding to give tribute to Caesar, saying himself to be Christ a king."

*John 18:33-38* Pilate, therefore, entered into the Praetorium again, and called Jesus, and said to him, "You are the King of the Jews?" Jesus answered him, "From yourself do you say this? or did others say it to you about me?"
Pilate answered, "Am I a Jew! your nation and the chief priests did deliver you up to me; what did you?"
Jesus answered, "My kingdom is not of this world; if my kingdom were of this world, my officers had struggled that I might not be delivered up to Jews; but now my kingdom is not from hence."
Pilate, therefore, said to him, "Art you then a king?" Jesus answered, "You do say it; because a king I am, I for this have been born, and for this, I have come to the world, that I may testify to the Truth; everyone who is of the Truth, does hear my voice." (The Church of Truth was the original name of the church R.7.29)
Pilate said to him, "What is truth?" and this having said, again he went forth unto the Jews, and said to them, "I do find no fault in him;"

## Chapter 48. (Friday, April 3, 33AD 7AM)
## Trial before Pilate (What is Truth?)

*Pilate has traveled by horse to arrive at dawn on the Jerusalem-Jericho Roman road which is about a 17-mile trip taking about three hours. He takes a seat in the Praetorium.*

Pilate says, "We have already dealt with that magician person Simon, who was guilty of sedition, why is this Jesus being brought in? I have heard that he is also a magician, having raised Simon from the dead, but magic is not a capital offense. What are the charges?"

Caiaphas says, "This one we found perverting the nation and forbidding to give tribute to Caesar."

James says to Pilate, "He helped to kill John the Baptist, the true Abijah priest, and sets himself up as the David king."
Pilate says, "I thought Herod Antipas killed John because his wife told him to." Then turning to Jesus, "Are you really the King of the Jews? I thought the Jews only recognize their priests. They have no respect for me as Prefect."

Jesus answers, "I am not a king of this world, but a king in the Church of Truth."

Pilate says, "How is it possible for a church to be based on truth when all men lie?" Pilate leaves to consult with his advisor."

*Luke 23:5-12 And they were the more urgent, saying -- "He does stir up the people, teaching throughout the whole of Judea -- having begun from Galilee -- unto this place." And Pilate having heard of Galilee, questioned if the man is a Galilean, and having known that he is from the jurisdiction of Herod, he sent him back unto Herod, he being also in Jerusalem in those days.*

*And Herod having seen Jesus did rejoice exceedingly, for he was wishing for a long time to see him, because of hearing many things about him, and he was hoping some sign to see done by him, and was questioning him in many words, and he answered him nothing. And the chief priests and the scribes stood vehemently accusing him, and Herod with his soldiers having set him at naught, and having mocked, having put around him gorgeous apparel, did send him back to Pilate,*

*And both Pilate and Herod became friends on that day with one another, for they were before at enmity between themselves.*

## Chapter 49. (Friday, April 3, 33AD 7:30AM)
### Trial before Agrippa

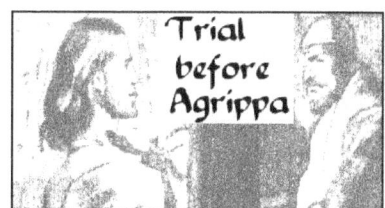

Pilate returns, saying, "I find no fault with this man Jesus."

Wanting to impress Pilate, Agrippa says, "He stirs up the people, teaching throughout the whole of Judea, having come from Galilee, unto Qumran."

Pilate says, "Galilee would be under the jurisdiction of Herod Antipas, is it not? Did not your uncle make you commissioner of markets in Tiberias in Galilee?" "Yes," says Agrippa.

Pilate smiles, "Good then; he is all yours."

Agrippa walks over to Jesus, "I am glad to finally meet you. I hear that you can heal the sick and raise the dead. Would you like to perform one of these feats of magic for us!"

*Jesus just stares at him.*

"You stand accused of being the King of the Jews. That is what I will become one day if my friend, 'Little Boots' becomes emperor."

*Jesus just stares at him.*

"You are not showing me any respect. Can one of the Sadducees lend him a crown of thorns, a purple robe, and the pine cone scepter." *They dress him up.*

"Behold, the king of the Jews!

Pilate comes forward and says, "Agrippa, you have amused me today. Why have we been at enmity, we must dine together."

*Tacitus Annals 15.44 Christus, the founder of the name, had undergone the death penalty in the reign of Tiberius, by sentence of the procurator Pontius Pilatus."*

*Mark 15:12-14 And Pilate answering, again said to them, "What, then, will you that I shall do to him whom you call king of the Jews?" and they again cried out, "Crucify him." And Pilate said to them, "Why -- what evil did he?" and they cried out the more vehemently, "Crucify him;"*

*Matt 27:15-17,20-25 And at the feast the governor had been accustomed to release one to the multitude, a prisoner, whom they willed, and they had then a noted prisoner, called Barabbas, they, therefore, having been gathered together, Pilate said to them, "Whom will you I shall release to you? Barabbas or Jesus who is called Christ?"*

*And the chief priests and the elders did persuade the multitudes that they might ask for themselves Barabbas, and might destroy Jesus; and the governor answering said to them, "Which of the two will you that I shall release to you?" and they said, "Barabbas." Pilate said to them, "What then shall I do with Jesus who is called Christ?" They all say to him, "Let be crucified!"*

*And Pilate having seen that it profits nothing, but rather a tumult is made, having taken water, he did wash the hands before the multitude, saying, "I am innocent of the blood of this righteous one; you shall see;" and all the people answering said, "His blood is upon us, and upon our children!"*

## Chapter 50. (Friday, April 3, 33AD 7:45AM)
## Trial before Pilate (Release Barabbas!)

Pilate asks the people, "What shall we do with this King of the Jews? I see no treason here."

*A third defendant, Theudas-Barabbas, is brought in.*

James comes forward, "'The Book of Leviticus (25:8-12) states that 'at seven times seven years at the jubilee that slaves and prisoners are to be freed.' Being that we began the 'Grand Jubilee' in 26AD when you took office, it would be customary to let Jesus and Barabbas go free."

Pilate says, "I did not come all this way to crucify one person, but I could respect your law. What does it say about Jesus?"

James says, "'The Book of Daniel (9:26) states that 'after sixty-two 'sevens', the Anointed King will be put to death'."

Pilate says, "I should only crucify those guilty of capital crimes, but I will allow you to choose one to be freed: the 'King of the Jews' or Barabbas?"

They all shout, "Free Barabbas."

Pilate says, "All right, Jesus' blood is on your hands."

*Matt 27:3-10 Then Judas -- he who delivered him up -- having seen that he was condemned, having repented, brought back the thirty pieces of silver to the chief priests, and to the elders, saying, "I did sin, having delivered up innocent blood;" and they said, "What -- to us? You shall see!" And having cast down the pieces of silver in the sanctuary, he departed, and having gone away, he did hang himself.*
*And the chief priests having taken the pieces of silver, said, "It is not lawful to put them to the treasury, seeing it is the price of blood;" and having taken counsel, they bought with them the field of the potter, for the burial of strangers; therefore was that field called, "Field of blood," unto this day. Then was fulfilled that spoken through Jeremiah the prophet, saying, " and I took the thirty pieces of silver, the price of him who has been priced, whom they of the sons of Israel did price, and gave them for the field of the potter, as the Lord did appoint to me."*

## Chapter 51. (Friday, April 3, 33AD 8:00AM)- Judas repents too late

Zacchaeus says, "The War Scroll (VII) declares that there be at least three leaders: Michael, Gabriel, and Sariel. You have condemned Simon and Jesus: a Michael and a Sariel, but you need a Gabriel."

Pilate laughs, "Are we crucifying angels or men?"

Zacchaeus says, "The Gabriel is Judas Iscariot."

Pilate says, "Bring me this Judas"...*Judas is brought in.*

Pilate says, "Are you the one who alerted me that the criminals were here?"... Judas answers, "Yes, it was I."

"I was told that you wanted thirty pieces of silver for this. What do you want from me?"

"I only desired to replace the leader Simon, but, now with Theudas released, you have made me responsible for the blood Jesus, to whom I once swore allegiance."

Pilate asks, "What does Jewish law say about betraying a fellow comrade?"

The people shout, "Betrayal is death; crucify him."

"All right, I will follow Jewish law again, but don't think I have chopped off my foreskin."

*The guards take Simon, Jesus, and Judas outside to be scourged and crucified. (It is important to note that they, being of priestly status, were not stripped naked, but kept their loin cloths.)*

## SECTION 8 (8:15AM to 3:05PM (crucified 9AM (3rd/6th hour), Friday, April 3, 33AD)
## The Crucifixion

Duccio di Buoninsegna (1255-1319)

*John 19:16,17* Then, therefore, he delivered him up to them, that he may be crucified, and they took Jesus and led him away, and bearing his cross(crossbar), he went forth to the place called Place of a Skull, which is called in Hebrew Golgotha;

*Mark 15:21,22* And they impress a certain one passing by (Jesus said, "Become passers-by." --Gospel of Thomas; thus a disciple) -- Simon, a Cyrenian, coming from the field, the father of Alexander (Theudas the disciple representing Therapeuts from Alexandria) and Rufus (Thomas the Twin, the disciple, having red hair like Esau had his birthright taken away by Herod the Great, his father, and given to the younger son, Herod Antipas, like Esau's was stolen by Jacob his twin brother)-- that he (Simon) may bear his (own) cross(bar), and they bring him to the place Golgotha, which is, being interpreted, "Place of a skull;" (in Qumran the skull was placed to mark the beginning of the latrine area, thus the impure area called the Salt)

*Luke 23:26* And as they led him away, having taken hold on Simon, a certain Cyrenian, coming from the field (on a mission; thus a disciple), they put on him the cross(bar), to bear it behind Jesus. (Simon is carrying his own crossbar behind Jesus)

*Matt 27:32,33* And coming forth, they found a man, a Cyrenian, by name Simon: him they impressed that he might bear his cross(bar); and having come to a place called Golgotha, that is called Place of a Skull,

*The Nag Hammadi Library - The Second Treatise of the Great Seth*
Yes, they saw me; they punished me. It was another, their father, who drank the gall and the vinegar; it was not I. They struck me with the reed; it was another, Simon, who bore the cross(bar) on his shoulder. I was another upon Whom they placed the crown of thorns. But I was rejoicing in the height over all the wealth of the archons and the offspring of their error, of their empty glory and laughing at their ignorance.

## Chapter 52. (Friday, April 3, 33AD 8:15AM)
## Carrying the Cross

*The soldiers bring Judas, Jesus, and Simon out of the building. First, the soldiers tie the crossbar to the back of Judas Iscariot, pushing him forward, then Jesus and then Simon Magus. Their path is a short journey south of the praetorium just beyond a skull on the ground, marking the toilet area called the Salt.*

An onlooker says, "Isn't that first person Judas, the one who betrayed Jesus?"

Another says, "I hear this second person Jesus was traded for the criminal Theudas Barabbas, the leader of the Therapeuts of Alexandria, Egypt."

"Isn't that last man his leader, Simon Magus, the one who took John the Baptist's place?"

"I heard he was from the far reaches of Cyrene. I wonder why he was standing in the field?"

"Not field, but mission. There he befriended Thomas, the deposed Herod called the twin having lost his inheritance like the red-haired Esau to Jacob?"

Another says, "It is amazing that they do not stumble with that great weight on their backs."

*Matt 27:34 they gave him to drink vinegar mixed with gall (here is revealed the poison -- Strong's Lexicon 5521 χολή - gall" or bile, i.e. (by analogy) poison or an anodyne (wormwood, poppy, etc.), being feminine suggesting the greenish hue. In all the other references, it is merely called vinegar with the added gall implied.), and having tasted, he would not drink.*

*(Jesus was now being given a choice: to take the poison now and to avoid crucifixion or to take it later at the ninth hour as planned and attempt the rescue plan to again save Simon Magus, his friend, father-in-law, step-father of Mary Magdalene, and Lazarus. In the Garden of Gethsemane, Jesus had struggled with the possibility of being placed on the cross, in spite of his innocence, to replace the aging Thaddeus-Theudas-Barsabbas, who was guilty. Having accepted the plan of taking the cup of poison, it was now growing clearer and clearer that every event was being fulfilled in each verse in Psalms 22:1-31 that would point to him as the prophesied Messiah. He thought about taking the poison ("tasted it"), but decided to proceed with the plan.)*

*Mark 15:23 and they were giving him to drink wine mingled with myrrh, and he did not receive. (Peter who was not present at the crucifixion has assumed that Jesus was given myrrh, but this is what was used later by Nicodemus. The "wine" is really spoiled wine: vinegar, later, Mark has the correct vinegar, but missing the gall.)*

## Chapter 53. (Friday, April 3, 33AD 8:45AM)
## Postponing the Poison

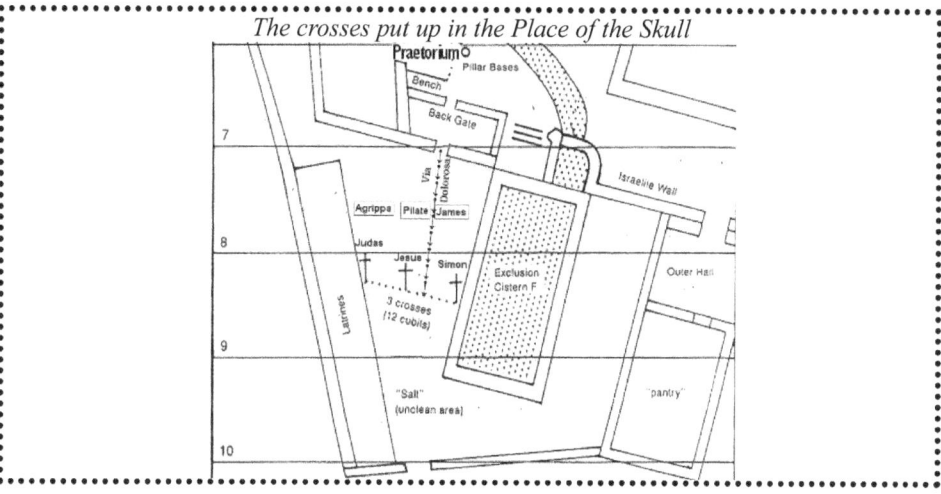
*The crosses put up in the Place of the Skull*

*As they are lying on the ground with their crossbars still tied to their backs awaiting the spikes to be driven into their wrists, Theudas gives them all an analgesic to ease the pain.*
To Jesus, he whispers, "You could take the poison now and appear to be dead and avoid crucifixion."

Jesus replies, "No, follow the plan at the ninth hour. It has the best chance of saving my father-in-law Simon. Here is the signal I will give from Psalm 22." He begins to sing it now:

> *"My God, my God, why have you forsaken me?*
> *Why are you so far from saving me, so far from my cries of anguish? My God, I cry out by day, but you do not answer, by night, but I find no rest."*

*The spikes are driven in all three wrists and the crossbars of the two are raised up by pulleys to the already erected posts and fitted into the slots. Jesus is still on the ground.*

Mark 15:25 And it was the **third hour**, and they crucified him;
John 19:14 and it was the preparation of the passover, and as it were the **sixth hour**, and he (Pilate) said to the Jews, "Lo, your king!"
It is important to point out that Mark 15:25 says it is the third hour for the hour when Jesus was placed on the cross and yet John 19:14 (although slightly out of place: when they were being sent out, yet Pilate's statement fits better here) has the sixth hour when Pilate released him to be crucified. This time discrepancy can only be explained by a time change that moved the clocks three hours forward. Peter would know the Essene time as he was in charge of the cock-crowing, but is giving the Pharisee time before the clocks change at noon, thus it is 9:00 AM Pharisee time (9:00 - 6:00(morning)) which is the third hour. John is showing the Essene time already adjusted that moved forward three hours after midnight coinciding with Peter's three denials thus it is 12 noon Essene time from midnight, but (12:00 minus 6:00(morning)) which is the sixth hour.

Matt 27:35a And having crucified him, Matt 27:38 Then crucified with him are two robbers, one on the right hand, and one on the left,
Mark 15:27 And with him they crucify two robbers, one on the right hand, and one on his left,
Luke 23:33b there they crucified him;
John 19:18 where they crucified him, and with him two others, on this side, and on that side, and Jesus in the midst.
GP 10a And they brought two malefactors, and they crucified the Lord between them.

Matt 27:37 and they put up over his head, his accusation written, "This is Jesus, the king of the Jews."
Mark 15:26 and the inscription of his accusation was written above -- "The King of the Jews."
Luke 23:38 And there was also a superscription written over him, in letters of Greek, and Roman, and Hebrew, "This is the King of the Jews."
John 19:19 And Pilate also wrote a title, and put it on the cross, and it was written, "the king of the Jews;" (John 19:20 ... written in Hebrew, in Greek, in Roman (Not likely since too many words and an illiterate addition: should have been Aramaic, Greek, Latin.)
John 19:21,22 The chief priests of the Jews said, therefore, to Pilate, "Write not -- The king of the Jews, but that one (James) said, I am king of the Jews;" Pilate answered, "What I have written, I have written."

## Chapter 54a. (Friday, April 3, 33AD 9AM)
## Placed on the Cross (9AM (3rd hour/6th hour)): King of the Jews

*Pilate is seated north of the Salt next to Agrippa to observe the crucifixion*
The centurion approaches Pilate saying, "James, Jesus' brother, tells me that Simon as the leader is supposed to be on the center cross. I assume you want Jesus there."
"Yes, and I want a sign above his crossbar saying 'King of the Jews'."
Agrippa says, "May I suggest that 'King of the Jews' is not technically accurate: he is just a prophet. James, over there is actually the 'King of the Jews' now, but also just a prophet."
Pilate replies, "He is not yours to crucify. My 'King of the Jews' is to stay. I want them to see how they humiliate and kill their own kings."

*The soldiers proceed to add the sign, saying "King of the Jews to the center cross and pull Jesus' crosspiece up to the center cross with a pulley. They bind the legs of all three with chains so that they do not die too quickly from suffocation because of stretched lungs. Jesus is in the center facing north so that Pilate can see him. Simon Magus is to Jesus' right and Judas Iscariot to his left by the latrine. The drugs have kicked in and they do not scream as blood drips from their wrists.*

After watching for an hour, Pilate is bored and says, "I was expecting Jesus to walk off the cross, but clearly he is just a man and not a God."
Agrippa says, "Pilate, shall we ride our horses down to the Dead Sea? The salt makes it so buoyant that Jesus is said to have walked on water."
*At the Dead Sea, Pilate tells his soldiers to try to walk on water, but they fall in.*

*Matt 27:44* With the same also the robbers, who were crucified with him, were reproaching him.
*Luke 23:33c* and the criminals, one on the right hand and one on the left.
*Luke 23:39* And one of the criminals, who were hanged, was speaking evil of him, saying, "If you be the Christ, save yourself and us."
*Luke 23:40-43* And the other answering, was rebuking him, saying, "Do you not even fear God, that you are in the same judgment? and we indeed righteously, for things worthy of what we did we receive back, but this one did nothing wrong;" and he said to Jesus, "Remember me, when you may come in your kingdom;" and Jesus said to him, "Verily I say to you, To-day with me you shall be in the paradise." *GP 13* And one of those malefactors reproached them, saying, 'We for the evils that we have done have suffered thus,

*PESHER ON NAHUM (4Q169) 1:4-6 (Nahum 2:12)* "The lion brings prey for his cubs, and strangles prey for his lionesses and he fills his cave with prey, and his den with torn prey." And this Young Lion of Wrath (Pontius Pilate) strikes the Simple Ones of Ephraim by means of his great men (the force of Rome) and the men of his Council (the Sanhedrin). And he executes revenge on the seekers-of-smooth-things (Simon's Essene Mission) and hangs men alive from a tree (the Crucifixion), to perform an abomination which was not done in Israel since earlier times. He declares, 'Behold I am against you, says the Lord of Hosts.'

## Chapter 54b. (Friday, April 3, 33AD 11AM)
## Two criminals talk to Jesus

*It is around the eleventh hour with Pilate still gone and the drugs have worn off and they groan in pain.*

The criminal Judas Iscariot on the cross to Jesus' left says, "You call yourself the Christ, all your fake miracles cannot save you now. Did peace bring the Restoration?"

The criminal Simon Magus to the right says, "Do you not even fear God's retribution for your betrayal? We both are guilty of treason, but Jesus is not. Jesus, I thank you for your loyalty and compassion. Remember me, when you come into your kingdom."

Jesus said to him, "Truly, I say to you, Today with me you shall be in the paradise."

"Simon adds, "And to you Judas, the fires of Gehenna will be your reward."

James' cousin Susanna goes over to James sitting alone "James, have you no remorse to have crucified your own brother?"
James answers, "I definitely regret all this, I never believed that Jesus would be crucified. You must be relieved that your father, Theudas, was saved."

Susanna says, "Can you be trusted to save your brother, Jesus?"

"Upon my mother's life, I promise."

She whispers, "Here is the plan: Jesus will take poison to make him appear to be dead. You must ask Pilate for his body. If you act quickly, Jesus can be revived in the cave that you are the gardener of."

"If there is a chance to save my brother, I will do it."

### The Four Marys at the Cross

|   | Mother Mary | Mary Magdalene | Helena (mother of Magdalene) | Susanna Mary daughter of Cleopas |
|---|---|---|---|---|
| Matt 27:56 | Mary the mother of James and of Joses[(1)] | Mary the Magdalene | the mother of the sons of Zebedee[(3)] | |
| Mark 15:40 | Mary of James [(1)] the less, and of Joses | Mary Magdalene | Salome [(3)] | |
| Luke 23:49 | the women who did follow him from Galilee | | | |
| John 19:25 | his mother[(1)] | Mary the Magdalene | his mother's sister[(3)] | Mary of Cleopas[(2)] |

### The Four Marys at the cave before the Resurrection

|   | Mother Mary | Mary Magdalene | Helena | Susanna |
|---|---|---|---|---|
| Matt 27:61 | | Mary the Magdalene | the other Mary | |
| Mark 15:47 | Mary of Joses[(1)] | Mary the Magdalene | | |
| Luke 23:55 | And the women also who have come with him out of Galilee having followed after | | | |

### The Four Marys at the cave after the Resurrection

|   | Mother Mary | Mary Magdalene | Helena | Susanna |
|---|---|---|---|---|
| Matt 28:01 | | Mary the Magdalene | the other Mary | |
| Mark 16:01 | Mary of James[(1)] | Mary the Magdalene | Salome[(3)] | |
| Luke 24:10 | Mary of James[(1)] | Mary Magdalene | Joanna[(3)] | the other women with them |
| John 20:11 | | Mary Magdalene | | |

(1) Mother Mary = his mother = Mother of "James (James the less" meaning younger Joseph, his father); Joses is James' brother so interchangeable.
(2) Susanna: Mary daughter of Cleopas, Jesus' uncle: (Road to Emmaus)
(3) Helena is a sister-in-law to Mother Mary through the marriage of her daughter Mary Magdalene; Salome, dancing at the The "Beheading" of John the Baptist; Joanna, female John the Baptist as the 30th of his group; consort of Zebedee (Simon Magus) who adopted James and John (Clementines)

## Chapter 54c. (Friday, April 3, 33AD 11:15AM)
## Four Marys and a possible son

Jesus looks down and sees the four Marys crying, saying, "My dearest mother of me and of James and Joses. Do not cry; I will conquer death."

Mother Mary replies, "May you at least go to a better place."

Jesus says "Helena, mother of my beloved wife, I have also saved a place in Paradise for Simon."

"You have a good heart. May you embrace in Paradise."

Jesus says, "Magdalene, my beloved, the mother of him inside your belly, behold our son! I will meet you in the garden of James. And dearest John Mark, please take care of this mother and child."

As Magdalene sobs loudly, Susanna says, "All is in place. James is sorry, he has promised to help."

*Those at the Crucifixion:*

1. Jesus - talks to Mary Magdalene about their baby inside her.
2. Mother Mary - "His mother", "Mary mother of James and Joses", "Mother of James the less and of Joses"
3. Helena - "Mother of the sons of Zebedee" (as the consort of Simon Magus she adopted sons James and John, the sons of Zebedee H.13.7 Justa, feminine of Justus), "Salome" (teacher of Herod's step-daughter, dancing at the "beheading" of John the Baptist and as Joanna, the female John the Baptist equaling Luna as the 30th position in the John the Baptist's group:Triacontad; Helena H.2.23), "His mother's sister" (sister-in-law to Mother Mary through the marriage of her natural daughter Mary Magdalene to Jesus H.2.20);
4. Mary Magdalene - wife of Jesus, mistakes Jesus for James "the Gardener" (John 20:11-18).
5. Susanna (unnamed here, mentioned in Luke 8:3 with Joanna) - daughter of Jesus' uncle Cleopas (James), who was on the Road to Emmaus Appearance (Luke 24:13-32). Judas Iscariot - to the right, first criminal, who makes fun of Jesus
6. Simon Magus - second criminal, who uses code word: Paradise for caves south of the Salt
7. Agrippa - later King of Judea (41-44AD), chatting with Pilate, goes with him to the Dead Sea
8. Zacchaeus - youngest son of High Priest Ananus runs over with a hyssop stalk with a sponge on top, laced with poison
9. Cornelius the centurion - uses a lancet to determine if Jesus is dead (he lies!), later guards the caves
10. Joseph of Arimathea - Joseph, brother of Jesus, asks for Jesus' body
11. Theudas Barabbas - (Barabbas is corrupted Barsabbas, the family name) his father Joseph's brother, Jesus' uncle, brings the poison and the antidote

*Time changes from 12 noon (sixth-hour) to 3 PM (the ninth-hour)*
Matt 27:45 *And from the sixth hour darkness came over all the land unto the ninth hour,*
Mark 15:33 *And the sixth hour having come, darkness came over the whole land till the ninth hour,*
Luke 23:44,45 *And it was, as it were, the sixth hour, and darkness came over all the land till the ninth hour, and the sun was darkened, and the veil of the sanctuary was rent in the midst,*
GP 15a *And it was noon, and darkness came over all Judaea:* GP 18 *And many went about with lamps, supposing that it was night, and fell down.* GP 22 *Then the sun shone, and it was found the ninth hour:*

## Chapter 54d. (Friday, April 3, 33AD 12 noon = 3PM)
### Darkness *(time moves 3 hrs)*

The crier calls out, "Sixth Hour."

*Fortuitously, Pilate and Agrippa returned at noon time but the first crier had just called out the 6th hour, and all they heard was the 9th hour.*

The crier calls out, "Ninth Hour."

Pilate remarked, "How could that be, is it that late already."

Agrippa says, "Let us be seated. It appears that they have been up there for sixth hours since the third hour, from 9:00AM until 3:00PM according to my calculation. Their end could be near."

Pilate replies, "Perhaps, but I have seen some stay alive for days."

*Matt 27:46-50 And about the ninth hour Jesus cried out with a great voice, saying, "Eli, Eli, lama sabachthani?" That is, "My God, my God, why did You forsake me?" And certain of those standing there having heard, said -- "Elijah he does call;" And immediately, one of them having run, and having taken a sponge, having filled it with vinegar, and having put it on a reed, was giving him to drink, but the rest said, "Let alone, let us see if Elijah does come -- about to save him."*
*And Jesus having again cried with a great voice, yielded the spirit;*

*Mark 15:34-37 And at the ninth hour Jesus cried with a great voice, saying, "Eloi, Eloi, lamma sabachthani?" which is, being interpreted, "My God, my God, why did You forsake me?" And certain of those standing by, having heard, said, "Lo, Elijah he does call;" And one having run, and having filled a sponge with vinegar, having put it also on a reed, was giving him to drink, saying, "Let alone, let us see if Elijah does come to take him down."*
*And Jesus having uttered a loud cry, yielded the spirit,*

*Luke 23:36 the soldiers, coming near and bringing vinegar to him,*
*Luke 23:46 And having cried with a loud voice, Jesus said, "Father, into your hands I commit my spirit;"*
*And having said this he breathed forth the spirit.*

*John 19:28-30 After this, Jesus knowing that all things now have been finished, that the Writing may be fulfilled, said, "I thirst;"*
*A vessel, therefore, was placed full of vinegar, and they having filled a sponge with vinegar, and having put it around a hyssop stalk, did put it to his mouth;*
*when, therefore, Jesus received the vinegar, he said, "It has been finished;" and having bowed the head, gave up the spirit.*

*GP 16 And one of them said, Give him to drink gall with vinegar. And they mixed and gave him to drink,*

## Chapter 54e. (Friday, April 3, 33AD 3:05PM)
## Requesting the poison

*Jesus sees that Pilate has arrived back and gives the pre-arranged signal for the poison that will make him appear to be dead.*

Jesus cries out, "My God, my God, why did You forsake me? I thirst."

*There is a vessel off to the side filled with vinegar and gall.*

*Zacchaeus runs over with a hyssop stalk with a sponge on top and dips it into the vessel and puts it to Jesus' lips.*

*In a few minutes, Jesus lowers his head and his body goes limp, appearing to be dead.*

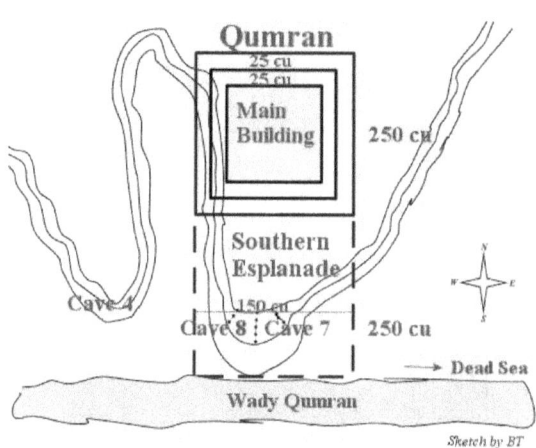

# SECTION 9 (3:05PM to midnight, Friday, April 3, 33AD)
## The Rescue

Michelangelo(1475-1564)

*The derivation of Arimathea is Hebrew: ariah - lion and mathētai - disciples (lion is "Lion of the tribe of Judah, the Root of David" Revelation 5:5) thus James, having taken Jesus' place.*
*Mark 15:43,44 Joseph of Arimathea, an honorable counselor, (a man good and Just, -- he was not consenting to their counsel and deed - Luke 23 50,51) (rich - Matt 27:57) who also himself was waiting for the kingdom of heaven, came, boldly entered in unto Pilate, and asked the body of Jesus; and (Pilate) having called near the centurion, did question him if he were long dead,*

*Pleural effusion from crucifixion trauma*

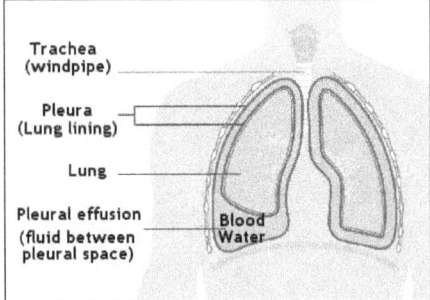

*John 19:34,35 but one of the soldiers (Cornelius the centurion later baptized as Luke) with a spear (lancet) did pierce his side, and immediately there came forth blood and water; and he who has seen has testified, and his testimony is true, and that one has known that true things he speaks, that you also may believe.*

*Mark 15:45 And having known it from the centurion, he granted the body to Joseph.*

*Luke 23:54 And the day was a preparation, and Sabbath was approaching (the evening having come Mark 15:42)*
*John 19:31 The Jews, therefore, that the bodies might not remain on the cross on the Sabbath, since it was the preparation, (for that Sabbath day was a great one,) asked of Pilate that their legs may be broken, and they taken away.*

*Deuteronomy 21:23 A body shall not remain all night upon the tree, but you shall bury him the same day, for a hanged man is accursed by God;*

## Chapter 55. (Friday, April 3, 33AD 3:15PM)
## Ask for the body, test for death, Sabbath excuse

James goes up to Pilate saying, "Esteemed Prefect, as the brother of Jesus, may I request the body of Jesus to bury him."

Pilate replies, "How could he be dead already! He has only been on the cross for six hours. Centurion, check if he is still alive.

Cornelius, being a surgeon and having examined crucifixion victims before, takes a lancet and puts it in the lower part of the lung cavity and out comes blood and water, which is the result of the trauma of crucifixion. He attests to his finding, saying "I say the truth that this man has died from crucifixion."

"Centurion, take down the King of the Jews."

James says, Thank you. Could I also request the removal of the other two crucified ones? Our laws in Deuteronomy say 'a crucified man cannot remain on a cross after sundown without causing insult to God and must be buried the same day.' Since Passover begins at sundown, it would be important not to offend our God."

"You Jews have too many rules. The other two are of little interest to him. Soldiers, make sure you pull the chains taut to break their legs; then, being unable to push up with the legs, their lungs will burst and they will die quickly. The Dead Sea was more lively than these crucifixions. If I hurry, maybe I could be home before dark."

*John 19:32,36,38 The soldiers, therefore, came, and of the first indeed they did break the legs, and of the other who was crucified with him, and having come to Jesus, when they saw him already having been dead, they did not break his legs;*
*For these things came to pass, that the Writing may be fulfilled, "A bone of him shall not be broken;"*
*(Joseph) came, therefore, and took away the body of Jesus,*
*Luke 23:53 And (Joseph) having taken the body down,*
*Matt 27:59 And (Joseph) having taken the body,*

*John 19:39 And Nicodemus also came -- who previously had come unto Jesus by night at the first -- bearing a mixture of myrrh and aloes, as it were, a hundred pounds.*

*The hundred pounds is probably not of its weight, but rather it cost, their expense is indicated by the fact that myrrh and frankincense were given with gold to the baby Jesus. The combination of myrrh and frankincense are used in Chinese medicine for "traumatic injuries with pain, swelling, and redness due to qi stagnation and blood stasis." Theophrastus, the successor to Aristotle in his 'Equiry of Plants IX.xx.2' states "Pepper is a fruit, ... both however are heating : wherefore these, as well as frankincense, are used as antidotes for poisoning by hemlock." Clearly, whatever the medicines, the goal was to vomit the poison that was given on the cross and administer an antidote for it.*

## Chapter 56. (Friday, April 3, 33AD 3:45PM)
## Taking down the bodies

*Meanwhile, Cornelius having carefully unwrapped the chains around Jesus' legs, uses the pulley to lower Jesus still nailed and roped to the crossbar with the help of Zacchaeus and they place Jesus gently on the ground. He takes a crowbar and yanks the two spikes from his wrists.*

A soldier says, "Why are you being so careful; he is already dead."

Cornelius replies, "We do not want the body to be defiled further. He is after all the Son of God."

The soldier mutters, "This Jewish God is not very powerful to let his son die."

*Theudas comes with a select quantity of myrrh, aloe, and antidote in a palanquin belonging to James. James and Theudas lift him onto the stretcher as the women apply the lotions to his wrists, keeping his body covered, so as not to reveal his faint breath.*

*The soldiers following Pilate's instructions, break the legs of the other two by yanking the chains around their legs, causing both to faint from the pain.* "What do we do next?" the soldiers ask.

Cornelius says, "I will lower those dead ones down." *Then Cornelius and Zacchaeus lower Simon and remove the spikes from his wrist. Then they do the same for Judas.*

*Jesus is taken away by James and Theudas; his mother and Magdalene follow. Helena stays behind to attend to Simon and Susanna for Judas.*

*Matt 27:59-61* Joseph wrapped the body in clean linen, and laid it in his new tomb, that he hewed in the rock, and having rolled a great stone to the door of the tomb, he went away; *Matt 27:61* and there were there Mary the Magdalene, and the other Mary (Helena, as all women were called Mary and she being the consort of Simon Magus who was on the 2nd cross), sitting opposite the sepulcher.

*Mark 15:46,47* And he, having brought fine linen, and having taken him down, wrapped him in the linen, and laid him in a sepulcher that had been hewn out of a rock, and he rolled a stone unto the door of the sepulcher, and Mary the Magdalene, and Mary of Joses (Mother Mary matching with 2nd woman at the cross in Mark and Matthew), were beholding where he is laid.

*Luke 23:53,55,56* Joseph wrapped the body in fine linen, and placed it in a tomb hewn out, where no one was yet laid. And the women also who have come with him out of Galilee having followed after, beheld the tomb, and how his body was placed, and having turned back, they made ready spices and ointments, and on the Sabbath, indeed, they rested, according to the command.

*John 19:40-42* They took, therefore, the body of Jesus, and bound it with linen clothes with the spices, according as it was the custom of the Jews to prepare for burial; and there was in the place where he was crucified a garden, and in the garden a new tomb, in which no one was yet laid; there, therefore, because of the preparation of the Jews, that the tomb was near, they laid Jesus.

*GP 24* And he took the Lord, and washed him, and wrapped him in a linen cloth, and brought him into his own tomb which was called the Garden of Joseph.

## Chapter 57. (Friday, April 3, 33AD 4PM)
## Wrapping the bodies and placing in the tomb

*The four Marys: Mother Mary, Mary Magdalene, Helena, and Susanna, having wrapped the bodies with linen as if to be buried, follow the men as they bring the three to the caves. one at a time on the stretcher.*

*There is a walkway that goes over the pinnacle of rock to the caves. Jesus is placed in first cave that is on the outside of the cliff being the cave of the prince (James) and Simon Magus and Judas in next cave of the king (opposite the chasm between the cave of Lazarus: (#4). Two stones that roll are used to seal up each cave. The stone for the front of Jesus' cave is rolled closed first, left slightly ajar, with Theudas hiding inside.*

*When it is almost sundown and the women return to the Queen's house, just across the Wadi Qumran.*

*Once Jesus is inside the cave, Theudas induces Jesus to vomit and gives him the antidote. He binds his wrist. To help the others, he rolls the stone door open. As he rolls the stone of the adjacent tomb where Simon Magus and Judas have been placed, it crashes down and breaks in two.*

Cave 7Q (Priest's tomb) where Simon Magus and Judas were placed
Archeologists' description in note form of Cave 7Q, found in 1955. (In Discoveries in the Judean Desert 3, Oxford, Clarendon Press 1962, in French)."At the extremity of the platform which extends south of the Khirbet (the southern esplanade). A rounded chamber of which the roof, the whole southern part and a part of the earthen floor have collapsed into the wady Qumran. It was reached by a staircase coming down from the edge of the platform, to the north-west of the chamber; only the lower steps of the staircase have been preserved. Most of the written fragments were collected on these steps. One of the texts, no 19, was written on papyrus and was preserved only by its impression on a block of mud . A shard covered with mud similarly carries the imprint of papyrus fibres and the trace of two Greek letters.... Possibility of habitation: yes, in its original state.... The total of ceramics appears to indicate that this cave was used during the two main periods of occupation of the Khirbet."

Cave 8Q (King's tomb) where Jesus was placed
Archeologists also describe Cave 8Q. "At the south-west of cave 7Q. The method of access has not been able to be determined and a part only of the chamber has been preserved. What remained of the ceiling was cracked and it was necessary to let it fall. The texts and objects were found immediately under the earthen floor. Possibility of habitation: probable, in its original state."

GP 28-33 But the scribes and Pharisees and elders being gathered together one with another, when they heard that all the people murmured and beat their breasts, saying. 'If by his death these most mighty signs have come to pass, see how just he is'. The elders were afraid and came to Pilate, beseeching him and saying, 'Give us soldiers, that we may guard his sepulcher for three days, lest his disciples come and steal him away, and the people suppose that he is risen from the dead and do us evil.'
And Pilate gave them (delete:Petronius) *(Cornelius -Luke)* the centurion with soldiers to guard the tomb. And with them came the elders and scribes to the sepulcher,
And having rolled a great stone together with the centurion *(Cornelius -Luke)* and the soldiers, they all together who were there set it at the door of the sepulcher; And they affixed seven seals, and they pitched a tent there and guarded it.

*Cornelius would be later baptized by Jesus as Luke and would help Jesus write that gospel in addition to being his doctor to help him with the wounds on his wrist which prevented him from having fully functional hands. Later Jesus would tell Peter that Cornelius was to be allowed at the Sacred Table, having passed down a tablecloth with embroidered animals to demonstrate that the animals of Noah on the ark were symbolic of all the tribes of Noah who were being welcomed.*

## Chapter 58. (Friday, April 3, 33AD 6PM)
## Guarding the tomb

*Given that it was possible for the Restoration to begin on Passover and thus God might raise them from the dead, Caiaphas asked Pilate to have the caves guarded. He feared that the disciples would steal the bodies and claim that they had been resurrected.*

The messenger from Pilate comes to the centurion Cornelius, "You are instructed by Pilate to guard the tombs."

Cornelius remarks, "Do the Jews think they are Egyptians now that they must block the dead from the afterlife?"

*The soldiers have camped farther out from the peak of the rock above the caves.* Having heard the crash, they are afraid to move, thinking that the gods have caused it, but Cornelius goes to look and calls out, "Who's there?"

Theudas appears from the tomb, where Jesus has been placed, with gold coins which he places in Cornelius' hand, saying with a wink, "The dead have no need of these."

Looking at the broken door stone, Cornelius says, "So you are the earthquake then that scared us!" Going back to the soldiers, he hands each a gold coin, saying, "No need for alarm."

*The Rich Man and Lazarus*
*Luke 16:19-31* "*And a certain man was rich, and was clothed in purple and fine linen, making merry sumptuously every day, and there was a certain poor man, by name Lazarus, who was laid at his porch, full of sores, and desiring to be filled from the crumbs that are falling from the table of the rich man; yea, also the dogs, coming, were licking his sores.*"

"*And it came to pass, that the poor man died, and that he was carried away by the angels to the bosom of Abraham -- and the rich man also died, and was buried; and in Hades having lifted up his eyes, being in torments, he does see Abraham afar off, and Lazarus in his bosom, and having cried, he said, Father Abraham, deal kindly with me, and send Lazarus, that he may dip the tip of his finger in water, and may cool my tongue, because I am distressed in this flame.*"

"*And Abraham said, Child, remember that you did receive your good things in your life, and Lazarus in like manner the evil things, and now he is comforted, and you are distressed; and besides all these things, between us and you a great chasm is fixed, so that they who are willing to go over from hence unto you are not able, nor do they from thence to us pass through.*"

"*And he said, I pray you, then, Father, that you may send him to the house of my father, for I have five brothers, so that he may thoroughly testify to them, that they also may not come to this place of torment.*"

"*Abraham said to him, They have Moses and the prophets, let them hear them; and he said, No, father Abraham, but if anyone from the dead may go unto them, they will reform.*"

*And he said to him, If Moses and the prophets they do not hear, neither if one may rise out of the dead will they be persuaded.*"

Hades was considered to be Gehenna, the area outside of Jerusalem where the fires were always lit, burning garbage. *In Qumran, it is the chasm between two caves: Cave 4 (priest's cave) where Simon and Judas were placed and Cave 8 (king's cave that James ('Gardener: Adam', also 'rich man', being in charge of burying the Church money there) buried Jesus in).*
In the parable of Lazarus died and had gone to heaven, presided over by Abraham *(being Hillel who taught the concept of turning the other cheek)* He was rewarded for leading a good life, although he was poor living on crumbs from the rich man's table. *(Helena's saying to Jesus)*
The rich man *(Caiaphas who had married the High Priest Ananus' daughter, being rich from collecting the Church tithes).* These five brothers *(sons of Ananus, also High Priest).* The rich man begs to be allowed to be resurrected to warn his sons.
*(This parable would inspire the catechism of the Catholic Church that says 'He descended into Hell and on the third day he rose again.')*

## Chapter 59. (Friday, April 3, 33AD 7PM)
## Jesus' dream

*Under the careful watch of Theudas, Jesus slept. He dreamed of being inside the parable he had told of 'Lazarus and the Rich Man'.*

Jesus calls up to Lazarus *(Simon Magus)* in heaven, "Father Abraham, I do not deserve to be scorched by the flames of Hell. Have I not cared for the poor!"

Helena, who is next to Simon above is saying, "No, I witnessed him treating women and Gentiles like dogs having to eat crumbs from the Sacred Table."

Jesus cries, "Your daughter was given the wine of the Sacrament at our wedding. Surely, that was kind."

Helena replies, "Yet, you did not invite her to the Last Supper; is John Mark the one you love then?"

"I have faithfully followed the rules of the Essenes. Help me, the fires are singeing my hands and feet!"

At around midnight Jesus wakes up from the dream screaming, "God has forsaken me!"

*Theudas comforts him and gets him to stand up, helping him to walk around. He lights an oil lamp and places it in the window to announce that Jesus has recovered.*

## SECTION 10 (Saturday, April 4 to May 6, 33AD)
## The Resurrection

Botticelli(1445-1510)

*John 20:1,2 And on the first of the Sabbaths, Mary the Magdalene does come early (there being yet darkness) to the tomb, and she sees the stone having been taken away out of the tomb, she runs, therefore, and comes unto Simon Peter, and unto the other disciple whom Jesus was loving, and said to them, "They took away the Lord out of the tomb, and we have not known where they laid him."*

*John 20:3-5 Peter, therefore, went forth, and the other disciple, and they were coming to the tomb, and the two were running together, and the other disciple did run forward more quickly than Peter, and came first to the tomb, and having stooped down, sees the linen clothes lying, yet, indeed, he entered not.*

*Luke 24:12 And Peter, having risen, did run to the tomb, and having stooped down he sees the linen clothes lying alone,*

*John 20:6-8 Simon Peter, therefore, comes, following him, and he entered into the tomb, and beholds the linen clothes lying, and the napkin that was upon his head, not lying with the linen clothes, but apart, having been folded up, in one place; then, therefore, entered also the other disciple who came first unto the tomb, and he saw, and did believe;*

*GP 35-38 And in the night in which the Lord's day was drawing on, as the soldiers kept guard two by two in a watch, there was a great voice in the heaven; And they saw the heavens opened, and*
***two men descend from thence with great light and approach the tomb.***
*And that stone which was put at the door rolled of itself and made way in part, and the tomb was opened, and both the young men entered in. When therefore those soldiers saw it, they awakened the centurion (Cornelius -Luke) and the elders, for they too were nearby keeping guard.*

# Chapter 60. (Saturday, April 3, 33AD Midnight)
## Magdalene gets Peter and John Mark

*On Passover Sabbath only Theudas, as a Therapeut physician, is allowed to be out and about. Magdalene, since she is pregnant is also free from the rules.*

*Magdalene sees the light up at the caves and goes up to see if Jesus had been revived. When she gets to the cave, she sees the broken stone door and immediately hurries down to wake Peter and John Mark.*

"Wake up Peter and John, the stone has been broken. Someone has stolen Jesus' body."

*In the early dawn, just light enough to see, Peter and John Mark jumped up and start running. John Mark is ahead. When he gets to Jesus' cave he looks in, seeing the linen clothes, but hesitates. Peter rushes in and sees also the napkin that he was buried in. They panic.*

John Mark says, "Wait, the fact that these are neatly folded means that his body was not been stolen."

Jesus overhears them, "My disciples, uncle Theudas is just helping me to wash. I have all the conveniences at hand in this priest toilet."

*Shortly, he appears to them, wearing only a loincloth, and in the dark flickering lamp light, it appears that he is unscarred with only his wrists wrapped; both embrace him and help him to put his linen gown on.*

*John 20:11-17 And Mary was standing near the tomb, weeping without; as she was weeping, then, she stooped down to the tomb, and beholds two angels in white, sitting, one at the head, and one at the feet, where the body of Jesus had been laid. And they say to her, "Woman, why do you weep?" she said to them, "Because they took away my Lord, and I have not known where they laid him;" and these things having said, she turns around, and sees Jesus standing, and she had not known that it is Jesus.*
*Jesus said to her, "Woman, why do you weep? whom do you seek;" she, supposing that he is the Gardener, said to him, "Sir, if you did carry him away, tell me where you did lay him, and I will take him away;" Jesus said to her, "Mary!"; having turned, she said to him, "Rabboni;" that is to say, "Teacher."*
*Jesus said to her, "Be not touching me, for I have not yet ascended unto my Father; and be going on to my brethren, and say to them, I ascend unto my Father, and your Father, and to my God, and to your God."*

*Matt 28:04 From the fear of him did the keepers shake, and they became as dead men. Mark 16:04 And having looked, they see that the stone has been rolled away -- for it was very great, Matt 27:54 And the centurion, and those with him watching Jesus, having seen the earthquake, and the things that were done, were exceedingly afraid, saying, "Truly this was God's Son."*
*Mark 15:39 and the centurion who was standing across from him, having seen that, having so cried out, he yielded the spirit, said, "Truly this man was Son of God."*

*GP 39-42 And, as they (the soldiers) declared what things they had seen, again* **they see three men coming forth from the tomb, and two of them supporting one,** *and a cross following them. And of the two the head reached unto the heaven, but the head of him that was led by them overpassed the heavens. And they heard a voice from the heavens, saying. 'Hast thou preached to them that sleep?' And a response was heard from the cross, 'Yea.'*

## Chapter 61. (Saturday, April 4, 33AD 1AM)
## Mary mistakes Jesus; He is taken down the hill

*Mary Magdalene had followed the two disciples back up the mountain, but obviously at a slower pace. Becoming confused, she looks in the other cave and sees two men in white. (Being Essene leaders they were called angels by tradition; the one at the far end is Judas Iscariot still sedated.)*

Simon asks, "Magdalene, why do you weep?"

Magdalene sobbing, "Because they took away my Lord, and I have not known where they laid him."

Hearing someone behind her, she turns, seeing a shadowy figure, says, "Gardener, did you take him?"
Jesus says, "Mary!"
"My Master! But you are standing?"

As she reaches to hug him, Jesus says, "Better not hug me. I am spiritually impure and I intend to return to monastery."
Magdalene says, "Only immersion in the baptismal pool can fix that. Martha kissed Lazarus and he stunk more." *She kisses him on the mouth.*

Just then Cornelius arrives and sees Jesus standing. In amazement he says, "Truly, you are God's Son! My lancet seemed to show that you were still alive on the cross, but I did not believe it possible."

Peter says to John Mark, "Let's help Jesus down to the Queen's house before it is light."

*They support Jesus between them and reach the top of the peak. The dawn sunlight is reflected in his hair, projecting like a cross. From the heavens, the angel chorus seems to say, 'Yes'.*

*Isaiah 29:6 "Thou shalt be visited of the Lord of hosts with thunder (Jonathan Annas See Formal Appointment of the Twelve Apostles: Mark 03:17), and with earthquake (Theudas), and great noise, with storm and tempest, and the flame of devouring fire (lightning: Simon Magus).*

*Mark 16:1,2 And the Sabbath having past,* **Mary the Magdalene, and Mary of James (Mother Mary), and Salome - Joanna Luke 24:10 (Helena)**, *bought spices, that having come, they may anoint him, and early in the morning of the first of the Sabbaths, they come unto the sepulcher, at the rising of the sun,*

*Matt 28:2,3 and lo, there came a great earthquake (Theudas), for an angel of the Lord, having come down out of heaven, having come, did roll away the stone from the door, and was sitting upon it, and his countenance was as lightning (Simon Magus).*

Jesus has gone down the mountain with Peter and John Mark, the women look into the other cave

- Matt 28:03 - "angel of the Lord; countenance was as lightning, and his clothing white as snow" *(Simon Magus dressed in his clean white garment as an Essene angel)*,
- Mark 16:05 - "a young man sitting on the right hand, arrayed in a long white garment" *(Simon Magus in his crucifixion position to the right of Jesus - young having been raised as Lazarus from excommunication)*
- Luke 24:04 - "two men stood by them in glittering apparel "*(In the second cave tomb were Simon Magus and Judas, who was heavily sedated, but still an Essene leader - thus an angel, propped up.)*
- GP 55 - "young man sitting in the midst of the tomb, beautiful and clothed in a garment exceeding bright" *(Simon Magus dressed in his clean white garment)*
- Note that Mark and Gospel of Peter show "young man" instead of "angel". Both are right as this is Simon Magus who is, as the leader by Essene designation, an angel like Simeon acting as the Gabriel at the Annunciation of Mary, but he is also Lazarus and raised up to initiate (young man) by Jesus having been excommunicated (dead). He was also the "young man" running away naked at the arrest of Jesus.

Mark 16:5-7 and having entered into the sepulcher, they saw a young man sitting on the right hand, arrayed in a long white garment, and they were amazed. And he said to them, "Be not amazed, you seek Jesus the Nazarene, the crucified: he did rise -- he is not here; lo, the place where they laid him! and go, say to his disciples, and Peter, that he does go before you to Galilee; there you shall see him, as he said to you."

## Chapter 62. (Saturday, April 4, 33AD 5AM)
## The women visit the tomb. Jesus is gone.

*Mary Magdalene had followed Jesus down and collected Mother Mary, Helena, and Susanna and headed back up the hill with them in the early dawn.*

Mother Mary says to Magdalene, "So you actually kissed my son in the flesh. That is a miracle indeed!"

Helena says, "How will we be able to move the stone from the other cave without Peter and John?"

Magdalene says, "Do not worry, Theudas, is there and he is not called 'Earthquake' for nothing."

*Having crossed over the top of the peak, their apprehension changes to awe as they see Simon Magus sitting on the blocking stone, fallen and cracked in two parts near the cave, his clean white linen, reflecting the sun.*

Helen running and caressing his head and face, kisses him, saying, "The Standing One still lives, sitting on a throne of stone. How are you?"
"Not standing quite yet."

Susanna ask, "What of the other angel?"

Magdalene looking into the cave, "Oh you mean Satan, he seems to be still alive."

Simon says, "All of you must listen carefully. It is important to say that Jesus was not here because he was resurrected. This story will play well with the converts and weaken Caiaphas. As the Church of the Resurrection, we will be worthy to have the 'seal of the living God' on our foreheads." (Rev 7:2)

*Rev 13:2-5 And the beast (Zealot) that I saw was like to a leopard (leader of military division such as Judas Iscariot), and its feet (the money jar for Church tithes at the feet) as of a bear (the Herods), and its mouth as the mouth of a lion (to speak on behalf of king), and the dragon (Caiaphas - the High Priest who followed Joazar Boethus in philosophy) did give to it his power, and his throne, and great authority.*
*And I saw one of its heads as slain to death, and its deadly stroke was healed (John the Baptist has been executed and replaced by Jesus) and all the earth did wonder after the beast, Rev 13:04 and they did bow before the dragon (Caiaphas) who did give authority to the beast, and they did bow before the beast, saying, 'Who is like to the beast? who is able to war with it?' And there was given to it a mouth speaking great things, and evil-speakings, and there was given to it authority to make war forty-two months, (In other words until the Restoration: the three and half years of Daniel: 3.5 years\*360 (12 months of 30 day months) or 42 months.)*

*Luke 23:39 And one of the criminals who was hanged (Judas), was speaking evil of him, saying, "If you be the Christ, save yourself and us."*

*Luke 24:3,4 and having gone in (to the tomb), they found not the body of the Lord Jesus. And it came to pass, while they are perplexed about this, that lo, two men stood by them in glittering apparel,(In the second cave tomb were Simon Magus and Judas, who was heavily sedated, but still an Essene leader - thus an angel, propped up.)*

*Acts 1:16-19 'Men, brethren, it behoved this Writing that it be fulfilled that beforehand the Holy Spirit did speak through the mouth of David, concerning Judas, who became guide to those who took Jesus, because he was numbered among us, and did receive the share in this ministration, this one, indeed, then, purchased a field out of the reward of unrighteousness, and falling headlong, burst asunder in the midst, and all his bowels gushed forth, and it became known to all those dwelling in Jerusalem, insomuch that that place is called, in their proper dialect, Aceldama, that is, field of blood,*

## Chapter 63. (Saturday, April 4, 33AD 6AM)
## Judas dies in a Field of Blood

*Jesus visits Simon Magus at Ein Feshkha, he is on crutches and his ankles are in castes.*

Jesus says, "Simon, I see you are recovering. As for me, I could walk all the way to Jerusalem."

"Don't rub it in, but it is still a small price to pay for life. I am truly indebted to you forever. It took great courage and sacrifice."

Jesus says, "It is your best magic trick ever."

Simon says, "I am sure that Thomas will never believe it."

"Where is Judas. I thought he was also rescued from the cross and the women saw him in your cave?"

Simon answers, "The leopard was a good lieutenant, who guarded the tithes faithfully, making sure that the Zealots got some of it, which you oppose; but betrayal is the greatest of all sins even for a Zealot."

Jesus, "Perhaps he was just carrying out God's will."

"Then it was God's will that on exiting the cave in the palanquin, Theudas lost his balance, tipping him headlong into the valley of Gehenna."

*Luke 24:13-15 And, lo, two of them were going on during that day to a village, distant sixty furlongs from Jerusalem, the name of which Emmaus, and Cleopas (the uncle) and another (James, the brother of Jesus) were conversing about all these things that have happened in Jerusalem(Qumran). And it came to pass in their conversing and reasoning together, that Jesus himself, having come near, was going on with them, and their eyes were held so as not to know him,*

*John 20:26,-29 And after eight days, again were his disciples within, and Thomas with them; Jesus comes, the doors having been shut, and he stood in the midst, and said, "Peace to you!" then he said to Thomas, "Bring your finger hither, and see my hands, and bring your hand, and put it to my side, and become not unbelieving, but believing." And Thomas answered and said to him, "My Lord and my God;" Jesus said to him, "Because you have seen me, Thomas, you have believed; happy those not having seen, and having believed."*

*John 21:1-6,10,41-43 After these things did Jesus manifest himself again to the disciples on the sea of Tiberias, and he did manifest himself thus: here were together Simon Peter, and Thomas who is called Didymus, and Nathanael from Cana of Galilee, and the sons of Zebedee, and two others of his disciples (John Mark, whom Jesus was loving, and Andrew (GP 60)). Simon Peter said to them, "I go away to fish;" they say to him, "We go also with you;" they went forth and entered into the boat immediately, and on that night they caught nothing. And morning being now come, Jesus stood on the shore, yet indeed the disciples did not know that it is Jesus; Jesus, therefore, said to them, "Men, have you any meat?" they answered him, "No;" and he said to them, "Cast the net on the right side of the boat, and you shall find;" they cast, therefore, and caught 153 fishes.*

*He (Jesus) said to them, "Have you anything here to eat?" and they gave to him part of a broiled fish, and of a honeycomb, and having taken, he did eat before them,*

*Mark 16:19,20 The Lord, then, indeed, after speaking to them, was received up to the heaven (back to monastery), and sat on the right hand of God; and they, having gone forth, did preach everywhere, the Lord working with them, and confirming the word, through the signs following. Amen.*

## Chapter 64. (April 5-12, 33AD 6AM)
## Emmaus, Thomas, and Broiled fish prove Jesus in the flesh

Jesus enters the church at Mird Minor which is near the convent of Asher, saying "Peace be unto you."
Thomas says, "Are you really human or a ghost. They say you died on the cross." Jesus says, "Touch the holes in my wrist and the place that I was pierced."

Thomas touches the scars on his wrist and chest and says, "You are my Lord, my God."

*Next morning Jesus joins his uncle Cleopas and his brother James on the walk from Emmaus to Jerusalem. It being midpoint of the 27-hour journey.*
Cleopas says, "Jesus, how does it feel to be invisible?" James says, "The women are ready to say that they saw an empty tomb and this will not be a lie because they came after your rescue."

Jesus says, "But why is my Resurrection necessary? It should be enough of a miracle that I am alive! Look at the journey I am now taking!"

*A week later Jesus goes to Mazin and eats broiled fish and honeycomb with the disciples.*

Jesus asks Peter, "Do you understand the difference between 'agapé' love and 'phileo' love?"
Peter says, "Please, explain it again, Teacher."

Jesus says, "We love each other, but love needs to include everyone as 'agapé' love does. There is no jealousy in 'agapé' love. It makes us all equal. Remember my lesson on washing each other's feet."

*(John Aquila writes:)*
*Rev 14:1-5 And I saw, and lo, a Lamb (Jesus having been sacrificed like a Pascal lamb) having stood upon the mount Sion (the Cenacle building on Mount Zion), and with him an hundred forty-four thousands (the 10 provinces with the monastics of Asher and Dan added each having 12,000 members), having the name of his Father written upon their foreheads (symbol of the cross: X, soon to be Chi Rho: ₽); and I heard a voice out of the heaven (Jesus not yet in the monastery on the higher platform), as a voice of many waters (all having been baptized), and as a voice of great thunder (those in monastery are welcome), and a voice I heard of harpers harping with their harps (those in the abbey: the Psalms played by David on his harp, hymns with musical accompaniment were popularized by Therapeuts as in Adoration by the Shepherds), and they sing, as it were, a new song before the throne, and before the four living creatures (Lion, Calf, Man, Eagle of Ezekiel 1:10), and the elders, and no one was able to learn the song except the hundred forty-four thousands, (Reviewing the two groups again: (1) who have been bought from the earth (from the mission of Peter, James and John where fees are paid); (2) the monastics (such as John Mark, Philip, and Andrew) these are they who with women were not defiled, for they are virgins; these are they who are following the Lamb whithersoever he may go; these were bought from among men, a first-fruit to God and to the Lamb and in their mouth there was not found guile, for unblemished are they before the throne of God.)*

*Acts 1:1-5,8-11 The former account, indeed, I made concerning all things, O Theophilus, that Jesus began both to do and to teach, until the day in which, having given command, through the Holy Spirit, to the apostles whom he did choose out, he was taken up, to whom also he did present himself alive after his suffering, in many certain proofs, through forty days being seen by them, and speaking the things concerning the reign of God. And being assembled together with them, he commanded them not to depart from Jerusalem(Qumran), but to wait for the promise of the Father, which, says he 'You did hear of me; because John, indeed, baptized with water, and you shall be baptized with the Holy Spirit, after not many days.'*
*And these things having said, they beholding, he was taken up, and a cloud did receive him up from their sight; and as they were looking steadfastly to the heaven in his going on, then, lo, two men (the second in the hierarchy: Jonathan Annas) stood by them in white apparel, who also said, 'Men, Galileans, why do you stand gazing into the heaven? This Jesus who was received up from you into the heaven (monastery), shall so come in what manner you saw him going on to the heaven.'*

## Chapter 65. (May 6, 33AD)
## Ascension to Monastery

Jonathan (in white apparel as the Son of God) introduces Jesus standing on a platform in the Cenacle building on Mount Zion in Jerusalem, "Behold the 'Lamb of God' who suffered for us, but is still here in Spirit."

Jesus speaks, "The span of time that I am allowed in the world is over tomorrow. My Spirit must return to Heaven. I have added two more provinces to the ten of the Diaspora namely Asher and Dan for the monastics. Since each of the twelve have 12,000 members, there are 144,000 represented here today." They shout "Amen".

Jesus continues, "Remember, we are all as one through the baptism of the Holy Spirit, but there is a need to establish two churches: an abbey church and a monastery. The abbey church is for those whose entrance fee is by donation to their ministers and teachers, joining together to sing hymns to God as the Therapeuts do. The monastery church is for those who remain chaste and pool their wealth as the Essenes do. Both are equal in God's eyes."

"I assure you that the Restoration will come. Perhaps in three or six years, God will allow me to return to continue his work. Meanwhile, I will not be far away. The Holy Spirit will reveal to you my plans for this new mission. For now, Peter, James, and John will oversee the creation of abbeys throughout the known world and John Mark, Philip, and Andrew will preach the benefits of chastity in the Marriage of the Lamb in the already flourishing monasteries."

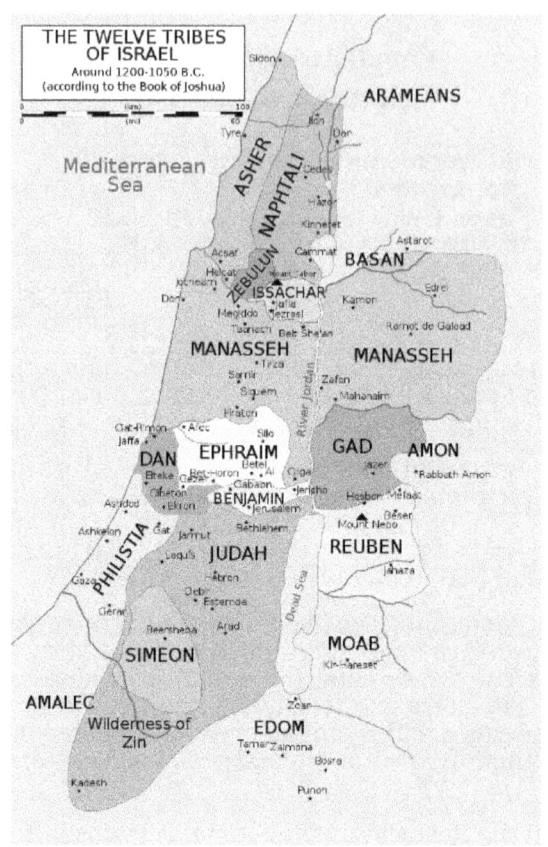

# SECTION 11 (May 24, 33AD to 37AD)
## The New Mission

King Abgar V (died 40AD) of Edessa, whose wife was Queen Helena of Adiabene, sent a letter to Jesus requesting a portrait to heal his leprosy. Jesus sent back a Mandylion (holy towel) with Ananias (Simon Magus) (Eccl Hist 1.13.1-10; The Doctrine of Addai; Antiq 20.1.3-4;Acts 5:1-11)

*Acts 1:12-15 Then did they return to Jerusalem from the mount that is called of Olives, that is near Jerusalem, a sabbath's journey; and when they came in, they went up to the upper room, where were abiding (eleven disciples) both Peter, and James, and John, and Andrew, Philip, and Thomas, Bartholomew (John Mark), and Matthew, James, of Alphaeus (Jonathan Annas)(Simon Magus with feet bandaged), and Judas of James (Theudas - Judas Thaddaeus - Judas ('brother of' rather than 'son of') Jesus' father Joseph thus Jesus' uncle - usage from Last Supper after Judas Iscariot left); these all were continuing with one accord in prayer and supplication, with women, and Mary the mother of Jesus, and with his brethren. (Mary Magdalene was not there because of the long walk, being pregnant.) In those days Peter stood up among the believers (a group numbering about a hundred and twenty).*

*Acts 1:23-26 And they set two, Joseph called Barsabas, who was surnamed Justus, and Matthias, and having prayed, they said, 'You, Lord, who are knowing the heart of all, show which one you did choose of these two to receive the share of this ministration and apostleship, from which Judas, by transgression, did fall, to go on to his proper place;' and they gave their lots, and the lot fell upon Matthias, and he was numbered with the eleven apostles.*

*R.1.60 After him Barnabas, who also is called Matthias, who was substituted as an apostle in the place of Judas.*

## Chapter 66. (May 24, 33AD)
## Choosing a replacement for Judas

*At the Cenacle Building on Mount Zion in Jerusalem, there are 121 people present.*

*Peter, leading the group, reads from Psalms 69 and 109* and begins his sermon, "See how many of these words of David have come true for Jesus, his descendant. In fact, these predictions have proved correct down to the details such as this Psalm (69:21): 'They also gave me poison for my food, and for my thirst they gave me vinegar to drink'."

After the sermon, he says, "As the next order of business we must now select a replacement for Judas, the traitor. The two men under consideration are ones who witnessed Jesus' second rising when he ascended to monastery. The first rising of his resurrection was witnessed only by myself and John Mark and then by the women, and technically by Theudas, who stayed with him in the burial cave. Let us salute him now."

"First, we have Jesus' younger brother James bar Sabbas and then his next younger brother Joses Matthias bar Sabbas, whom you call Barnabas." *They cast lots* and Peter reads, "Chosen is Barnabas."

After the meeting, James complains to Uncle Cleopas, "Father would have insisted that I be chosen."
Theudas replies, "Perhaps, you are forgetting that you were ready to be Caiaphas' lackey?"
"But I did get Pilate to release his body."

"Thank God for that, yet Peter was ready to literally cut off your ear in the Garden."

*Acts 3:1-6;4:22 And Peter and John were going up at the same time to the temple, at the hour of the prayer, the ninth hour, and a certain man, being lame from the womb of his mother, was being carried, whom they were laying every day at the gate of the temple, called Beautiful, to ask a kindness from those entering into the temple, who, having seen Peter and John about to go into the temple, was begging to receive a kindness. And Peter, having looked steadfastly toward him with John, said, 'Look at us;' and he was giving heed to them, looking to receive something from them; and Peter said, 'Silver and gold I have none, but what I have, that I give to you; in the name of Jesus Christ of Nazareth, rise up and be walking.' For above forty years of age was the man upon whom had been done this sign of the healing.*

*Acts 3:11-21 And as the lame man who was healed held Peter and John, all the people ran together unto them in the porch called Solomon's -- greatly amazed, and Peter having seen, answered unto the people, 'Men, Israelites! why wonder you at this? or on us why look you so earnestly, as if by our own power or piety we have made him to walk? 'The God of Abraham, and of Isaac, and of Jacob, the God of our fathers, did glorify His child Jesus, whom you delivered up, and denied him in the presence of Pilate, he having given judgment to release him, and you the Holy and Righteous One did deny, and desired a man -- a murderer -- to be granted to you, and the Prince of the life you did kill, whom God did raise out of the dead, of which we are witnesses; and on the faith of his name, this one whom you see and have known, his name made strong, even the faith that [is] through him did give to him this perfect soundness before you all. And now, brethren, I have known that through ignorance you did it, as also your rulers; and God, what things before He had declared through the mouth of all His prophets, that the Christ should suffer, He did thus fulfill; reform you, therefore, and turn back, for your sins being blotted out, that times of refreshing may come from the presence of the Lord, and He may send Jesus Christ who before has been preached to you, whom it behooves heaven, indeed, to receive till times of a **Restitution** of all things, of which God had spoken through the mouth of all His holy prophets from the age. (Luke 4:21 Great Jubilee cycle (50\*12)=600 from Ezekiel + 7 (29AD) is 36AD). (This year is code for Jesus returning to renew his marriage three years later. It will be shown later that the girl's name is Tamar.)*

*Acts 17:34 And certain men having cleaved to him (Paul), did believe, among whom is also Dionysius the Areopagite, and a woman, by name Tamar (Phoebe, daughter of Jesus), and others with them.*

## Chapter 67. (September 33AD)
## Peter heals James and explains that Jesus has a daughter

*Peter sees James, Jesus' brother, sitting outside Solomon's porch.*

"James, are you sulking that you were not appointed to the twelve?"

"I am unhappy, yes, because the silver and gold of leadership should have been mine from heredity. As I waited two years ago to be the chosen one to lead Joshua's crossing of the River Jordan, it is now the 40th year and it is my duty to be ready."

John Mark says, "Even Theudas does not agree with your prophesied year, but rather favors 44AD."

Peter says, "Your lameness serves no purpose. Just as your brother Joses was cured of blindness, so can you be cured of your lameness. Jesus has already forgiven you and has expressed his desire to make you bishop of Jerusalem." *He reluctantly gets up and the crowd, that has gathered, cheers.*

Peter speaks to the crowd, "In 29AD Jesus announced a new Mission corresponding to the Great Jubilee cycle of 600 which allows 12 Jubilee cycles of 50 years, as prophesied by Ezekiel. In seven years in 36AD we will see the fulfillment of the Restitution of Days when Jesus will return."

The crowds having dispersed, James says, "From your announcement, I see that Jesus' three year return from monastery is to conceive a son, having fathered Tamar. No doubt she was named after the daughter of David, who was dishonored by her step-brother. I suppose this is because my father dishonored Mary."

*Acts 4:5-13,15-17 And it came to pass upon the morrow, there were gathered together of them the rulers, and elders, and scribes, to Jerusalem, Acts 04:06 and Ananus the (previous) chief priest, and Caiaphas, and John (Jonathan Annas), and Alexander (subordinate of Simon Magus Mark 15:21, being Nicodemus on the council), and as many as were of the kindred of the chief priest, and having set them in the midst, they were inquiring, 'In what power, or in what name did you do this?' Then Peter, having been filled with the Holy Spirit, said unto them: 'Rulers of the people, and elders of Israel, if we today are examined concerning the good deed to the ailing man, by whom he has been saved, be it known to all of you, and to all the people of Israel, that in the name of Jesus Christ of Nazareth, whom you did crucify, whom God did raise out of the dead, in him has this one stood by before you whole. 'This is the stone that was set at naught by you, the builders, that became head of a corner; and there is not salvation in any other, for there is no other name under the heaven that has been given among men, in which it behooves us to be saved.'*
*And beholding the openness of Peter and John, and having perceived that they are men unlettered and plebeian, they were wondering and having commanded them to go away out of the Sanhedrin, they took counsel with one another, saying, 'What shall we do to these men? because that, indeed, a notable sign has been done through them, to all those dwelling in Jerusalem is manifest, and we are not able to deny it; but that it may spread no further toward the people, let us strictly threaten them no more to speak in this name to any man.'*

*According to Antiq 18.6.2-4, Agrippa plans to leave for Rome: Herod Antipas makes fun of Herod Agrippa and Agrippa goes to his friend Flaccus in 34AD, but quarrels with him and begins a journey to Rome trying to borrow money from the disciple Peter, being freedman of Agrippa's mother Bernice, who under her will had become a retainer of Antonia, refuses him as he had already defrauded by him. (He is called 'Protos'- correctly assumed by the translator Whiston to be Peter) - because he had this title as one of the Seven Church Leaders Chosen June 37AD representing Sunday, the first day of the week.) Agrippa is detained by Herennius Capito for debts, but escapes to Alexandria asking Alexander the alabarch for the money. He will give it only to his wife Cypros, who returns home. He then writes to Tiberius at Capri asking to visit and is invited, but when news arrives about his debt Tiberius sends him away At this time Philip Herod dies and his kingdom of Trachonitis and Gaulanitis, and of the nation of the Bataneans has no heir. Finally, Agrippa succeeds in borrowing money from Antonia in 35AD and Tiberius has him watch over his grandson Tiberius Gemellus, son of Drusus, which results in a valuable friendship with Caligula who will become the next Emperor.*

## Chapter 68. (September 33AD)
## Peter and John Mark are arrested by Caiaphas, but released; Agrippa leaves for Rome

*Peter and John Mark are arrested and brought to the Council. Present are Ananus the previous chief priest and his sons Jonathan and Matthew, also Theudas as Nicodemus to the Council.*

Caiaphas says, "Now that Jesus is out of the way in monastery, what is the point of you preaching his words?"

Peter answers, "He still directs us as the Holy Spirit."
John Mark adds, "Already Jesus has made Herod's Church accessible to all; its momentum continues to increase without him"
Jonathan says, "The Gentiles are providing a large revenue."

Ananus says, "But Peter and John need to stop pretending that Jesus was resurrected."

Nicodemus says, "To Jesus, it was a resurrection. It was fortunate that I was able to revive him even though his vital signs were close to death."

Caiaphas said, "So would you be willing to be a witness that his resurrection was a pretence?"
'No, I will not devalue the great suffering you brought on him."

As Peter is released, Agrippa accosts him saying, "Peter, I need for you to give me some of my late mother Bernice's money to get back to Rome"

Peter replies, "You defrauded me of that last amount. I cannot in good conscience, give you more. You will have to ask Marsyas."
Agrippa storms off, saying "I will not have Herod Antipas calling me a worthless vagabond."

It is 34AD. James Niceta begins Revelation *(later moved to Rev 8:2-11:19)* by writing a brief review of the years 2BC to 48AD in seven year sets, each ascribed to an angel. His name is not specified like his brother John Aquila who continues writing after that.

*Rev 9:1-4 And the fifth angel (Theophilus Annas: High Priest 37- 41AD); his older brother Jonathan Annas: High Priest 36-37 was discredited: Stoning of Stephen) did sound, and I saw a star out of the heaven having fallen to the earth, and there was given to it the key of the pit of the abyss, and he did open the pit of the abyss (Jesus' Resurrection), and there came up a smoke out of the pit as smoke of a great furnace, and darkened was the sun and the air, from the smoke of the pit.(The smoke in the pit is magician's smoke: the lie about the Resurrection: allows Simon Magus' magic to attract followers.)*

*and out of the smoke came forth locusts to the earth (John the Baptist living on locusts in the wilderness,) and there was given to them authority, as scorpions of the earth have authority, (A scorpion is synonymous with the Eagle, one of the four living creatures of Ezekiel that represent the mission: Eagle is Rome, Calf is Antioch, Lion is Alexandria, Man is Babylon. Thus Simon Magus, as Pope in John the Baptist's place, controls the western part of the mission.)*

Ezekiel 1:15-21 And I see the living creatures, and lo, one wheel is in the earth, near the living creatures, at its four faces. The appearance of the wheels and their works is as the color of beryl, and one likeness is to them four, and their appearances and their works are as it were the wheel in the midst of the wheel. On their four sides, in their going they go, they turn not round in their going. As to their rings, they are both high and fearful, and their rings [are] full of eyes round about them four. And in the going of the living creatures, the wheels go beside them, and in the living creatures being lifted up from off the earth, lifted up are the wheels. Whither the spirit is to go, they go, thither the spirit is to go, and the wheels are lifted up over-against them, for a living spirit is in the wheels. In their going, they go; and in their standing, they stand; and in their being lifted up from off the earth, lifted up are the wheels over-against them; for a living spirit is in the wheels.

*and it was said to them that they may not injure the grass of the earth, nor any green thing, nor any tree,(Jesus commanding the multitudes to recline upon the grass" (5,000/4,000); trees: bishops). but -- the men only who have not the seal of God upon their foreheads,(Simon's symbol 'X' represents entry into the Church)*

*Rev 9:8 and they had hair as hair of women (their best converts: persuading their husbands like Colvis of the Gauls & Constantine of the Romans)*

*Rev 9:11 and they have over them a king -- the angel of the abyss -- a name is to him in Hebrew, Abaddon, and in the Greek, he has a name, Apollyon. (Jesus having been resurrected)*

*Acts 4:36,37 And Joses, who was surnamed by the apostles Barnabas -- which is, having been interpreted, Son of Encouragement -- a Levite, of Cyprus by birth, a field being his, having sold it, brought the money and laid [it] at the feet of the apostles.*

## Chapter 69. (May 16, 34AD)
## Pentecost 34AD

### The Mission (figure by BT)

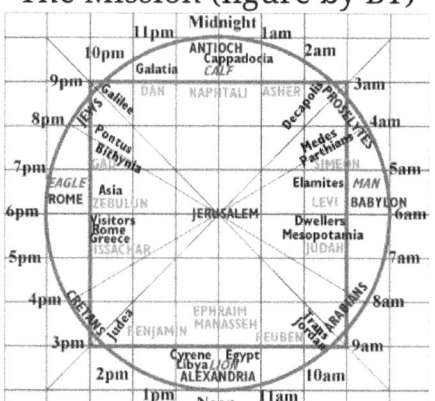

> *And in the day of the Pentecost being fulfilled, they were all with one accord in the same place, and there came suddenly out of the heaven a sound as of a bearing violent breath, and it filled all the house where they were sitting, and there appeared to them divided tongues, as it were of fire; it sat also upon each one of them, and they were all filled with the Holy Spirit, and began to speak with other tongues, according as the Spirit was giving them to declare. (Acts 2:1-4)*

Peter addresses the representatives of the Diaspora, "Let us give a toast to Alexander and Caesar to allow us to communicate in Greek and Latin. No, we are not drunk, for we drink new wine. Our spirits are high, but it is the Spirit that fills us." *They laugh.*

Then Peter and John Mark give many well-rehearsed sermons featuring selections from Joel 2, Psalm 16, and Psalm 101 that foretold Jesus' Crucifixion and Resurrection.

Simon Magus is next, "I am honored that you have re-elected me as Pope, having 'great power' and I have ordained John Mark as bishop, having 'great grace'." (Acts 4:33)

Joses is next, "As the twelfth disciple, I want merely to be your equal, so I am giving up all my goods to be held in common by entering a monastery in Cypress."

*Antiq 20.1.3-4 At the same time Helena, queen of Adiabene and her son Izates became converts to Judaism. Now during the time when Izates resided at Charax Spasini, a certain Jewish merchant (code for missionary) named Ananias visited the king's wives and taught them to worship God after the manner of the Jewish tradition. It was through their agency that he was brought to the notice of Izates, whom he similarly won over with the co-operation of the women. When Izates was convinced that he needed to be circumcised by Eleazar, who came from Galilee, Ananias (Simon Magus) opposed the need of it.*

*Acts 5:1-11 And a certain man, Ananias by name, with Sapphira his wife, sold a possession, and did keep back of the price -- his wife also knowing -- and having brought a certain part, at the feet of the apostles he laid it. And Peter said, 'Ananias, therefore did Satan (Zealot cause) fill your heart, for you to lie to the Holy Spirit, and to keep back of the price of the place? While it remained, did it not remain yours? and having been sold, in your authority was it not? why [is] it that you did put in your heart this thing? you did not lie to men, but to God;' and Ananias hearing these words, having fallen down, did expire, and great fear came upon all who heard these things. And having risen, the younger men wound him up, and having carried forth, they buried him. And it came to pass, about three hours after, that his wife, not knowing what has happened, came in, and Peter answered her, 'Tell me if for so much you sold the place;' and she said, 'Yes, for so much.' And Peter said unto her, 'How was it agreed by you, to tempt the Spirit of the Lord? lo, the feet of those who did bury your husband [are] at the door, and they shall carry you forth;' and she fell down presently at his feet, and expired, and the young men having come in, found her dead, and having carried forth, they buried her by her husband; and great fear came upon all the assembly, and upon all who heard these things.*

*This was the beginning of the rift prophesied at the Crucifixion:*
*Matt 27:51-53 "And lo, the veil of the sanctuary was rent in two from top unto bottom (two churches: abbey for the common folk and monastery for "the saints"), and the earth did quake (those married ones: the 5000), and the rocks (Peter the rock) were rent, and the tombs were opened, and many bodies of the saints who have fallen asleep (monastics at prayer), arose, and having come forth out of the tombs (monastery) after his rising, they went into the holy city, and appeared to many." (Simon is in control of the monasteries (the saints) and when Peter removes him as Pope, he still keeps them.)*

## Chapter 70. (36AD)
## Ananias & Sapphira excommunicated by Peter

Peter asks Simon Magus, "Was your mission to Adiabene as the assistant to the priest Ananias successful?"
Simon answers, "Yes it was. I was able to convert Queen Helena and her son Izates, but unable to prevent his circumcision. I brought with me a small painting of Jesus that I gave to King Abgar of Edessa, her husband, to help cure his leprosy."
"No image of Jesus is to be given out and certainly not for sale. Given your history, from now on, your actions should be named after you as 'simony'."
"Would you prefer that I give all of the generous donation to the Zealots and none to the Church?"

"I have the ear of the Holy Spirit and Jesus condemns you for this."
Simon retorts, "As Pope, I have the power of Ananius; the Holy Spirit is merely of third rank."
*At the later meeting of the females and acolytes, Peter asks the same question to Helena.*
Helena answers, "As Simon's consort, I am second to Simon who is the Pope and thus matching the sapphire on the second row of pews, thus you could call me Sapphira. The infallibility of the Pope is clear."

"You realize, Sapphira, that you and Ananius have to be excommunicated by our council for this."
Helena walking away, "That is funny. Are we doing the 'Lazarus raised' thing again then!"

*Antiq 18.4.6 About this time (34AD) it was that Philip, Herod's ' brother, departed this life, in the twentieth year of the reign of Tiberius, after he had been tetrarch of Trachonitis and Gaulanitis, and of the nation of the Bataneans also, thirty-seven years.*

*Antiq 18.6.4 Agrippa was no way daunted at Caesar's anger, but entreated Antonia, the mother of Germanicus, and of Claudius, who was afterward Caesar himself, to lend him those three hundred thousand drachmae, that he might not be deprived of Tiberius's friendship; so, out of regard to the memory of Bernice his mother, (for those two women were very familiar with one another,) and out of regard to his and Claudius's education together, she lent him the money; and, upon the payment of this debt, there was nothing to hinder Tiberius's friendship to him.*

*Antiq 18.6.5,6 Now Eutychus, was Agrippa's freedman (Eutychus is John Mark's name before he was baptized in the Church as seen in Acts 20:7-12 with Paul March 58AD), and drove his chariot, heard these words: Agrippa said to Nero, 'Oh that the day would once come when this old fellow Tiberius would die and name you for emperor of the habitable earth! Thus his grandson would have no hindrance and that earth would be happy, and I happy also.' Now Eutychus, who was Agrippa's freed-man, and drove his chariot, heard these words, and at that time said nothing of them; but when Agrippa accused him of stealing some garments of his, [which was certainly true,] (Eutychus confessed these statemnents to Tiberius who put him Agrippa in chains.) For certain," said Tiberius, "This is the man I meant to have bound is Agrippa." Upon which Agrippa betook himself to make supplication for himself, putting him in mind of his son, with whom he was brought up, and of Tiberius [his grandson] whom he had educated; but all to no purpose; for they led him about bound even in his <u>purple garments.</u>*

*The deposing of Stephen:*
*Acts 7:57,58 And they, having cried out with a loud voice, stopped their ears, and did rush with one accord upon him (Stephen), and having cast him forth outside of the city, they were stoning him -- and the witnesses did put down their garments at the feet of a young man called Saul (Paul)" (Acts 7:57-58)*

*Clue to St. Paul's identity (also called Saul) when he was imprisoned in Jerusalem. Salome is the daughter of Herodias who married Herod Antipas, thus Paul is Herod Antipas' son by his previous wife.*
*Acts 23:16 And the son of Paul's sister (Tychicus, son of Salome, Paul's sister-in-law) having heard of their lying in wait, having gone and entered into the castle, told Paul.*

## Chapter 71. (36AD-37AD)
## Agrippa is imprisoned then released with a kingdom

*Agrippa finally makes it to Rome at the palace.*

Agrippa says to Caligula, "Son of Germanicus and future emperor, it is good to be back! Thanks to your grandmother Antonia who was a friend of my mother, I have paid my debts and Tiberius, who hides from Rome, has let me back and we can be friends again."
Caligula says, "That doddering fool Tiberius would be better off dead."
Agrippa says, "Let's drink to that!" *Eutychus (John Mark) his charioteer, overhears.*

*Agrippa accuses Eutychus of stealing 'some garments' of his and had him arrested. These were not an ordinary garments, but the ones that Agrippa took from Jesus at the crucifixion. Eutychus, to escape punishment, tells Tiberius about Agrippa's traitorous remark. For this, Agrippa is put in chains, but in the next year, Tiberius had died (certainly poisoned by Caligula's mother). Becoming emperor in March 37AD, Caligula frees Agrippa, giving him a golden chain and the land of Philip, Herod Antipas' brother, who had died without heirs.*

Hearing of this, Herodias says to her husband Herod Antipas, "Caligula has made Agrippa a king. This title is rightly yours as his uncle and especially after you gave him a job when he was about to commit suicide because of his debts."
Antipas replies, "Dearest Herodias, Tiberius' death already creates a problem because, Vitellius was going to avenge my loss to King Aretas when he attacked because I divorced his daughter to marry you. To complain to Caligula now could cost me my tetrarchy. If I am exiled, will you come with me?"
"Of course."

*Antiq 18.5.3; 19.6.2 Vitellius came into Judea, and went up to Jerusalem; it was at the time of that festival which is called the Passover ... Besides which, he also deprived Joseph, who was also called Caiaphas, of the high priesthood, and appointed Jonathan the son of Ananus (36-37AD), the former high priest, to succeed him. So Vitellius prepared to make war with Aretas. Whereupon he ordered the army to march along the great plain, while he himself, with Herod the tetrarch and his friends, went up to Jerusalem to offer sacrifice to God, an ancient festival of the Jews being then just approaching; and when he had been there, and been honorably entertained by the multitude of the Jews, he made a stay there for three days, within which time he deprived Jonathan of the high priesthood, and gave it to his brother Theophilus.*

Paul trying to prove he is a Jew but his heredity is 1/8 Edomite (forcibly converted to Judaism by John Hyrcanus c. 125BC) from his great grandfather Antipater + 1/8 Nabataean-Arab from his great grandmother Cypros + 1/4 Samaritan (resettled by Sargon II king of the Assyrians) from his grandmother Malthace, wife of Herod the Great) + 1/2 Nabataean-Arab from mother Phasaelis, Herod Antipas' wife. *(Paul would have been circumcised to emphasize Jewish heritage and be able to claim that he was from the tribe of Benjamin from his Samaritan grandmother.)*
Acts 22:3 "I indeed, am a man, a Jew, having been born in Tarsus of Cilicia, and brought up in this city at the feet of Gamaliel, having been trained up a child (paideúō from país), according to the exactitude of a law of the fathers, being zealous of God, as all you are today."
2Cor 11:22: "Are they Hebrews? So am I. Are they Israelites? So am I. Are they offspring of Abraham? So am I."
Acts 23:6 "I am a Pharisee, the son of Pharisees."
Phil 3-5 "Circumcised the eighth day, of the nation of Israel, of the tribe of Benjamin, a Hebrew of Hebrews; as to the Law, a Pharisee;" *(It appeared to be Herodian policy to erase any foreign influence by requiring circumcision thus required Sylleus, who poisoned Obodas, king of Arabia, to be circumcised before marrying Herod the Great's sister Salome (Antiq 16:7:6). In addition his grandfather Herod the Great's father Antipater was an Idumaean and, when John Hyrcanus subdued all the Idumeans, he only "permitted them to stay in that country, if they would circumcise their genitals, and make use of the laws of the Jews" (Antiq 13:9:1).)*
Acts 26:4 "My manner of life from my youth, spent from the beginning among my own nation and at Jerusalem(*Qumran*), is known by all the Jews. They have known for a long time, if they are willing to testify, that according to the strictest party of our religion the Pharisees."
Gal 1:14 "I advanced in Judaism beyond many of the same age, for I was far more zealous for the traditions of my ancestors."
Acts 22:25-27 "Paul said to the centurion who was standing by, 'Is it lawful for you to flog a man who is a Roman citizen and uncondemned?' When the centurion heard this, he went to the tribune and said to him, 'What are you about to do? This man is a Roman citizen.' So the tribune came and said to him, 'Tell me, are you a Roman citizen?' He said, 'Yes.'

# Chapter 72. (37AD)
# Jonathan's attempt to merge conservatives and liberals fails (martyred as Stephen)

*When Caiaphas imprisoned the disciples, governor Vitellius deposed him and made Jonathan Annas High Priest (36-37AD). Believing in Priest Kings, he was known as Stephen from the Greek: 'stephanas' meaning crown. As head of the Feeding of the 4,000 under James, where 7 loaves were handed out, his 7 priests were: himself, Philip (one of the Twelve), Prochorus, Nicanor, Timon, Parmenas, and Nicolaus (later rewarded for poisoning Agrippa).*

*Stephen is made to appear before the Sanhedrin. The conservative faction wanted him removed, except for Gamaliel, the grandson of Hillel, who trained Paul as a child. He says, "I do not find fault with your non-violent revolution, but the changes you suggest are too radical." Saul listens in silence.*

> *Stephen's defense: "Like Abraham of old, Hillel has already modified Jewish law with the addition of the Golden Rule. Like his son Isaac, Menahem the Essene, having gained favor with Herod by successfully predicting Herod's kingship and duration, convinced him to reach out to the Diaspora. (Antiq 15.10.5). And you, Gamaliel, as Jacob, like Heli, the grandfather of Jesus, and his son Joseph like Joseph in Egypt could help to spread the seed of non-violence throughout the pagan lands of Rome. Filling Moses' sandals, Nicodemus of the Council could lead Therapeuts to The Promised Land of the known world where the Mediterranean becomes the Jordan River. In his tradition, Jesus as David and Solomon can build temples that contain altars for the Holy of Holies for all people of the known world."*

*The Council is furious, blaming him of blasphemy and wanting to stone him, but since he was the High Priest they requested that the governor depose him and substitute his younger brother, Theophilus.*

*Acts 6:7-13 And the **word of God** did increase, and the number of the disciples did multiply in Jerusalem exceedingly; a great multitude also of the priests were obedient to the faith.*
*This is code for the birth of Jesus' son. His name, Jesus Justus, will be mentioned by Paul has one of his co-workers, specifically saying that he is Jewish:*
*Col 4:11 And Jesus who is called Justus. These are the only men of the circumcision among my fellow workers for the kingdom of God, and they have been a comfort to me.*

*Samaria having received the 'word of God' shows that Jesus is with Simon and Philip and also Magdalene: Acts 8:14,15 And the apostles in Jerusalem(Qumran) having heard that Samaria has received the word of God, did send unto them Peter and John, who having come down did pray concerning them, that they may receive the Holy Spirit,*

*Antiq 18.4.2 But when this tumult was appeased, the Samaritan senate sent an embassy to Vitellius, a man that had been consul, and who was now president of Syria, and accused Pilate of the murder of those that were killed; for that they did not go to Tirathaba in order to revolt from the Romans, but to escape the violence of Pilate. So Vitellius sent Marcellus, a friend of his, to take care of the affairs of Judea, and ordered Pilate to go to Rome, to answer before the emperor to the accusations of the Jews. So Pilate, when he had tarried ten years in Judea, made haste to Rome, and this in obedience to the orders of Vitellius, which he durst not contradict; but before he could get to Rome Tiberius was dead.*

*Now, in the second year of the reign of Caligula Caesar, Agrippa desired leave to be given him to sail home, and settle the affairs of his government; and he promised to return again, when he had put the rest in order, as it ought to be put. So, upon the emperor's permission, he came into his own country, and appeared to them all unexpectedly as asking, and thereby demonstrated to the men that saw him the power of fortune, when they compared his former poverty with his present happy affluence.*

## Chapter 73. (September 37AD)
## Magdalene has given birth to a son: Jesus Justus

*It is September 37AD, Mary Magdalene knocks on the door of the monastery in Caesarea Maritima with a baby in her arms and a four-year-old daughter holding on to her garment.*

Magdalene says, "It is Jesus, I seek." Coming to the door, Jesus says, "Greetings dear wife and beautiful daughter Tamar. And what have we here?"
"It is your heir and he shall have your name."

Jesus looks into the bundle and says, "My dear Magdalene, He is so divine, my new crown prince Jesus Justus." Then he stoops down to hug his daughter, "So what do you think of your brother?"
Magdalene says, "Now you can rest easy knowing that our son can bear the heavy burden of your mission on his shoulders when he is a man."

"I am so pleased that I can officially take the 'Justus' title from James. I will have the phrase 'the word of God has increased' added to the Acts of the Apostles; for, in the gospel of John, Simon wrote, 'In the beginning was the Word'; thus I became the 'Word'."

Magdalene says, "Oh yes, I see, so, if there was no announcement of our daughter's birth, everyone is supposed to know that she was just a girl."

Jesus stoops down again to Tamar, "You are not just a girl, are you? You shall be a deacon of the Church."

*The true description of Simon Magus is given:*
*Acts 8:9-11 And a certain man, by name Simon, was before in the city using magic, and amazing the nation of Samaria, saying himself to be a certain great one, to whom they were all giving heed, from small unto great, saying, 'This one is the great power of God;' and they were giving heed to him, because of his having for a long time amazed them with deeds of magic.*

*Acts 8:5-8;12 And Philip having gone down to a city of Samaria, was preaching to them the Christ, Acts 8:6 the multitudes also were giving heed to the things spoken by Philip, with one accord, in their hearing and seeing the signs that he was doing, for unclean spirits came forth from many who were possessed, crying with a loud voice, and many who have been paralytic and lame were healed, and there was great joy in that city. And when they believed Philip, proclaiming good news, the things concerning the reign of God and the name of Jesus Christ, they were baptized both men and women; and Simon also himself did believe, and, having been baptized, he was continuing with Philip, beholding also signs and mighty acts being done, he was amazed.*

*Acts 8:26-38 And an angel of the Lord (Simon) spoke unto Philip, saying, 'Arise, and go on toward the south, on the way that is going down from Jerusalem to Gaza,'-- this is desert. Acts 08:27 And having arisen, he went on, and lo, a man of Ethiopia (Titus-Marsyas), a eunuch, a man of rank, of Candace the queen of the Ethiopians, who was over all her treasure, who had come to worship to Jerusalem; he was also returning, and is sitting on his chariot, and he was reading the prophet, Isaiah. And the Spirit (Jesus' directions) said to Philip, 'Go near, and be joined to this chariot;' and Philip having run near, heard him reading the prophet Isaiah, and said, 'Do you then know what you do read?' and he said, 'Why, how am I able, if someone may not guide me?' he called Philip also, having come up, to sit with him. And the contents of the Writing that he was reading was this: 'As a sheep unto slaughter he was led, and as a lamb before his shearer dumb, so he does not open his mouth; in his humiliation, his judgment was taken away, and his generation -- who shall declare? because taken from the earth is his life.' And the eunuch answering Philip said, 'I pray you, about whom does the prophet say this? about himself, or about some other one?' and Philip having opened his mouth, and having begun from this Writing, proclaimed good news to him: Jesus. (He did not know that Jesus was alive.) And as they were going on the way, they came upon a certain water, and the eunuch said, 'Lo, water; what does hinder me to be baptized?' And Philip said, 'If you do believe out of all the heart, it is lawful; 'and he answering said, 'I believe Jesus Christ to be the Son of God;' and he commanded the chariot to stand still, and they both went down to the water, both Philip and the eunuch, and he baptized him (as bishop);*

# Chapter 74. (September 37AD)
# Philip sent to the Ethiopian of Ham

*Simon Magus arrives.* Magdalene says, "Oh great power of God, Simon the Magician. I have heard much of you from Samaria of how you are using magic to amaze the crowds."
Simon answers, "I see Philip has been filling your head with tall tales."

Turning to Jesus he says, "Pilate has been recalled!"
Jesus says, "So I do not have to hide anymore."
Magdalene says, "Admit it, Jesus, you clearly like it in monastery."

Jesus says to Simon, "It seems I must constantly raise you from the dead: once as Lazarus and then I had to send my bishop, Philip, to have your excommunication from Peter removed. I guess with all your deaths, you remain the Standing One. I love you Simon, but you know I cannot condone the selling Church positions or supporting the Zealots."

Simon says, "You cannot run a Church with paupers as donors and the donkeys need a carrot. Speaking of that, I am sending Philip to Titus of the Ethiopians of Ham. My plan is to make this 'big fish', Marsyas, a bishop. Perhaps we can use him as an ally against Agrippa, and his money is always welcome."
Jesus says, "Peter had that right: 'simony'."
"My legacy increases!"

Magdalene interjects, "Enough you two! Talking business in front of our innocents. I am leaving."

Jesus goes over to the baby and kisses him and looks into Magdalene's eyes, "Thank you for the great joy that you have given me. I am sad that I will not be allowed to be with you for six years, but I cherish the time we have had together."

# SECTION 12 (37AD to 44AD)
## Ascendency of Peter & Paul and rise and fall of Herod Agrippa 40-44AD

This was the model for the Blinding on the Road to Damascus
Mark 10:46-50 And they come to Jericho (tribe of Benjamin), and as he is going forth from Jericho, with his disciples and a great multitude, a son of Timaeus -- Bartimaeus *(son of Gamaliel)* the blind *(of the level similar to Joses when he was healed)* -- was sitting beside the way begging, and having heard that it is Jesus the Nazarene, he began to cry out, and to say, "The Son of David -- Jesus! deal kindly with me;" and many were rebuking him, that he might keep silent, but the more abundantly he cried out, "Son of David, deal kindly with me." And Jesus having stood, he commanded him to be called, and they call the blind man, saying to him, "Take courage, rise, he does call you;" and he, having cast away his garment, having risen, did come unto Jesus. And answering, Jesus said to him, "What will you I may do to you?" and the blind man said to him, "Rabboni, that I may see again;" and Jesus said to him, "Go, your faith has saved you;" and immediately he saw again, and was following Jesus in the Way *(the Church)*.
Matt 20:29 And they going forth from Jericho, there followed him a great multitude, and lo, two blind men *(Saul = Paul)* sitting by the Way...

Acts 9:1-6,10-18 And Saul, yet breathing of threatening and slaughter to the disciples of the Lord, having gone to the chief priest, did ask from him letters to Damascus, unto the synagogues, that if he may find any being of The Way, both men and women, he may bring them bound to Jerusalem. And in the going, he came near to Damascus, and suddenly there shone round about him a light from the heaven, and having fallen upon the earth, he heard a voice saying to him, 'Saul, Saul, why do you persecute me?' And he said, 'Who are you, Lord?' and the Lord said, 'I am Jesus whom you do persecute; hard for you at the pricks to kick;' trembling also, and astonished, he said, 'Lord, what do you wish me to do?' and the Lord [said] unto him, 'Arise, and enter into the city, and it shall be told you what it behooves you to do.' And the men who are journeying with him stood speechless, hearing indeed the voice but seeing no one, and Saul arose from the earth, and his eyes having been opened, he beheld no one, and leading him by the hand they brought him to Damascus, and he was three days without seeing, and he did neither eat nor drink.
And there was a certain disciple in Damascus, by name Ananias, and the Lord said unto him in a vision, 'Ananias'; and he said, 'Behold me, Lord;' and the Lord said unto him, 'Having risen, go on unto the street that is called Straight, and seek in the house of Judas, one by name Saul of Tarsus, for, lo, he does pray, and he saw in a vision a man, by name Ananias, coming in, and putting a hand on him, that he may see again.' And Ananias answered, 'Lord, I have heard from many about this man, how many evils he did to Your saints in Jerusalem, and here he has authority from the chief priests, to bind all those calling on Your name.' And the Lord said unto him, 'Be going on, because a choice vessel to Me is this one, to bear My name before nations and kings -- the sons also of Israel; for I will show him how many things it behooves him for My name to suffer.' And Ananias went away, and did enter into the house, and having put upon him his hands, said, 'Saul, brother, the Lord has sent me -- Jesus who did appear to you in The Way in which you were coming -- that you may see again, and may be filled with the Holy Spirit.' And immediately there fell from his eyes as it were scales, he saw again also presently, and having risen, was baptized.

Shows that Paul was 40 and thus he was born in November 16AD
Acts 19:22 Having sent to Macedonia two of those ministering to him -- Timothy and Erastus -- he himself stayed a period (Gr. 'chronon' as 40 years) in Asia.
Gal 1:17 "Nor did I go up to Jerusalem to those who were apostles before me, but I went away into Arabia (Tarsus - for training), and returned again to Damascus."

## Chapter 75. (September 37AD)
## Paul is blinded, Jesus speaks to him

*When Jonathan Annas (Stephen) gave his speech at his metaphoric stoning, Paul was an acolyte under Gamaliel, having held their garments and still holding the conservative view against Jonathan's liberal ideas. The Council sends him to Caesarea Maritima to arrest Simon Magus (Ananias).*
Simon Magus greets him, "Is this the Saul who ridicules us in the infamous Habakkuk Pesher."

Saul says, Although the Council sent me to attempt to shut down your mission, I have been reconsidering Stephen's defense. Maybe, his vision is correct."
"Ah yes, Jonathan can ramble at times, but he was brave to attempt to use his position as High Priest to gain recognition of our path that we call the 'Way'. So, now that you doubt the purpose of your mission, let me discuss with you a greater mission to the Diaspora. Afterwards, I will take you along the narrow street called 'Straight' and see if the Holy Spirit is willing to talk with you?"
Saul says, "You seem to be implying that this is an actual person." "We shall see."

*They enter in the church and sit down. As Saul looks up above at a raised platform, the blinding light from the open roof illuminates a figure that to Paul seems to be the resurrected Christ and he sobs.*

"The figure says, "My dearest Paul, be no more Saul, David's enemy. Agree to be persecuted rather than to persecute, to love rather than to hate, to prepare the people for the coming Resurrection?"
"Yes, even to the cross, my Lord."
"Then I will have Ananias secure a place for you in the monastery in Tarsus."

*Antiq 18.6.11 Now, in the second year of the reign of Caligula Caesar, Agrippa desired leave to be given him to sail home, and settle the affairs of his government (tetrarchy of Herod Philip who had died earlier); and he promised to return again, when he had put the rest in order, as it ought to be put. So, upon the emperor's permission, he came into his own country, and appeared to them all unexpectedly as asking, and thereby demonstrated to the men that saw him the power of fortune, when they compared his former poverty with his present happy affluence.*

*Antiq 18.7.1 But Herodias, Agrippa's sister, who now lived as wife to that Herod who was tetrarch of Galilee and Peres, took this authority of her brother in an envious manner, particularly when she saw that he had a greater dignity bestowed on him than her husband had; since, when he ran away, it was because he was not able to pay his debts; and now he came back, he was in a way of dignity, and of great good fortune. She was therefore grieved and much displeased at so great a mutation of his affairs; and chiefly when she saw him marching among the multitude with the usual ensigns of royal authority, she was not able to conceal how miserable she was, by reason of the envy she had towards him; but she excited her husband, and desired him that he would sail to Rome, to court honors equal to his; for she said that she could not bear to live any longer, while Agrippa, the son of that Aristobulus who was condemned to die by his father, one that came to her husband in such extreme poverty, that the necessaries of life were forced to be entirely supplied him day by day; and when he fled away from his creditors by sea, he now returned a king. Antipas being, the son of a king, and a greater claim to the throne, but he sat still, and was contented with a private life.*

Vatican Museum: Nabatean Sepulchral Inscription: "referring to the 46th year of King Aretas" (37AD: Paul's conversion).

2Cor 11:32-33 "In Damascus, the governor under King Aretas (9BC-40AD) - his daughter and mother of Paul was divorced by Herod Antipas which started a war between them) had the city of the inhabitants of Damascus guarded in order to arrest me. But I was lowered in a basket from a window in the wall and slipped away."

Acts 9:19-27 "And having received nourishment" (three years in Tarsus monastery), "was strengthened, and Saul was with the disciples in Damascus certain days, and immediately in the synagogues, he was preaching the Christ, that he is the Son of God. And all those hearing were amazed, and said, 'Is not this he who laid waste in Jerusalem those calling on this name, and, hither to this intent had come, that he might bring them bound to the chief priests?' And Saul was still more strengthened, and he was confounding the Jews dwelling in Damascus, proving that this is the Christ.

# Chapter 76. (38-39AD)
# Agrippa takes Philip's Tetrarchy / Antipas will soon will lose his / Paul escapes Damascus in a basket

*At Caesarea Maritima Herod Agrippa lands to take over the lands of Herod Philip.*

Agrippa says to Herodias, "Greetings sister. Your husband Uncle Antipas once treated me like a pauper and now I am rich as a king. He is just a feeble tetrarch unable to defend himself from the incense traders of Petra."

Herodias says, "With an emperor like Caligula, your fortunes could be bankrupt just as easily."
Agrippa laughs. "Caligula is my friend. He wants me to be another Herod the Great."
Herodias says, "I would rather lose these lands than to be king under you!"
"We shall see."

The next year, Paul is speaking to the governor of Damascus, "I wish an audience with my grandfather."

The governor says, "King Aretas has disowned you since your father Herod Antipas divorced and disgraced your mother Phasaelis to marry Herodias."

Paul answers, "But now that I have graduated at level seven from the monastery of Tarsus in the Church of the Way, I wanted to tell him the news of Christ crucified and resurrected and that he bids us all to love our enemies."
"We worship other gods, you should leave."

*Paul stays, gathering large crowds, but fearing arrest, he escapes by being lowered down in a basket.*

**R.1.43** *We sought for a fitting opportunity, a week of years was completed from the passion of the Lord (7 years + 33AD = 40AD), the Church of the Lord which was constituted in Jerusalem was most plentifully multiplied and grew, being governed by most righteous ordinances by* **James [the Just], who was ordained bishop in it by the Lord.**
*Acts 9:31-35 Then, indeed, the assemblies throughout all Judea, and Galilee, and Samaria, had peace, being built up, and, going on in the fear of the Lord, and in the comfort of the Holy Spirit, they were multiplied. And it came to pass that Peter passing throughout all quarters, came down also unto the saints who were dwelling at Lydda, and he found there a certain man, Aeneas by name -- for eight years laid upon a couch (James had finished eight years of study since Peter had invited him to enter the Church 33AD+8= 41AD) -- who was paralytic (humorous allusion to the fact that he was always on his knees), and Peter said to him, 'Jesus the Christ does heal you, Aeneas; arise and take up your bed;' and immediately he rose, and all those dwelling at Lydda, and Saron saw him, and did turn to the Lord. (The name Aeneas being a Greek-Roman name shows that James agrees to exempt circumcision.)*

*Antiq 19.6.2 (Agrippa having been made king of Judea 41AD) And when Agrippa had entirely finished all the duties of the Divine worship, he removed Theophilus, the son of Ananus, from the high priesthood, and bestowed that honor of his on Simon the son of Boethus, (41- 43AD)*
*Antiq 19.6.4 And now king Agrippa took the high priesthood away from Simon Cantheras, and put Jonathan, the son of Ananus, into it again, and owned that he was more worthy of that dignity than the other. But this was not a thing acceptable to him, to recover that his former dignity. So he refused it, and said, "O king! I rejoice in the honor that thou hast for me, and take it kindly that thou would give me such a dignity of your own inclinations, although God hath judged that I am not at all worthy of the high priesthood. I am satisfied with having once put on the sacred garments; for I then put them on after a more holy manner than I should now receive them again. But if thou desirest that a person more worthy than myself should have this honorable employment, give me leave to name you such a one. I have a brother that is pure from all sin against God, and of all offenses against yourself; I recommend him to you, as one that is fit for this dignity." So the king was pleased with these words of his, and passed by Jonathan, and, according to his brother's desire, bestowed the high priesthood upon Matthias (43).*

## Chapter 77. (40AD)
## Peter tells James, brother of Jesus, about his appointment to Bishop of Jerusalem

At Lydda, Peter approaches James, who is knelling in prayer, saying, "Sorry to disturb you, but I bring news from High Priest Theophilus. Recognizing your transformation from the crippled man looking for the year of Exodus, previously healed by Jesus and me, having completed eight years of study, and taken the name of Aeneas, the forefather of the Romans, demonstrating that you will now accept Gentiles, His Excellency would like you to appear before him to be ordained as Bishop of Jerusalem."

James replies, "I am surprised and honored! With Caligula, having confiscated Herod Antipas' tetrarchy, and soon to become a King as powerful as Herod the Great, Theophilus must fear that he will be replaced by High Priest Boethus' son, who is against us."

Peter says, "Yes, let us use your new position to bring us closer to a reconciliation with your Jewish Christian factions in opposition to King Agrippa."

James says, "I have read the ten books of the debates between you and Simon Magus that cover the time, two years ago, when you were chasing Simon Magus from Tyre and Sidon, Beirut, Byblos, Tripolis, and Aradus. I commend Father Jonathan, James son of Alphaeus, for requesting Clement to compile them. These Clementines have kept our two groups focused against heresy and could be the basis of an excellent story."

*Promotion of Mother Mary to Mother Superior like Anna, who blessed Jesus*
*Acts 9:36-42 And in Joppa there was a certain female disciple, by name Tabitha, (which interpreted, is called Dorcas,) this woman was full of good works and kind acts that she was doing; Acts and it came to pass in those days she, having ailed, died, and having bathed her, they laid her in an upper chamber, and Lydda being near to Joppa, the disciples having heard that Peter is in that place, sent two men unto him, calling on him not to delay to come through unto them.*
*And Peter having risen, went with them, whom having come, they brought into the upper chamber, and all the widows stood by him weeping, and showing coats and garments, as many as Dorcas was making while she was with them.*
*And Peter having put them all forth without, having bowed the knees, did pray, and having turned unto the body said, 'Tabitha, arise; and she opened her eyes, and having seen Peter, she sat up, and having given her his hand, he lifted her up, and having called the saints and the widows, he presented her alive, and it became known throughout all Joppa, and many believed on the Lord;*

*Rev 09:13,14 And the sixth angel (Matthew Annas) did sound, and I heard a voice out of the four horns of the altar of gold that is before God (Theophilus Annas as high priest), saying to the sixth angel who had the trumpet, 'Loose the four angels who are bound at the great river Euphrates; and loosed were the four angels, who have been made ready for the hour, and day, and month, and year, that they may kill one third.' (1. priests, 2. laity, and 3. nonbelievers-who are already dead or made dead by excommunication)*
*The Church now has four factions that needed to join together against the great threat of King Agrippa who would now be as powerful as Herod the Great:*

1. *James, the brother of Jesus, made Bishop of Jerusalem in 40AD (later called Jewish Christians)*
2. *Simon's monastery in Caesarea Maritima being called "Seekers of Smooth Things" in the Damascus Document of the Dead Sea Scrolls*
3. *the monastery of Qumran for Gentiles where Peter would train to be archbishop*
4. *the Church of Damascus and Antioch connected to Diaspora missions of Peter and Paul*

*Theophilus Annas placed his younger brother, Matthew, Angel 4, in charge a new Church in a Herod House in Caesarea Maritima with the goal of reconciliation. Matthew Annas would be High Priest in 43AD. The area was considered in the territory of Babylon and therefore "The Great River Euphrates." ("To kill" is merely to have the power to excommunicate.)*

## Chapter 78. (40AD)
## Peter helps Mother Mary (Tabitha) to adjust to her new role as Mother Superior

*Peter and John Mark arrive at Joppa. Mother Mary is in bed exhausted.*
Peter says, "Mary, are you all right?"

Seeing them, she arose quickly saying, "Yes I am fine. I am glad that you have come on my 65th birthday."
John Mark says, "You look exhausted Tabitha."

"Yes, I have been looking back on my life since my birth in December 26BC and being married at seventeen, then widowed at 23AD. Although Jesus survived, no mother should have to watch her son be crucified on a cross. These past years I have enjoyed my many years as a seamstress with my sister nuns and now it is so hard to say goodbye to them to become Mother Superior of the Church in Ephesus."

John Mark says, "I will be glad to accompany you on your journey. After all, I promised Jesus when he was on the cross to care for you and Magdalene."

Peter says, "That should be a good way for you to avoid the wrath of Herod Agrippa, as he has not forgotten those chains you put him in." *They laugh.*

Mother Mary says, "Now that he is king over the lands of Herod Antipas, I wonder if he is already suffering from his grandfather's insanity."

John Mark says, "Certainly his benefactor Caligula also seems to be a victim of the royal inbreeding."

*(Acts 09:40-42 And Peter ... he presented her (Tabitha) alive, Acts 09:42 and it became known throughout all Joppa, and many believed on the Lord;) Acts 09:43 and it came to pass (three years later), that he ("the Lord" - carried over from v. 42 - not Peter) remained many days in Joppa, with a certain one, Simon a tanner.*

Caligula (Caius) was assassinated in January 41AD. Agrippa was in Rome and negotiates with the Senate to install Claudius as emperor.

Antiq 20.4.1. Now Claudius, though he was sensible after what an insolent manner the senate had sent to him yet did he, according to their advice, behave himself for the present with moderation; but not so far that he could not recover himself out of his fright; so he was encouraged to claim the government partly by the boldness of the soldiers, and partly by the persuasion of king Agrippa, who exhorted him not to let such a dominion slip out of his hands, when it came thus to him of its own accord. Now this Agrippa, with relation to Caius, did what became one that had been so much honored by him; for he embraced Caius's body after he was dead, and laid it upon a bed, and covered it as well as he could, and went out to the guards, and told them that Caius was still alive; but he said that they should call for physicians, since he was very ill of his wounds. But when he had learned that Claudius was carried away violently by the soldiers, he rushed through the crowd to him, and when he found that he was in disorder, and ready to resign up the government to the senate, he encouraged him, and desired him to keep the government;

Antiq 19.5.1 Now when Claudius had taken out of the way all those soldiers whom he suspected, which he did immediately, he published an edict, and therein confirmed that kingdom to Agrippa which Caligula had given him, and therein commended the king highly. He also made an addition to it of all that country over which Herod, who was his grandfather, had reigned, that is, Judea and Samaria; and this he restored to him as due to his family.

Antiq 10.1.2 Upon the presentation of your ambassadors to me (emperor Claudius) by Agrippa, my friend, whom I have brought up, and have now with me, and who is a person of very great piety, who are come to give me thanks for the care I have taken of your nation, and to entreat me, in an earnest and obliging manner, that they may have the holy vestments, with the crown belonging to them, under their power, - I grant their request, as that excellent person Vitellius, who is very dear to me, had done before me. And I have complied with your desire, in the first place, out of regard to that piety which I profess, and because I would have everyone worship God according to the laws of their own country; and this I do also because I shall hereby highly gratify king Herod, and Agrippa, junior, whose sacred regards to me, and earnest good-will to you: **Cornelius, the son of Cero,**

## Chapter 79. (43AD)
## Jesus is out of monastery to renew his marriage; decides to write another gospel

*Jesus leaves the monastery to ask Simon Magus for approval to renew his marriage.*

Jesus says, "Hello my friend, I was told there was a tanner who lives here."

Simon exclaims, "Could it be Jesus or is it just his Spirit! Yes, I prefer being simply a 'tanner' to Judas' tester label of 'Satan'. You have missed all the action with Caligula assassinated and Claudius made emperor with the help of Caligula's turncoat friend: none other than our favorite person King Herod Agrippa, owning now as much territory as Herod the Great. Let me guess you want my blessing to renew your marriage. My answer is 'yes'. You are most productive in both senses of the word when you are out of monastery. God may be happy to have you to himself, but we need you. I fear that King Agrippa will start putting us all to the sword next."

Jesus says, "I am concerned that Mathew's intended detailed gospel will eclipse our Gospel of John. I will need to put together a similar version that empathizes my teachings."

Simon says, "I have the perfect person to be your scribe. You will remember him as the centurion Cornelius who used the lancet at your Crucifixion to confirm your death."
"Yes, he is perfect!"

*Acts 10:1-6 And there was a certain man in Caesarea, by name Cornelius, a centurion from a band called Italian, pious, and fearing God with all his house, doing also many kind acts to the people, and beseeching God always, he saw in a vision manifestly, as it were the ninth hour of the day, an angel of God coming in unto him, and saying to him, 'Cornelius;' and he having looked earnestly on him, and becoming afraid, said, 'What is it, Lord?' And he said to him, 'Your prayers and your kind acts came up for a memorial before God, and now send men to Joppa, and send for a certain one Simon, who is surnamed, Peter, this one does lodge with a certain Simon a tanner, whose house is by the sea; this one shall speak to you what it behooves you to do.'*

*Acts 10:9-16 And on the morrow, as these are proceeding on The Way, and are drawing near to the city, Peter went up upon the house-top to pray, about the sixth hour, and he became very hungry and wished to eat; and they making ready, there fell upon him a trance, and he does behold the heaven opened, and descending unto him a certain vessel, as a great sheet, bound at the four corners, and let down upon the earth, in which were all the four-footed beasts of the earth, and the wild beasts, and the creeping things, and the fowls of the heaven, and there came a voice unto him: 'Having risen, Peter, slay and eat.' And Peter said, 'Not so, Lord; because at no time did I eat anything common or unclean;' and there is a voice again a second time unto him: 'What God did cleanse, you, declare not you common and this was done thrice, and again was the vessel received up to the heaven.*

*19.7.4. However, there was a certain man of the Jewish nation at Jerusalem, who appeared to be very accurate in the knowledge of the law. His name was Simon. This man got together an assembly, while the king was absent at Caesarea, and had the insolence to accuse him as not living holily, and that he might justly be excluded out of the temple, since it belonged only to native Jews. But the general of Agrippa's army informed him that Simon had made such a speech to the people. So the king sent for him; and as he was sitting in theater, he bid him sit down by him, and said to him with a low and gentle voice, "What is there done in this place that is contrary to the law?" But he had nothing to say for himself, but begged his pardon. So the king was more easily reconciled to him than one could have imagined, as esteeming mildness a better quality in a king than anger, and knowing that moderation is more becoming in great men than passion. So he made Simon a small present, and dismissed him.*

# Chapter 80. (43AD)
## Jesus associates with Cornelius (Luke); tells Peter to give equal standing to Gentiles

*Jesus stands on the third story of the Church at Joppa. He passes down a tablecloth with the beasts from Ezekiel: "four-footed beasts of the earth" (calf), "and the wild beasts" (lion), "and the creeping things" (snake: man), "and the fowls of the heaven" (eagle). He says "Slay and eat."*

Peter looking toward the light that is coming through from the open shutter on the roof, says "Is this Matthew Annas that guides me?"

Jesus answers, "No, it is the Holy Spirit."

"My teacher, are you implying that I must include all peoples to the Holy table?"

"Yes, Peter, Gentiles and Jews are to be equal."

Peter, turning to the congregation, calls out, "Cornelius I invite you to join me on the second level."

*Jesus comes down and sits with them.*

Cornelius says, "I saw you risen, you who were dead. To share the sacrament with you is a third miracle."

Jesus asks, "Will you be my scribe for my new gospel?"

"I will do anything you need of me."

"Thank you." Then turning to Peter, "My sympathies on your wife's death. As a widower, you will be eligible to be an archbishop next year. Also, you must reconcile with Herod Agrippa. You are a pillar of my Church and his son, Agrippa II, whom Paul has trained, could be another."

Acts 12:1-2 And about that time, Herod the king put forth his hands, to do evil to certain of those of the assembly, and he killed James, the brother of John, with the sword. (excommunication)
Agrippa intends to publicly depose Peter in a mock Crucifixion trial told as a composite of Peter's graduation as an archbishop at Qumran
Acts 12:3-11 And having seen that it is pleasing to the Jews, he added to lay hold of Peter also -- and they were the days of the unleavened food -- whom also having seized, he did put in prison, having delivered him to four quaternions of soldiers to guard him, intending after the Passover to bring him forth to the people.
Peter, therefore, indeed, was kept in the prison, and fervent prayer was being made by the assembly unto God for him, and when Herod was about to bring him forth, the same night was Peter sleeping between two soldiers, having been bound with two chains, guards also before the door were keeping the prison,(The two chains are a metaphor for the chains for Agrippa's chains when in prison in Rome.)
And lo, an angel of the Lord (Matthew Annas) stood by, and a light shone in the buildings, and having smitten Peter on the side, he raised him up, saying, 'Rise in haste', and his chains fell from off his hands. The angel also said to him, 'Gird yourself, and bind on your sandals; 'and he did so; and he said to him, 'Put your garment round and be following me;' and having gone forth, he was following him, and he knew not that it is true that which is done through the angel, and was thinking he saw a vision, (Peter had been studying to become an archbishop and Matthew Annas (the angel), having freed him, begins his graduation ceremony. He instructs him on how to dress as the leader of the missionaries rather than the priests in the monastery: not in bare feet, but sandals; not to be belt-less, but having a belt. He is struck on the side as a symbol of Jacob wrestling with the angel (Genesis 32:25) . Then the levels are described from the highest to the lowest, back into the Street (The Way) that Peter had graduated through under the direction of Matthew Annas (the angel), sending him forth as an archbishop.)
and having passed through a first ward, and a second, they came unto the iron gate that is leading to the city, which of its own accord did open to them, and having gone forth, they went on through one Street, and immediately the angel departed from him.
And Peter having come to himself, said, 'Now I have known of a truth that the Lord did send forth His angel, and did deliver me out of the hand of Herod, and all the expectation of the people of the Jews;'
(Peter was initially bound to Herod by his mother-in-law, Glaphyra, who was of the Herod family. Now that his wife had passed on, he is not bound.)

## Chapter 81. (44AD)
## Herod Agrippa shows signs of insanity; Peter ordained archbishop

King Herod Agrippa, beginning to show signs of the madness, summons James Niceta and Peter to appear before him. "James, you are accused of plotting against me with Zealots. Get me my sword!"

Blastus, his servant, whispers to him, "O king, the sword is only a metaphor for excommunication."

"At least let me hold it while I excommunicate him!"

Agrippa says, "Now Peter, I hear that you have accused me of not acting in a holy manner. Turning to the imaginary crowd, Shall we crucify him or Barabbas?"

Peter replies, "I apologize. Your incarceration of me coincided with my graduation as an archbishop and my release from my prison cell in Qumran became a metaphoric ceremony of my graduation. I hope for your blessing."

Agrippa says, "Out of our previous friendship, you have my blessing. Next, I will visit Procurator Fadus to see Theudas Barabbas' head on a spike. He foolishly tried to cross the Jordan River with his followers as Joshua." *(He gets up and walks out.)*

Peter stares at Niceta shocked. "Jesus' will be sad to lose his uncle Cleopas after replacing him on the cross."

*Acts 12:19-23 (Herod Agrippa) having gone down from Judea to Caesarea, he was abiding there. And Herod was highly displeased with the Tyrians and Sidonians, and with one accord they came unto him, and having made a friend of Blastus, who is over the bed-chambers of the king, they were asking peace, because of their country being nourished from the king's; and on a set day, Herod having arrayed himself in kingly apparel, and having sat down upon the tribunal, was making an oration unto them, and the populace were shouting, 'The voice of a god, and not of a man;' and presently there smote him an angel of the Lord, because he did not give the glory to God, and having been eaten of worms, he expired.*

*Antiq 19.8.2. Now when Agrippa had reigned three years over all Judea, he came to the city Caesarea, which was formerly called Strato's Tower; and there he exhibited shows in honor of Caesar, upon his being informed that there was a certain festival celebrated to make vows for his safety. At which festival a great multitude was gotten together of the principal persons, and such as were of dignity through his province. On the second day of which shows he put on a garment made wholly of silver, and of a texture truly wonderful, and came into the theater early in the morning; at which time the silver of his garment being illuminated by the fresh reflection of the sun's rays upon it, shone out after a surprising manner, and was so resplendent as to spread a horror over those that looked intently upon him; and presently his flatterers cried out, one from one place, and another from another, (though not for his good,) that he was a god; and they added, "Be thou merciful to us; for although we have hitherto reverenced you only as a man, yet shall we henceforth own you as superior to mortal nature." Upon this, the king did neither rebuke them, nor reject their impious flattery. But as he presently afterward looked up, he saw an owl sitting on a certain rope over his head, and immediately understood that this bird was the messenger of ill tidings, as it had once been the messenger of good tidings to him; and fell into the deepest sorrow. A severe pain also arose in his belly, and began in a most violent manner. He, therefore, looked upon his friends, and said, "I, whom you call a god, am commanded presently to depart this life; while Providence thus reproves the lying words you just now said to me; and I, who was by you called immortal, am immediately to be hurried away by death. But I am bound to accept of what Providence allots, as it pleases God; for we have by no means lived ill, but in a splendid and happy manner." When he said this, his pain became violent. Accordingly, he was carried into the palace, and the rumor went abroad everywhere, that he would certainly die in a little time ... he departed this life, at age 54, the 7th year of his reign.*

## Chapter 82. (44AD)
## King Herod Agrippa is poisoned by Simon Magus

The eunuch Blastus-Nicolaus speaking to Simon Magus, "I am concerned about King Herod Agrippa's sanity. He seems to have lost touch with reality, becoming paranoid and suspecting everyone."

Simon Magus says, "Nicolaus, would it not be a duty to put a mad dog down?"
Blastus says, "I understand what you are saying, but he once was great. It is such a tribute to him that he succeeded in restoring his grandfather Herod the Great's kingdom piece by piece."

Simon says, "He did inherit Herod's conniving and callous nature, that is sure. If you help us, I could ordain you as bishop of the Church of Laodicea."

"Just give me the poison and I will put it in his drink."

*In Caesarea Maritima on the second day of the festival, King Agrippa entered theater wearing a silver garment. It was early in the morning so that the sun's reflection made him look like a god. As the crowds were gasping in amazement, he happened to look up at a rope above him and saw the owl, the portent that had been foretold of his death when he was in captivity in Rome. Blastus had given him the poison earlier. He doubled over in pain and was carried away. He died at the age of 54, in the 7th year of his reign.*

*March 44AD Magdalene is three months pregnant; Bartholomew, the other disciple, 'the disciple Jesus loved' is finally revealed as John Mark:*
*Acts 12:12-17 Also, having considered, he came unto the house of Mary (Mother Mary), the mother of **John, who is surnamed, Mark**,*
*[John 19:26 Jesus, then perceiving the mother (Mary Magdalene) and **the disciple standing by, whom Jesus loved**, is saying to the mother of him...*
*Acts 03:01 And Peter and **John** were going up at the same time to the temple, at the hour of the prayer, the ninth hour, and a certain man, being lame from the womb of his mother ...]*
*And Peter having knocked at the door of the porch, there came a damsel to hearken, by name Rhoda, and having known the voice of Peter, from the joy she did not open the porch, but having run in, told of Peter standing before the porch, and they said unto her, 'You are mad;' and she was confidently affirming it to be so, and she said 'It is an angel' and Peter was continuing knocking, and having opened, they saw him, and were astonished, and having beckoned to them with the hand to be silent, he declared to them how the Lord brought him out of the prison (made him an archbishop), and he said, 'Declare to James (son of Alphaeus = Jonathan) and to the brethren these things;' and having gone forth, he (Peter) went on to another place (Rome).*

*September 44AD*
*Acts 12:24 And the **word of God** did grow and did multiply*

*Mark 10:11,12 Jesus said to them, "Whoever may put away his wife, and may marry another, does commit adultery against her; and if a woman may put away her husband, and is married to another, she commits adultery." Paul's justifications for Magdalene's divorce:*
*1Cor 7:10-15 To the married I give this charge (not I, but the Lord): the wife should not separate from her husband (but if she does, she should remain unmarried or else be reconciled to her husband), and the husband should not divorce his wife. To the rest, I say (I, not the Lord) that if any brother has a wife who is an unbeliever, and she consents to live with him, he should not divorce her. If any woman has a husband who is an unbeliever, and he consents to live with her, she should not divorce him. For the unbelieving husband is made holy because of his wife, and the unbelieving wife is made holy because of her husband. But if the unbelieving partner separates, let it be so. In such cases, the brother or sister is not enslaved. God has called you to peace.*

## Chapter 83. (September 44AD)
## Magdalene gives Jesus a second son; asks for divorce

Peter knocks, Rhoda announces him

Magdalene, arriving at Simon's house in Lydda, hands the bundled baby to Jesus saying "Now I have given you an heir and a spare. Let's call him Joseph."

Jesus says, "Another boy, he is beautiful!"

Magdalene says, "I have something important to say to you, I am concerned that you and Peter and Paul have taken the view that Simon Magus is somehow evil. They pretend that he alone was responsible for the poisoning of Agrippa. You know that my mother Helena owes her life to him and I love him as if he was my natural father. It appears that I am forced to choose sides. Although I still hold you dear, I believe that I have no choice, but to ask you for a divorce."

Jesus answers, "I also hold you dear, but I do not see how the Church will survive without the support of Agrippa II. Simon relies on 'simony', but we rely on freely given offerings and the people are poor. I hear that Peter shortly after his ordination, tried for reconciliation, but they just laughed at him"

Magdalene says, "I am sorry that I did not let Peter into your mother's church. At first, I did not let him as he was dressed in black as an archbishop, and I did not know if he was supposed to be with me at the three-month viability point of my pregnancy with our child. They were already calling me Rhoda as I had told them I was planning to go with John Mark to Simon Magus' territory of Rhodes and Cypress. I am sorry about that. Politics can be cruel. I just want to be free of it."

Jesus says, "I understand, I accept your divorce. Paul will find a way to justify it."

*St. Peter's Cave Church near Antakya (Antioch), Turkey*

Acts 11:19-25 Those, indeed, therefore, having been scattered abroad, from the tribulation that came after Stephen, went through unto Phoenicia, and Cyprus, and Antioch, speaking the word to none except to Jews only; and there were certain of them men of Cyprus and Cyrene (included Agrippa II, the son of King Agrippa, being groomed to lead the Church), who having entered into Antioch, were speaking unto the Hellenists, proclaiming good news. The Lord Jesus (carried over from Acts 11:20, showing Jesus is there), and the hand of the Lord (Peter) was with them, a great number also, having believed, did turn unto the Lord.

And the account was heard in the ears of the assembly that is in Jerusalem concerning them, and they sent forth Barnabas to go through unto Antioch, who, having come, and having seen the grace of God, was glad, and was exhorting all with purpose of heart to cleave to the Lord, because he was a good man, and full of the Holy Spirit, and of faith, and a great multitude was added to the Lord.

And Barnabas went forth to Tarsus, to seek for Saul, and having found him, (in March going to Qumran for the famine relief, then in September) he brought him to Antioch, and it came to pass that they a whole year did assemble together in the assembly, and taught a great multitude, the disciples also were **first divinely called "Christians" in Antioch, Syria**

Acts 12:25;13:1 And Barnabas and Saul returned from Jerusalem, having fulfilled the ministry, having taken also with them John, who was surnamed. Mark. And there were certain in Antioch in Syria, in the assembly there, prophets and teachers; both Barnabas, and Simeon who is called Niger (Peter wearing black robe of an archbishop), and Lucius the Cyrenian (Luke to be assigned to Cyrene and Libya), Manaen (the close friend and freedman of King Herod Agrippa named (Marsyas-Titus), also Herod the tetrarch's foster-brother: Saul (spurious: 'and') thus Antipas Herod's son).

# Chapter 84. (October 44AD)
## In Antioch, Syria they are first called Christians

*Jesus, John Mark, and Peter disembark from the ship from Caesarea Maritima to Seleucia, the port of Antioch, Syria. They are greeted by Joses-Barnabas, Paul, and Marsyas-Titus.*

Jesus kisses Joses, Paul, and Titus and says "I am excited that we are now to be called Christians."

Paul says, "Our old name of the 'Way' was always difficult to explain. Peter, congratulations on gaining the the black robe and suggesting our new name.

Peter says, "Do not forget that I was the first to call Jesus, the Christ."

Paul says, "I believe that was the seer Daniel."

Jesus says, "Yes, he said I, the Anointed One, would be 'cut off', yet here I am, and the plant root is blossoming into Christianity."

John Mark says, "And from Magdalene's womb: one daughter and two sons."

Joses asks, "Are you going to name him after our father like I was?"

"Yes, we are. He will replace James as Joseph of Arimathea."

Jesus says, "I hear that Paul is planning a Missionary Journey with you and John Mark, stopping first in Cypress. I would like to go with you. As you see, I have left the monastery and have decided that I can travel incognito as no one knows what I look like anymore. From there I will go with John Aquila to Patmos."

## Paul's First Missionary Journey (44-46AD) with Barnabas

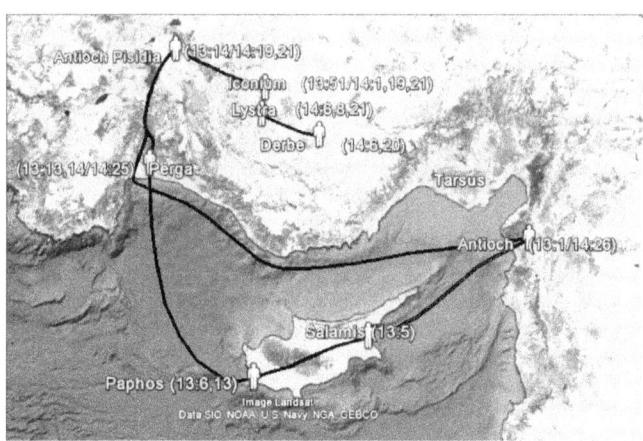

(Antioch .. Seleucia .. Salamis .. Paphos .. Perga .. Antioch of Pisidia .. Iconium .. Lycaonia .. Lystra .. Derbe .. backtrack)

# SECTION 13 (44AD to 46AD)
## Paul's First Missionary Journey with Barnabas

Raffael(1483-1520)

*Acts 13:2-5 and in their ministering to the Lord and fasting, the Holy Spirit (Jesus) said, 'Separate you to me both Barnabas and Saul to the work to which I have called them,' then having fasted, and having prayed, and having laid the hands on them, they sent them away. These, indeed, then, having been sent forth by the Holy Spirit, went down to Seleucia, thence also they sailed to Cyprus, and having come unto Salamis, they declared the word of God in the synagogues of the Jews, and they had also John (Mark) as a ministrant;*

*Acts of Barnabas*
*Since from the descent of the presence of our Saviour Jesus Christ, the unwearied and benevolent and mighty Shepherd and Teacher and Physician, I beheld and saw the ineffable and holy and unspotted mystery of the Christians, who hold the hope in holiness, and who have been sealed; and since I have zealously served Him, I have deemed it necessary to give account of the mysteries which I have heard and seen. I John (Mark), accompanying the holy apostles Barnabas and Paul, being formerly a servant of Cyrillus the high priest of Jupiter (a disguised position for servant of Herod Agrippa"), but now having received the gift of the Holy Spirit through Paul and Barnabas and Silas, who were worthy of the calling, and who baptized me in Iconium. After I was baptized, then, I saw a certain man standing clothed in white raiment (Jesus!); and he said to me: Be of good courage, John, for assuredly your name shall be changed to Mark, and your glory shall be proclaimed in all the world. The darkness in you has passed away from you, and there has been given to you understanding to know the mysteries of God.*

*Acts 13:6-12 and having gone through the island unto Paphos, they found a certain Magian, a false prophet, a Jew, whose name is Bar-Jesus (Simon Magus under Jesus); who was with the proconsul Sergius Paulus (Agrippa II having filled in for him), an intelligent man; this one having called for Barnabas and Saul, did desire to hear the word of God, and there withstood them Elymas the Magian -- for so is his name interpreted -- (Elymas means "Wise" in Arabic and stands from Simon Magus) seeking to pervert the proconsul from the faith. And Saul -- who also is Paul -- having been filled with the Holy Spirit, and having looked steadfastly on him, said, 'O full of all guile, and all profligacy, son of a devil, enemy of all righteousness, will you not cease perverting the right ways of the Lord? and now, lo, a hand of the Lord is upon you, and you shall be blind, not seeing the sun for a season;' and presently there fell upon him a mist and darkness, and he, going about, was seeking some to lead by the hand; then the proconsul having seen what has come to pass, did believe, being astonished at the teaching of the Lord. (Paul affirms Simon's excommunication #3)*

## Chapter 85. (October 44AD)
## Paul, Barnabas, John Mark and Jesus sail to Cyprus

*The group having sailed to Cyprus from Antioch arrive in the harbor of Salamis. Simon Magus and John Aquila welcome them as they disembark. Jesus kisses them both. Aquila and Jesus return to the ship to continue on to the Isle of Patmos. The others visit the house of Agrippa II.*

Agrippa II says, "It is an honor to have so many important disciples of Jesus here. Simon Magus has explained to me the Church of the Way and I am anxious to ask you more about your lord Jesus Christ. The Emperor Claudius has sent me here to learn of governorship while the proconsul is away and I will be returning to Rome in a few months."

Paul says, "Agrippa the Younger, I have been your tutor for many years and, unfortunately, I would be wary of this distinguished Magian Simon as his words are poison. This, your father could attest to, if he were still alive."

Agrippa II says, "Are you implying that the rumors are true that he was poisoned?"

Simon replies, "His sickness was congenital and similar to his grandfather Herod the Great."

Paul says, "That is not the consensus. Simon has already been reduced to the level that we designate as blind for his transgression."

Simon Magus says, "Talk about the blind leading the blind." *Paul glares at him.*
*Paul and Barnabas leave Cypress for Perga as John Mark separates from them; then to Antioch of Pisidia.*

*Acts 13:13 And those about Paul having set sail from Paphos, came to Perga of Pamphylia, and John having departed from them, did turn back to Jerusalem(Qumran). (John Mark being the "one whom Jesus loved" was Magdalene's guardian and his abrupt departure is an indication that the divorce from Jesus has begun.)*

*Acts 13:44,45,48,50-52 And on the coming sabbath, almost all the city of Antioch of Pisidia was gathered together to hear the word of God, And when the Gentiles heard this, they were glad, and glorified the word of the Lord: and as many as were ordained to eternal life believed. But the Jews having seen the multitudes, were filled with zeal, and did contradict the things spoken by Paul -- contradicting and speaking evil and did raise persecution against Paul and Barnabas, and did put them out from their borders; they having shaken off the dust of their feet against them, came to Iconium, and the disciples were filled with joy and the Holy Spirit.*

*Acts of Paul - Paul and Thecla #1 (1-3) This apocryphal story fits very well at this point to the flight of Paul and Barnabas from Antioch of Pisidia to Iconium. It shows a monastic version of Christianity which was thought to come later on, but actually, having been derived from the monastic Essenes, it really came first.*
*When Paul went up unto Iconium after he fled from Antioch of Pisidia , there journeyed with him Demas (Barnabas, later Ananus the Younger; Demas: "the people") and Hermogenes the coppersmith (person collected the copper coins),*
*And a certain man named Onesiphorus, (Onesiphorus was clearly the head of the Christian monastery in Iconium as Paul refers to him in his letter in 62AD:2Tim 1:16-18) "May the Lord grant mercy to the household of Onesiphorus, for he often refreshed me; he was not ashamed of my chains, but when he arrived in Rome he searched for me eagerly and found me -- may the Lord grant him to find mercy from the Lord on that Day -- and you well know all the service he rendered at Ephesus.") when he heard that Paul had come to Iconium, went out with his children to meet him, that he might receive him into his house: for Titus had told him what manner of man Paul was in appearance; for he had not seen him in the flesh, but only in the spirit.*
*And he went by the king's highway that leadeth unto Lystra and stood expecting him, and looked upon them that came, according to the description of Titus. And he saw Paul coming,*

## Chapter 86. (March 45AD)
## Acts of Paul - Paul and Thecla

*Paul and Barnabas are walking toward Iconium.*

Onesiphorus speaking to his two children, "Look for a man little of stature, thin-haired upon the head, crooked in the legs, of good state of body, with eyebrows joining, and nose somewhat hooked."
His wife says, "The man in the distance walks gracefully."
Onesiphorus greets Paul, "You are as Titus described to me. Let me introduce my family." His wife says, "Yes you do have a face like an angel."

"Barnabas and I appreciate your welcome after being thrown out of Antioch of Pisidia."
*They take them to the plaza. Many are assembled. Paul begins to preach Jesus resurrected. A young girl Thecla, who is soon to be married, hears this:*

> "For I would that all men were even as I myself. But every man hath his proper gift of God, one after this manner, and another after that. I say therefore to the unmarried and widows, it is good for them if they abide even as I. But if they cannot contain, let them marry: for it is better to marry than to burn.with passion.(1Cor 7:7-9)."

*Due to the crowd complaints, the governor put Paul in prison, but Thecla gave her silver bracelets to the jailer to be allowed to speak with him. She kisses his chains and sits at his feet as he tells her the wonderful works of God. She is miraculously saved from being burned at the stake by a huge deluge and escapes with Paul and Barnabas. Later as a nun, she looks for Paul in Rome, but finds he is dead.*

*Acts 14:4-7 And the multitude of the city was divided, and some were with the Jews, and some with the apostles, and when there was a purpose both of the nations and of the Jews with their rulers to use them despitefully, and to stone them, they having become aware, did flee to the cities of Lycaonia, Lystra, and Derbe, and to the region round about, and there they were proclaiming good news.*

*Jesus' youngest brother Simon-Silas (lame man) at the age of 23 has come to Lystra to join the monastery there and is initiated by Paul at age 23.*

*Acts 14:8 And a certain man in Lystra, impotent in the feet, was sitting, being lame from the womb of his mother -- who never had walked, this one was hearing Paul speaking, who, having steadfastly beheld him, and having seen that he has faith to be saved, said with a loud voice, 'Stand up on your feet upright; and he was springing and walking,*

*At Lystra, the people remembering Ovid's Ovid's Metamorphose Book VIII (the story of Philemon and Baucis) where the gods Jupiter (Zeus) and Mercury (Hermes) visit Phrygia disguised as human travelers. They go from house to house in search of food and lodging, but are refused by everyone except old Baucis and Philemon, who show the two visitors their best hospitality. They prepare the finest meal they could, given their poverty, and are astonished at one point to see the wine replenishing itself. Realizing that their guests are divine, they attempt to offer their only goose as a sacrifice, but Jupiter and Mercury stop them. Then the gods destroy the town except for these two.*

*Acts 14:11-20 and the multitudes having seen what Paul did, did lift up their voice, in the speech of Lycaonia, saying, 'The gods, having become like men, did come down unto us;' they were calling also Barnabas Zeus, and Paul Hermes, since he was the leader in speaking.*

*And the priest of the Zeus that is before their city, oxen and garlands unto the porches having brought, with the multitudes did wish to sacrifice, and having heard, the apostles Barnabas and Paul, having rent their garments, did spring into the multitude, crying and saying, 'Men, why these things do you? and we are men like-affected with you, proclaiming good news to you, from these vanities to turn unto the living God, who made the heaven, and the earth, and the sea, and all the things in them; who in the past generations did suffer all the nations to go on in their ways, though, indeed, without witness He did not leave himself, doing good -- from heaven giving rains to us, and fruitful seasons, filling our hearts with food and gladness;' and these things saying, scarcely did they restrain the multitudes from sacrificing to them.*

*And there came thither, from Antioch of Pisidia and Iconium, Jews, and they having persuaded the multitudes, and having stoned Paul, dragged him outside of the city, having supposed him to be dead; and the disciples having surrounded him, having risen he entered into the city, and on the morrow he went forth with Barnabas to Derbe.*

# Chapter 87. (March 45AD)
## At Lystra Barnabas and Paul are mistaken for gods

Simon-Silas says, "Greetings, my brother Joses."

Barnabas says, "Greetings, Silas, I cannot believe that my younger brother, Simon, is now age 23."

On the next day, Paul baptizes him, "Be lame no more and achieve the priesthood at this monastery of Lystra. I will look forward to having you accompany me in the future."

*The crowds have started to grow, hearing that Paul cured a lame man, and Paul begins to preach.* They start talking to each other, "Could this be the gods visiting as Ovid has told us? Will they destroy us if we do not offer them hospitality?" They address Barnabas, "I assume you are Zeus as the oldest; that eloquent one must be Hermes."

Paul tries to dissuade them, "There is only one living God whom we serve. These gods of yours are merely the reflection of all your vanities. As servants of the son of God, we ask merely for food and lodging."

*They bring cows dressed in garlands, offering them to Barnabas and Paul; the people become even more agitated. Paul and Barnabas slip away to Derbe.*

*Acts 15:1-21 And certain having come down from Judea, were teaching the brethren -- 'If you be not circumcised after the custom of Moses, you are not able to be saved 'there having been, therefore, not a little dissension and disputation to Paul and Barnabas with them, they arranged for Paul and Barnabas, and certain others of them, to go up unto the apostles and elders to Jerusalem about this question, they (Paul and Barnabas) indeed, then, having been sent forward by the assembly, were passing through Phoenicia and Samaria, declaring the conversion of the nations, and they were causing great joy ("Great joy" is Jesus' daughter Tamar (Phoebe) coming of age at 12 and one-half in March 46) to all the brethren. And having come to Jerusalem, they were received by the assembly, and the apostles, and the elders, they declared also as many things as God did with them; and there rose up certain of those of the sect of the Pharisees who believed, saying, 'Circumcision should be required according to the law of Moses.'*

*Council of Jerusalem*
*And there were gathered together the apostles and the elders, to see about this matter, and there having been much disputing,*
***Peter having risen up said unto them**, 'Men, brethren, you know that from former days, God among us did make choice, through my mouth, for the nations to hear the word of the good news, and to believe; and the heart-knowing God did bare them testimony, having given to them the Holy Spirit, even as also to us, and did put no difference also between us and them, by the faith having purified their hearts; now, therefore, why do you tempt God, to put a yoke upon the neck of the disciples, which neither our fathers nor we were able to bear? but, through the grace of the Lord Jesus Christ, we believe to be saved, even as also they.'*
*And all the multitude did keep silence, and were **hearkening to Barnabas and Paul**, declaring as many signs and wonders as God did among the nations through them; and after they are silent,*
***James answered**, saying, 'Men, brethren, hearken to me; Simeon (Simeon called Niger: Peter) did declare how at first God did look after to take out of the nations a people for His name, and to this agree the words of the prophets, as it has been written: After these things I will turn back, and I will build again the tabernacle of David, that is fallen down, and its ruins I will build again, and will set it upright -- that the residue of men may seek after the Lord, and all the nations, upon whom My name has been called, said the Lord, who is doing all these things. 'Known from the ages to God are all His works; therefore I judge: not to trouble those who from the nations do turn back to God, but to write to them to abstain from the pollutions of the idols, and the whoredom, and the strangled thing; and the blood; for Moses from former generations in every city has those preaching him -- in the synagogues every sabbath being read.'*

## Chapter 88. (March 46AD)
## The Council of Jerusalem

*Having been called to the Council of Jerusalem, Paul and Barnabas stop at the convent in Lydda.*

Barnabas says, "Hello, my niece Tamar, you have grown into a beautiful young girl."
"Thank you, Uncle Joses."

Paul kissing her on the cheek says, "Now that you are twelve we must perform your Bat Mitzvah."
"I would like to be baptized as Phoebe to honor my grandmother."

Proceeding to the Council of Jerusalem, Paul confides to Barnabas, "Do you think that Jesus would allow me to be married to Phoebe in the Essene way that he practices?" "It would certainly join us all together."

At the Council, Peter speaks, "In my vision, that clearly came from Jesus, he passed down a cloth that showed the need to make Gentiles equal with Jews. We now accept Jews and Gentiles at our table. Circumcision should not be an issue."

Paul speaks, "I have found the Gentiles ready to believe in the resurrected Jesus, but the detailed instructions of Moses serve no purpose for them."

Barnabas says, "The Gentiles clearly are attached to their Greco-Roman beliefs. It is hard enough to convince them that we are not heathen gods."
James seeking reconciliation, says, "You are right to concentrate on getting them to give up their gods, animal sacrifices and bestiality."

*The council votes to adopt James' concept and to exempt circumcision.*

## Section 14 (46AD to 48AD) John Mark and Barnabas Mission to Cypress;
## Paul's Second Missionary Journey (47-48(54)) with Silas

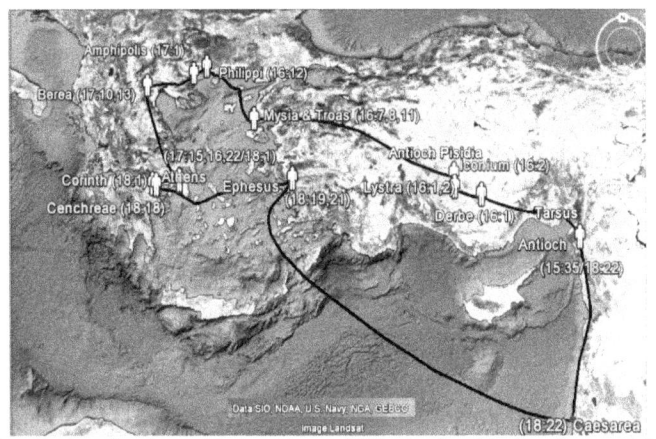

(Antioch .. Derbe .. Lystra .. Iconium .. Mysia .. Troas .. Philippi .. Amphipolis .. Berea .. Athens .. Corinth .. Cenchreae .. Ephesus .. Caesarea)

*Acts 15:22-35 Then it seemed good to the apostles and the elders, with the whole assembly, chosen men out of themselves to send to Antioch with **Paul and Barnabas**: **Judas called Barsabas**(the family name just like James), and **Silas**youngest brother Simon ('sehlah') meaning rock similar to Peter's 'Cephas', leading men among the brethren -- having written through their hand thus: 'The apostles, and the elders, and the brethren, to those in Antioch, and Syria, and Cilicia, brethren, who are]of the nations, greeting; seeing we have heard that certain having gone forth from us did trouble you with words, subverting your souls, saying to be circumcised and to keep the law, to whom we did give no charge, it seemed good to us, having come together with one accord, chosen men to send unto you, with our beloved Barnabas and Paul: men who have given up their lives for the name of our Lord Jesus Christ. We have sent, therefore, Judas and Silas, and they by word are telling the same things. 'For it seemed good to the Holy Spirit, and to us, not to lay further burden on you, except to abstain from things offered to idols, and blood, and a strangled thing, and whoredom; from which keeping yourselves, you shall do well; be strong!'*

*They then, indeed, having been let go, went to Antioch, and having brought the multitude together, did deliver the epistle, and they having read, did rejoice for the consolation; Judas also and Silas, being themselves also prophets, through much discourse did exhort the brethren, and confirm, and having passed some time, they were let go with peace from the brethren unto the apostles. And Paul and Barnabas continued in Antioch, teaching and proclaiming good news -- with many others also -- the word of the Lord;*

*Acts 15:36-39 and after certain days, Paul said unto Barnabas, 'Having turned back again, we may look after our brethren, in every city in which we have preached the word of the Lord -- how they are.' And Barnabas counseled to take with them John called Mark, Acts 15:38 and Paul was not thinking it good to take him with them who withdrew from them from Pamphylia, and did not go with them to the work; there came, therefore, a sharp contention, so that they were parted from one another,*

**Acts of Barnabas** *And I (John Mark) found Paul in bed in Antioch from the toil of the journey, who also seeing me, was exceedingly grieved on account of my delaying in Pamphylia. And Barnabas coming, encouraged him, and tasted bread, and he took a little of it. (Taking the sacrament.) And they preached the word of the Lord, and enlightened many of the Jews and Greeks. And I only attended to them, and was afraid of Paul to come near him because he was quite enraged against me. And I gave repentance on my knees upon the earth to Paul, and he would not endure it. And when I remained for three Sabbaths in entreaty and prayer on my knees, I was unable to prevail upon him about myself; for his great grievance against me was on account of my keeping several parchments in Pamphylia.*

## Chapter 89. (June 46AD)
## Brothers in Antioch; Magdalene's divorce papers

Paul says, "This is an amazing time for Jesus' four brothers to be present together in one place."

Jude says, "I am sad to be leaving James as I have looked up to him to guide me on many of the Jewish principles that I still believe in."

Barnabas says, "Jude, what is important now is that we are not warring against each other. As Jesus said 'A house divided against itself cannot stand'."

Jude says, "Tell me brothers, why is it that I am the only one without a nickname? They are so confusing to the people. Joses, yours of Barnabas makes you sound like a farmer and your Pentecost name Matthias is even more confusing. Simon, your nickname Silas, derived from 'sehlah' meaning rock, makes you appear to be a challenger to Peter's Cephas. Then there was Uncle Theudas: Barabbas. Perhaps we can finally all be called Bar-sabbas as true sons of Sabbas."

Barnabas says, "Paul, on our Second Missionary Journey, I beg that you consider John Mark to accompany us. He had to leave your first journey, because he promised at the cross to watch over Mary Magdalene and her children. Now that he has her divorce papers with him, he is free to join us."

Paul, says, "I cannot condone this divorce. Jesus himself once said that it was illegal. To support it is to be aligned with Simon Magus. I am sorry, but you should leave us at Cypress." "Silas, will you go with me?" *"Of course!"*

Barnabas says, "This saddens me, as deeply as the wounds we endured together."

Acts 15:39 and Barnabas having taken Mark, did sail to Cyprus,
The Acts of Barnabas: And thence we sailed past the Anemurium (the southernmost point of Asia Minor, only 64 km from Cyprus); and having gone into it, we found two Greeks. And coming to us, they asked whence and who we were. And Barnabas said to them: If you wish to know whence and who we are, throw away the clothing which you have, and I shall put on you clothing which never becomes soiled; for neither is there in it anything filthy, but it is altogether splendid. And being astonished at the saying, they asked us: What is that garment which you are going to give us? And Barnabas said to them: If you shall confess your sins, and submit yourselves to our Lord Jesus Christ, you shall receive that garment which is incorruptible for ever. And being pricked at heart by the Holy Spirit, they fell at his feet, entreating and saying: We beseech you, father, give us that garment; for we believe in the living and true God whom thou proclaims. And leading them down to the fountain, he baptized them into the name of Father, and Son, and Holy Ghost. And they knew that they were clothed with power and a holy robe. And having taken from me one robe, he put it on the one; and his own robe he put on the other. And they brought money to him, and straightway Barnabas distributed it to the poor. And from them also the sailors were able to gain many things. And they, having come down to the shore, he spoke to them the word of God; and he having blessed them, we saluted them, and went on board the ship. And the one of them who was named Stephanos (Jonathan Annas) wished to accompany us, and Barnabas did not permit him. And we, having gone across, sailed down to Cyprus by night; and having come to the place called Crommyon Promontory, Cyprus, we found Timon (one Seven Deacons Chosen in June 37AD) and Ariston (Aristobulus - husband of Salome) the temple servants, at whose house also we were entertained. And Timon was afflicted by much fever. And having laid our hands upon him, we straightway removed his fever, having called upon the name of the Lord Jesus. **And Barnabas had received documents from Matthew, a book of the word of God, and a narrative of miracles and doctrines.** This Barnabas laid upon the sick in each place that we came to, and it immediately made a cure of their sufferings ... And we met a certain Jew, by name Barjesus (name used for Simon Magus in confrontation with Paul in Cyprus), coming from Paphos, who also recognized Barnabas, as having been formerly with Paul. He did not wish us to go into Paphos; but having turned away, we came to Curium. And we found that a certain abominable race (many women and men naked) on the road near the city and Barnabas turning, rebuked it ... the rest fled to the temple of Apollo, And when we came near the temple, a great multitude of Jews who were there, having been put up to it by Barjesus, stood outside of the city, not allowing us to enter, so we rested under a tree near the city for the night.

## Chapter 90. (September 46AD)
## Acts of Barnabas; the Gospel of Matthew

*Barnabas & John leave Paul*

*John Mark and Barnabas arrive in Cypress.* While disembarking, the sailors ask, "Why did you travel to this island of Cypress?" "What place did you come from."

Barnabas says, "These are questions that we all ask, but if you discard your clothing, you can put on clothing which never becomes soiled."

They exclaim, "Are you suggesting us to be part of the naked race of men and women that is happening in Curium sponsored by Bar-Jesus?"

Barnabas says, "No, but confess your sins, and submit to our Lord Jesus Christ and you shall receive the Holy Spirit." *They throw off their clothes and are baptized and Barnabas and John give them their cloaks. They are greeted by Timon, one of the Seven Deacons Chosen in June 37AD, and Aristobulus, the husband of Salome.*

Timon says, "I fear that we have been corrupted by Bar-Jesus. Would you also baptize us."
Barnabas says, "Not only will I baptize you in water, but also with the Gospel of Matthew."

Aristobulus asks, "Is this Matthew who was the High Priest in 43AD, being the son of Ananus the High Priest who judged Jesus with Caiaphas?"

John Mark says, "Yes it is and it will be part of four Gospels to be canonized next year, the first of which I, John, scribed for Jesus and Simon Magus."

Timon says "How is it possible for a Gospel written by Bar-Jesus to be included?"
John Mark answers, "This is yet to be decided between Matthew and Jesus."

*Acts 15:40,41 and Paul having chosen Silas, who having been handed over by the grace of God (Barnabas, the crown prince) to be the younger brother, went forth; and he went through Syria and Cilicia confirming the assemblies.*

Paul officiates at Timothy's Bar Mitzvah.
*Acts 16:1,2 And he came to Derbe and Lystra, and lo, a certain disciple was there, by name Timothy son of a certain woman, a believing Jewess (Salome, daughter of Thomas and Herodias, adopted daughter of Herod Antipas present at the "Beheading" of John the Baptist), but of a father, a Greek (Aristobulus, the son of Herod of Chalcis thus technically from Idumea like his great-grandfather Herod the Great, but now associated with the Greeks), who was well testified to by the brethren in Lystra and Iconium; this one did Paul wish to go forth with him, and having taken him, he circumcised him (merely symbolic for Bar Mitzvah), because of the Jews who are in those places, for they all knew his father -- that he was a Greek.*

Aristobulus & Salome

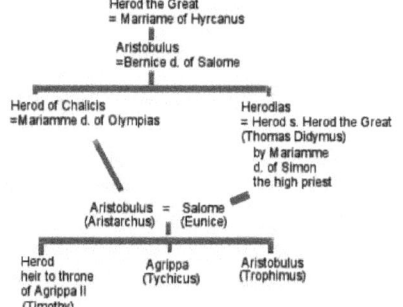

*Acts 16:6,7 Paul and Silas, having gone through Phrygia and the region of Galatia, having been forbidden by the Holy Spirit to speak the word in Asia, having gone toward Mysia, they were trying to go on toward Bithynia, and the Spirit did not suffer them (Jesus prevented Paul from going to Ephesus for the canonizing of the Gospels as there are still some factions who do not agree with Paul's teaching), and having passed by Mysia, they came down to Troas.*

# Chapter 91. (47AD)
## Paul's Second Journey with Silas begins

*Having come from Antioch through Tarsus, Paul and Silas came again to Derbe and then Lystra to perform Timothy's Bar Mitzvah.*

Salome greets Simon-Silas, "Look at how grown you are Simon." He replies, "And you Salome, are as beautiful as I remember you."

Aristobulus says, "I just got back from Cypress having been with Barnabas in his struggles with Simon Magus, who is now estranged from us."

Paul says, "Aristobulus, my friend, is the mission going well there? I do miss Barnabas."

"Having an early copy of the gospel of Matthew, he gains many followers."

"I have begged Jesus to let me attend the canonizing in Ephesus, but he says that I cannot."

"Yes, Matthew is already walking a tightrope between the factions and unfortunately you have many enemies given your early history and your strong advocacy for Gentiles. I am sure one day you will become an equal to Peter. You are certainly loved and respected here."

Timothy appears and Paul kisses him, saying "Timothy Herod, today, you become a man and I hope one step closer to being Agrippa's heir."

Timothy says, "I am already nervous, do not scare me with the future." Salome says, "The congregation is assembled. Let us go inside the church."

*After this, Paul and Silas go through Iconium to Mysia and Troas.*

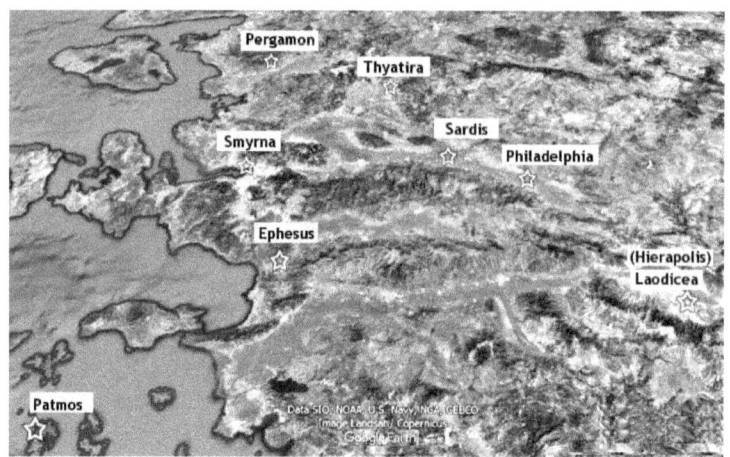
Seven Churches

# SECTION 15 (47AD to April 48AD)
## Canonizing of the Gospels

JanvanEyck(1390-1441)

*Rev 1:7-9 Lo, he does come with the clouds (reference to position 3, the position that Jesus held as Holy Spirit. See Trial of Jesus before Caiaphas (Mark 14:62) where Jesus said, "You shall see the Son of Man sitting on the right hand of the power, and coming with the clouds, of the heaven."), and see him shall every eye, even those who did pierce him, and wail because of him shall all the tribes of the land. Yes! Amen! 'I am the Alpha and the Omega, beginning and end', says the Lord, who is, and who was, and who is coming -- the Almighty. (Alpha to Omega are the graduation stages of Jesus' church with omega the last letter of the Greek alphabet replacing Tau, the last letter of the Hebrew. This is similar to Simon Magus' designations Samekh (60) Resh (200) Tau (400) = 660+6= 666.) I, John, who also am your brother, and fellow-partner in the tribulation, and in the reign and endurance, of Jesus Christ, was in the isle that is called Patmos, because of the word of God, and because of the testimony of Jesus Christ;*

*Rev 1:10-18 I was in the Spirit on the Lord's-day, and I heard behind me a great voice, as of a trumpet, saying, 'I am the Alpha and the Omega, the First and the Last and, what you do see, write in a scroll, and send to the seven assemblies that are in Asia; to Ephesus, and to Smyrna, and to Pergamon, and to Thyatira, and to Sardis, and to Philadelphia, and to Laodicea.' And I did turn to see the voice that did speak with me, and having turned, I saw seven golden lamp-stands, and in the midst of the seven lamp-stands, one like to a Son of Man, clothed to the foot (a long linen gown like a Zadokite priest as prescribed by Ezekiel 44:17: "When they enter the gates of the inner court, they shall wear linen garments; they shall have nothing of wool on them, while they minister at the gates of the inner court, and within."), and girt round at the breast with a golden girdle (Since a belt is not worn in the sanctuary it represents Jesus' position amongst the people), and his head and hairs white, as if white wool -- as snow, and his eyes as a flame of fire (Like the Ancient of Days in Daniel 7:9 I kept looking until thrones were set up and 'the Ancient of Days" took His seat; His vesture was like white snow And the hair of His head like pure wool. His throne was ablaze with flames, Its wheels were a burning fire.); and his feet like to fine brass, as in a furnace having been fired, (The money jar his feet not needing tithes of gold like Judas collected, but copper coins as freewill offerings) and his voice as a sound of many waters(baptism), and having in his right hand seven stars (his son Jesus Justus), and out of his mouth a sharp two-edged sword is proceeding (having authority over east and west), and his countenance is as the sun shining in its might (using the solar calendar). And when I saw him, I did fall at his feet as dead, and he placed his right hand upon me, saying to me, 'Be not afraid; I am the First and the Last, and he who is living, and I did become dead, and, lo, I am living to the ages of the ages. Amen! and I have the keys of the Hades and of the death (Jesus's resurrection).*

## Chapter 92. (47AD)
## Jesus' Letters to the Seven Churches

*Patmos, March, 48AD Jesus dictating to John Aquila*
To Archbishop Peter who leads the Mother Church at Ephesus, 'Your works, your labor, and your endurance are exceptional. Give up your impatience and realize that only agape love can overcome all differences.'

To Bishop James Niceta who leads the second Church at Smyrna, 'Resist your anger that almost got you killed by King Agrippa, and explain to the Jews who want to recognize the Day of Atonement on the 10th of the month that I, as the Lamb, have atoned for all sin. The faithful will have eternal life at death.'

To Bishop Clement, the third brother with James and John, who leads the Church at Pergamon, 'Use only the white stones *(the square cornerstones to be used in Christian Church)* and refrain from the black *(the Jewish temple stones representing Jewish laws)* and the half black *(the laws of Jewish Christians, like the requirement of circumcision)* as the Shepherd of Hermes has shown.'

To Bishop Lydia, who leads the Church at Thyatira, 'Avoid the influence of Bernice, the twin sister of Agrippa II, who is like Ahab's wife, Jezebel, using sexual practices of adultery and incest to manipulate men, causing them to pervert the Church.'

To Bishop Zacchaeus, the youngest son of the High Priest Ananus, who leads the Church at Sardis, 'I encourage you to reject the strict rules of the Sadducees and Essenes and to follow the Nazarite practice that I did when out of the monastery.'

To Bishop James, my brother, who leads the Church at Philadelphia and Jerusalem, 'I am glad that you no longer try to replace me. You are one of the pillars of the New Jerusalem.'

To Bishop Nicolaus-Blastus, who leads the Church of Laodicea, 'Choose Christian values, thus the warmer season Easter than Atonement in the colder. The Lamb forgives all sins.'

*(John Aquila writes:)* Rev 4:1,2 After these things I saw, and lo, a door opened in the heaven, and the first voice that I heard is as of a trumpet speaking with me, saying, 'Come up hither, and I will show you what it behooves to come to pass after these things;' *(The upper platform of the church had trapdoor that was opened to let the light shine through.)* and immediately I was in the Spirit, and lo, a throne was set in the heaven, and upon the throne is one sitting, *(John was seated stage right of the center throne as the witness to the coronation of Agrippa II)*
Ezekiel 1:26 And above the expanse that is over their head, as an appearance of a sapphire stone, is the likeness of a throne, and on the likeness of the throne a likeness, as the appearance of man upon it from above.
Rev 4:3 and He who is sitting was in sight like a stone, jasper and sardine: and a *(not ἶρις: rainbow)* was around the throne in sight like an emerald. *(The first row of the pews.)*
Rev 4:4 And around the throne are thrones twenty and four, and upon the thrones I saw the twenty and four elders sitting, clothed in white garments, and they had upon their heads crowns of gold; *(The twenty-four elders are wearing gold crowns and therefore they must have been temporal kings rather than elders of the Church. There are twenty-four kings of Judah from King David: Solomon, Rehoboam, Abijah, Asa, Jehoshaphat, Jehoram, Ahaziah, Athaliah, Jehoash, Amaziah, Uzziah, Jotham, Ahaz, Hezekiah, Manasseh, Amon, Josiah, Jehoahaz, Jehoiakim, Jeconiah, Zedekiah (up to the destruction of the First Temple) (Then from the reconstruction of the Second Temple by Herod) Herod, Agrippa I, Agrippa II (Archelaus was not a king). However, since they are wearing white garments and many were evil kings, it is clear that Agrippa II, the twenty-fourth king, is the one king sitting on the throne. He wears the white garment as Herod did because he holds the supreme position in the Church. From this it can be seen that this event is the Coronation of Agrippa.)*

Rev 10:7,11 but in the days of the voice of the seventh angel, when he may be about to sound, and the secret of God may be finished, as He did declare to His own servants, to the prophets. and he said to me, 'It behooves you again to prophesy about

- peoples (members of the Church paying no dues, John the scribe for Jesus and Simon Magus) - Gospel of John
- nations (foreign countries of the uncircumcised taught by Paul in Acts; Luke the scribe of Jesus) - Gospel of Luke
- tongues (Peter was the spokesman for Jesus and Pentecost bishops, Mark was his scribe) - Gospel of Mark,
- kings (like the Sadducee Jonathan Annas: Stephen (stephanos: crown); his brother Matthew and King Agrippa II, the nominal head of the Church) - Gospel of Matthew

## Chapter 93. (47AD)
## Matthew intends to canonize the Four Gospels

*Jesus arrives in Ephesus with John Aquila.*
Matthew kisses Jesus and says, "Having read your description that you sent from Patmos and having not seen you since your ministry, I feared our meeting."

Jesus answers, "Eyes of flame and tongue of sword could intimidate, yet my white wool hair should have calmed you. I bow to your seven Thunders."

Matthew says, "We both knew that a New Testament was essential, but there was a problem of merging the poetry of your Gospel, scribed by John Mark and Simon Magus, with the simplicity of Peter, scribed by the other Mark. There needed to be a more elaborate Gospel and you led the way with the Gospel scribed by Luke and I also contributed my Gospel. Each Gospel seemed to stand on its own, so we decided to keep four independent Gospels for the peoples, the tongues, the nations, and the kings."

Jesus says, "Yes, these four gospels could represent Ezekiel's vision of the Zodiacal Cross. The Gospel of John does represent all peoples in the congregation, and, since it emphasizes my death and resurrection, it would be Scorpio with its companion sign: Eagle. The Gospel of Mark with Peter, my spokesman as 'tongues', represents the bishops with the courage of the sign Leo, the lion."

"And the Gospel of Luke would represent the nations of the Gentiles and being also the vehicle for the monastic way modeled on the Essenes: requiring the yoke of the monastic or Nazarite path, possessing superhuman strength to resist sexual temptation, and thus the sign of Taurus, the ox. The Gospel of Matthew, represents the merging of kings, namely Agrippa II, the nominal head of the Church, with the priestly lines: the Winged Man *(angel)*: Aquarius."

*Rev 13:17,18 And that no one may be able to buy, or to sell, except he who is having the mark, or the name of the beast, or the number of his name. Here is the wisdom! He who is having the understanding, let him count the number of the beast, for the number of a man it is, and its number is 666.*

*(James Niceta writes:)*
*Rev 10:1-10 And I saw another strong angel coming down out of the heaven, arrayed with a cloud, and (hair not ἶρις: rainbow) upon the head (hair white as a lamb Rev 01:13), and his face as the sun, and his feet as pillars of fire, and he had in his hand a little scroll opened (Gospel of John), and he did place his right foot upon the sea, and the left upon the land (having studied in Rome at Tiber Island and the homeland), and he cried with a great voice, as a lion does roar (lion signifies a king), and when he cried, speak out did the seven thunders their voices (Matthew Annas the seventh angel speaks with authority); and when the seven thunders spoke their voices, I was about to write, and I heard a voice out of the heaven saying to me, 'Seal the things that the seven thunders spoke; you may not write these things.' And the angel whom I saw standing upon the sea, and upon the land, did lift up his hand to the heaven, and did swear in Him who does live to the ages of the ages, who did create the heaven and the things in it, and the land and the things in it, and the sea and the things in it -- that time shall not be yet,*
*And the voice that I heard out of the heaven is again speaking with me, and saying, 'Go, take the little scroll that is open in the hand of the angel who has been standing upon the sea, and upon the land:' and I went away unto the angel, saying to him, 'Give me the little scroll;' and he said to me, 'Take, and eat it up, and it shall make your belly bitter, but in your mouth it shall be sweet -- as honey.' And I took the little scroll out of the hand of the angel, and did eat it up, and it was in my mouth as honey -- sweet, and when I did eat it -- my belly was made bitter; (referring to the sections showing Simon Magus - he having poisoned King Agrippa)*

# Chapter 94. (47AD)
## The bitterness of the Gospel of John is removed

Matthew says, "Jesus, I want to assign James Niceta, to solve the problem of the prominence of Simon Magus in your Gospel of John. That he was once the Pope after John the Baptist is a true fact, but now he is viewed by most as an enemy, even Satan."

Jesus says, "It is true that after King Agrippa was poisoned, we decided to stay with the Herodian Dynasty because we believed that his son, Agrippa II, could be shaped to our cause. Unfortunately, after Paul revealed the truth to him of the poisoning of his father by Simon, it was impossible to collaborate with him. I have great regret over this situation as he is still my dear friend. This dispute has even cost me my marriage with Magdalene, but I do understand her decision. Yes, I did warn Simon, 'It is easier for a camel to go through the eye of a needle, than for a rich man to enter into the kingdom of God'. In my metaphor, I used the letter of Qof being the eye of a needle which is the symbol for the fourth position of cardinal, making it impossible for the letter Gimel being a camel, two levels below to show that money and 'simony' corrupts."

Matthew says, "The rift is especially unfortunate because Simon's path of 660, which many call the path of Satan 666, is exactly the same as ours. Tau has a Gematria value of 400, Resh is 200, and Samekh is 60. Added together they are 660 being all positions that one graduates to."

*Rev 05:11,12 And I saw, and I heard the voice of many angels around the throne, and the living creatures, and the elders -- and the number of them was myriads of myriads, and thousands of thousands -- saying with a great voice, 'Worthy is the Lamb that was slain to receive the power, and riches, and wisdom, and strength, and honor, and glory, and blessing !'*

The seven ministers under the Lamb (Jesus) for the seven days of the week:

1. Power (dunamis) - Atomos the Magus acting for Agrippa II
2. Riches (ploutos) - Aristobulus, the father of Timothy, as assistant to Power
3. Wisdom (sophia) - Salome the mother of Timothy
4. Strength (ischys) - Jesus Justus acting for his father as Adam (who must work to survive outside of Eden)
5. Honor (timé) - Timothy, the crown prince (His name being formed from 'timé' with its literal meaning: price; therefore the one who received the Herodian fees for initiation.) (Prior to this ceremony, Agrippa II, who was childless and possibly a homosexual, has adopted Timothy, his cousin, as his son following the pattern of the Roman Emperors (Paul officiated at Timothy's Bar Mitzvah Sept 47AD).
6. Glory (doxa) - Apollos as the 'Moses'; Therapeut leader (replacing Theudas)
7. Blessing (eulogia) - Matthew Annas as abbot

# Chapter 95. (April 48AD)
## Worthy is the Lamb to unseal the Gospels

*Agrippa II sits on the throne on the third level of the abbey in Ephesus; John is seated at the edge of the second level.* Matthew Annas, on the second level, calls out, " 'Who is worthy to open the scrolls and to loose the seals of it?" *There is silence.* Matthew calls out again "'Is no one in heaven or on earth, able to open the scrolls, or to behold them?"
Jesus calls out, "Yes, there is one from the tribe of Judah, the root of David, who is worthy to open the scrolls, and to loose the seven seals. I am the Lamb who shed his blood for all our sins here on this Day of Atonement."
*As Jesus, in white, walks forward to the center of the middle level and the trap door above opens to illuminate him.*
The congregation shouts, "Hallelujah, Alleluia"

Seven ministers call out their symbols as they form a semi-circle around the Lamb: Atomos the Magus, "power", Aristobulus, "riches", Salome, "Sophia", Jesus Justus, "strength", Timothy, "price", Apollos, "doxa", and Matthew, "eulogia".

*There are six pedestals. Jesus walks forward and opens the seal to Matthew's gospel and steps aside. (Also, he opens the other five, after each is read.)*
1. Matthew, dressed in the white chasuble of a High Priest, comes forward and reads the first chapter of his gospel; 2. Peter, dressed in the red chasuble of a cardinal, comes forward and reads the first chapter from his gospel Mark; 3. John Mark, dressed in the black chasuble of an archbishop, reads from Jesus' gospel of Luke; 4. Jesus, in white chasuble with a green sash, stays and reads from his gospel of John; 5. Thomas, in a brown chasuble with a pink sash, reads from his gospel; 6. Philip, in a purple chasuble with a gold sash, reads from his gospel; 7. John Aquila, dressed in a purple chasuble, stands at his seat off to the side and reads from Revelation.

Matthew calls out, "Salvation is to Him who is sitting upon the throne -- to our God, and to the Lamb!" The congregation says, "Amen."

# SECTION 16 (49AD to September 51AD)
## Jesus Second Marriage to Lydia

Berea: The Altar of the Apostle Paul

*Acts 16:9-12 And a vision through the night appeared to Paul -- a certain man of Macedonia (Luke) was standing, calling upon him, and saying, 'Having passed through to Macedonia, help us;'-- (This first use of 'us' by Luke meaning Luke together with Jesus and the use of 'vision' confirms this to be Jesus' message.) and when he saw the vision, immediately we (plural: meaning Luke acting on Jesus' behalf) endeavored to go forth to Macedonia, assuredly gathering that the Lord has called us to preach good news to them'. (The 'Lord' is Jesus and preaching "good news" is a hint that Jesus needs to have Paul to come to baptize Lydia who will soon be his second wife.)*
*Having set sail, therefore, from Troas, we came with a straight course to Samothracia, on the morrow also to Neapolis, thence also to Philippi, which is a principal city of the part of Macedonia -- a colony. And we were in this city abiding certain days,*

*Acts 16:13,14 on the sabbath-day (March 50AD) also we went forth outside of the city, by a river, where there used to be prayer, and having sat down, we were speaking to the women who came together, and a certain woman, by name Lydia, a seller of purple, of the city of Thyatira, worshipping God,*
*(In the first part of the sentence "worshipping God (theos)" shows that "Lord (kurios)" is definitely Jesus. Jesus was already acquainted with Lydia, having sent a letter to her as the bishop of the fourth Church at Thyatira in March 48AD. There he asked her not to allow Bernice into the church due to the allegations of incest with her twin brother Agrippa II. That she wore purple indicates that she was a bishop and the fact that she sold church positions shows that she was part of Simon Magus' Church that practiced simony.) was hearing, whose heart the Lord did open, to attend to the things spoken by Paul; (the preparation of baptism and the explanation of the Essene rules of marriage) and when she was baptized, and her household, she did call upon us, saying, 'If you have judged me to be faithful to the Lord, having entered into my house, remain;' and she constrained us. (Indicating her betrothal and preparation for sexual relations in October.)*

## Chapter 96. (49AD)
## Luke fetches Paul; Lydia betrothed to Jesus

*Jesus with Luke, approaches the Church in Thyatira, one of the Seven Churches. Lydia and her congregation are there to greet them.*

Jesus kisses Lydia. "I am so pleased to meet you. The purple vestments of bishop suit you."

Lydia says, "Paul is making me aware of the differences between the two churches, especially in the elimination of 'simony'. Tomorrow, he will baptize me into your Christian church. I hope also that you will find me worthy of being your virgin vessel for the continuation of King David's line. Many of the congregation are curious about your resurrection and whether the true Resurrection is yet to come."

Jesus says, "My death was by poison; revived by antidote, but a resurrection to me. As to the true Resurrection, I believe that Paul can speak more eloquently on it.

Paul, seeing the crowds, starts to preach, "Surely, Christ has been raised from the dead and therefore there is a resurrection of the dead? If Christ has not been raised, then our preaching is in vain and your faith is in vain." (1Cor 15:12-14)

Luke smiles, "Paul's logic appears to rely on faith."

*Ignoring Jesus, the crowd swarms around Paul.*
*Jesus takes Lydia's hand; they walk along the river.*

*Philippi October 50AD Acts 16:16-34 And it came to pass in our going on to prayer, a certain maid, having a spirit of Python (Bernice, the twin sister of Agrippa II now age 22 - Antiq 19.9.1 Bernice was sixteen at the time of her father's death 44AD = birthdate 28AD), did meet us, who brought much employment to her masters by soothsaying (i.e. converting new members to the Church of Simon Magus and extracting fees), she having followed Paul and us, was crying, saying, 'These men are servants of the Most High God, who declare to us a way of salvation;' and this she was doing for many days, but Paul having been grieved, and having turned, said to the spirit, 'I command you, in the name of Jesus Christ, to come forth from her;' and it came forth the same hour. And her masters having seen that the hope of their employment was gone (angers his brother Agrippa II), having caught Paul and Silas, drew them to the market-place, unto the rulers, and having brought them to the magistrates, they said, 'These men do exceedingly trouble our city, being Jews; and they proclaim customs that are not lawful for us to receive nor to do, being Romans.' (They beat Paul and Silas and throw them in prison. This event is treated as a metaphor for Ananus the Younger (being the jailor this time) graduating to archbishop like Peter's imprisonment under King Herod Agrippa, now it is his son Agrippa II.) And at midnight Paul and Silas praying, were singing hymns to God, and the prisoners were hearing them, and suddenly a great earthquake came (similar to Theudas at Resurrection, now Apollos head of Therapeuts), so that the foundations of the prison were shaken, opened also presently were all the doors, and all the bands were loosed; and the jailor (Ananus the Younger) having come out of sleep, and having seen the doors of the prison open, having drawn a sword, was about to kill himself, supposing the prisoners to be fled, and Paul cried out with a loud voice, saying, 'You may not do yourself any harm, for we are all here.' And, having asked for a light, he sprang in, and trembling he fell down before Paul and Silas, and having brought them forth, said, 'Sirs, what must I do that I may be saved?' and they said, 'Believe on the Lord Jesus Christ, and you shall be saved: you and your house' (church); and they spoke to him the word of the Lord, and to all those in his household (congregation); and having taken them, in that hour of the night, he did bathe him from the blows, and was baptized, himself and all his presently, having brought them also into his house, he set food before them, and was glad with all the household, he having believed in God. (baptized and sharing the Eucharist; the prison is now the Church.).*

*Acts 16:40b And they (used for Jesus without Luke) entered into Lydia (note: 'house' is left out) and having seen the brethren (having knowledge of in the biblical sense), they comforted them (all a euphemism for the sexual phase of Jesus and Lydia' marriage), and went forth.*

## Chapter 97. (November 50AD)
## Jesus' marriage is consummated

Bernice confronting Paul, "Why have you and Jesus forbidden me from this Church at Philippi. Lydia claims that I am a Jezebel. I hear she got this from one of Jesus' letters to the Churches."

Paul says," You are not really blameless here? What about the stories that you have committed incest with your brother Agrippa II?"
Bernice replies, "My twin brother has not married and is 'asexual' as are many monastics, perhaps like you, who proclaim celibacy, being sexually inadequate themselves. Is it my fault that I was married by my father King Agrippa to impotent old men!"

Paul answers, "Your anger already confirms my belief that 'women should remain silent in the churches and not be allowed to speak and be in submission as the law says'. (1Cor. 14:34) Jesus is too liberal."
Bernice rages at him, "I do not need to be a seer to know you are closet misogynist!" *She storms off.*

Zacchaeus arrives saying, "I am sorry, but Bernice has ordered me to arrest you, Paul, and Silas."
*He puts them in bonds and locks them in prison.*

Calling Zacchaeus over, Paul places his hands on his shoulders through the bars, saying "Ananus the Younger, I will call you 'Demas' as you are of the people. I anoint you, cardinal." *They sing hymns.*

*This time an Earthquake being Apollos as Theudas' replacement, releases them from prison. He having connections with Bernice's brother Agrippa..*

*Jesus and Lydia are holding hands.* Lydia kisses Jesus and says, "It is that time." Jesus says, "Yes my beloved." *They walk off together.*

*Acts 17:1-10 And having passed through Amphipolis, and Apollonia, they came to Thessalonica, where was the synagogue of the Jews, and according to the custom of Paul, he went in unto them, and for three sabbaths he was reasoning with them from the Writings, opening and alleging, 'That the Christ it behoved to suffer, and to rise again out of the dead, and that this is the Christ -- Jesus whom I proclaim to you.' And certain of them did believe, and attached themselves to Paul and to Silas, also of the worshipping Greeks a great multitude, of the principal women also not a few.*
*And the unbelieving Jews, having been moved with envy, and having taken to them of the loungers certain evil men, and having made a crowd, were setting the city in an uproar; having assailed also the house of Jason (Jason from the Argonauts to the Greeks being Japheth, son of Noah, the title of third division of the Fish being the Gentile group, originally John Mark, but now Luke), they were seeking them to bring them to the populace, and not having found them, they drew Jason and certain brethren unto the city rulers, calling aloud -- 'These, having put the world in commotion, are also here present, whom Jason has received; and these all do contrary to the decrees of Caesar, saying another to be king -- Jesus.' And they troubled the multitude and the city rulers, hearing these things, and having taking security from Jason and the rest, they let them go. And the brethren immediately, through the night, sent forth both Paul and Silas to Berea, who having come, went to the synagogue of the Jews; (The original mission to the Diaspora tried to incorporate pagan practices to aid their proselytizing. Jason was the substitute for Noah and the baptisms were done on the ocean where converts would swim to the boat and be blessed by the priest.)*

*September 51AD Lydia gives Jesus another son*
*Acts 17:13 And when the Jews from Thessalonica knew that also in Berea was the* **Word of God** *declared by Paul, they came thither also, agitating the multitudes;*

*1Cor 7:9 "But if they cannot control themselves, they should marry, for it is better to marry than to (burn with desire)."*
*Phil 4:3 "And I entreat you also, true yoke-fellow, help those women which labored with me in the gospel, with Clement also, and with other my fellow laborers, whose names are in the book of life."*

*Acts 17:14,15 and then immediately the brethren sent forth Paul, to go on as it were to the sea, but both Silas and Timothy were remaining there. And those conducting Paul, brought him unto Athens, and having received a command unto Silas and Timothy that with all speed they may come unto him, they departed;*

## Chapter 98. (September 51AD)
## Luke as Jason; Lydia presents Jesus with a son

In Thessalonica, Paul was preaching by the shore "The anointed one, the Christ, was prophesied to suffer, and to rise again out of the dead, and it is this Christ who is Jesus whom I proclaim to you now. Our very own Jason of the Argonauts, known to us as Japheth, the son of Noah, is ready to baptize you."

*Luke, acting as Jason, takes a group out in a boat. They jump off and are fished out of the sea in a big net. On the jetty, Simon-Silas baptizes them.*

After the ceremony, a messenger from Jesus hands him a letter. Paul reads it aloud to Silas and Luke, "Jesus says that Lydia has given him a son! He also invites me to Athens to visit with his daughter Phoebe as she will soon be of marrying age."

Simon says, "Looks like I may soon be an uncle."
Paul nervously says, "I guess I will have to stop hiding in celibacy and actively keep myself from 'burning' with the hellfire of sexual desire."
Simon says, "I am sure that Jesus is granting you a great privilege to be part of the exception to the Essene rules of celibacy as a future member of the David line for its continuation. The monastics do not understand that our paths are harder because the temptation is greater when balancing both states. My father knew that."
"I pray that Phoebe will accept me, so that we can be yoked together as two oxen harnessed to the plow of the Lord, as Taurus the bull in Ezekiel."

Simon says, "May the Word' be planted! Timothy and I can join you shortly. Be off in haste."

# SECTION 17 (November 51AD to March 54AD)
## Paul and Phoebe meet; betrothed, married, and with child

Grimoire of Armadel

Acts 17:16-21 and Paul waiting for them in Athens, his spirit was stirred in him, beholding the city wholly given to idolatry, therefore, indeed, he was reasoning in the synagogue with the Jews, and with the worshipping persons, and in the market-place every day with those who met with him. And certain of the Epicurean and of the Stoic philosophers, were meeting together to see him, and some were saying, 'What would this babbler wish to say?' and others, 'Of strange demons he does seem to be an announcer;' because Jesus and the rising again he did proclaim to them as good news, having also taken him, unto the Areopagus they brought him, saying, 'Are we able to know what is this new teaching that is spoken by you, for certain strange things you do bring to our ears? We wish, then, to know what these things would wish to be;' and all Athenians and the strangers sojourning, for nothing else were at leisure but to say something, and to hear some newer thing.

Acts 17:22-31 And Paul, having stood in the midst of the Areopagus, said, 'Men, Athenians, ....

Letter 1. SENECA TO PAUL, greeting I believe, Paul, that you have been informed of the talk which I had yesterday with my Lucilius about the apocrypha (or possibly the secret mysteries) and other things; for certain sharers in your teaching were with me. For we had retired to the gardens of Sallust (Gardens in Rome), where, because of us, those whom I speak of, going in another direction, saw and joined us. Certainly, we wished for your presence, and I would have you know it. We were much refreshed by the reading of your book, by which I mean some of the many letters which you have addressed to some city or capital of a province, and which inculcate the moral life with admirable precepts. These thoughts, I take it, are not uttered by you but through you, but surely sometimes both by you and through you: for such is the greatness of them and they are instinct (warm) with such nobility, that I think whole generations (ages) of men could hardly suffice for the instilling and perfecting of them. I desire your good health, brother.

Letter 2. PAUL TO SENECA, greeting I received your letter yesterday with delight, and should have been able to answer it at once, had I had by me the youth I meant to send to you. For you know when, and by whom, and at what moment, and to whom things ought to be given and entrusted. I beg, therefore, that you will not think yourself neglected, when I am respecting the dignity of your person. Now in that you somewhere write that you are pleased with my letter (or, write that you are pleased with part of my letter) I think myself happy in the good opinion of such a man: for you would not say it, you, a critic, a sophist, the teacher of a great prince, and indeed of all -unless you spoke truth. I trust you may long be in health.

## Chapter 99. (November 51AD)
## Speech on the Unknown God; Meets Seneca

Paul, standing on 'Ares Rock' near the Acropolis in Athens, says: "Men of Athens, As I passed along and observed the objects of your worship, I found also an altar with this inscription, 'To an Unknown God.' This God that you worship as unknown, I proclaim to you as the God who made the world and everything in it, being Lord of heaven and earth, who does not live in shrines made by man, nor is he served by human hands, not needing anything, since He gives to all men life, breath, and all things. From one ancestor he made all nations to inhabit the whole earth, and he allotted the times of their existence and the boundaries of the places where they would live, so that they would search for God and perhaps grope for him and find him, though indeed he is not far from each one of us. For in him we live and move and have our being. While God has overlooked our ignorance, now he commands all people everywhere to repent, because he has fixed a day on which he will have the world judged in righteousness by a *man* whom he has appointed, and of this, he has given assurance to all by raising him from the dead."

One person calls out, "No one can be resurrected from the dead. Where is this man?" Paul answers, "The prophet Daniel says, 'He is like unto the Son of Man, coming with the clouds of heaven'." (Dan 7:13)

Afterwards, an elderly man comes up to Paul, "That was an excellent oration. Let me introduce myself. I am Seneca the Younger, friend of the Emperor. Let's correspond by epistles." *Phoebe also was there.*

Acts 17:34a *and certain men having cleaved to him, did believe, among whom is also Dionysius the Areopagite,* (Bishop of Athens (Eccl Hist 3.4.11) (Curiously the name of Dionysius the Areopagite was successfully used as a pseudonym by Christian theologian and philosopher writing before 532, giving him great authority to spell out the orders of angels.) Paul clearly recognizes the seven orders of Angels: Angels, Archangels, Virtues, Powers, Principalities, Dominions, Thrones, Cherubim and Seraphim in his letters: Eph 1:21 "That power (God's) is the same as the mighty strength he exerted when he raised Christ from the dead and seated him at his right hand in the heavenly realms, far above all rule ('archēs': Power) and authority ('potestates'/'exousias': Principalities), wheels ('dynameōs': Power/Wheels/Virtues) and dominion ('kyriotētos'/'dominationes': Dominions), and every name that is invoked, not only in the present age but also in the one to come."
Col 1:16 "For by Him all things were created, both in the heavens and on earth, visible and invisible, whether thrones ('thronoi': Thrones) or dominions ('kyriotētes': Dominions) or rulers ('archai': Powers) or authorities ('exousiai' Principalities) - all things have been created through Him and for Him."

Acts 17:34b *and a woman, by name Damaris* (Tamar-Phoebe), *and others with them* (Luke and Jesus). (Tamar was the name of the virgin daughter of King David; its Greek form is Damaris. With Jesus, the descendant of David, this would certainly be the name given to the daughter of Jesus and Mary Magdalene who was born in September 33 after the Crucifixion. She would take the name of Phoebe, her grandmother's real name before she took the name of Helena (See the Clementines), being known also as Salome, Martha, and Luna (also in the Clementines).)

Acts 18:1,2a,c,3 *And after these things, Paul having departed out of Athens, came to Corinth, and having found a certain Jew, by name Aquila, of Pontus by birth, lately come from Italy, and Priscilla his wife. Paul came to them, and because of being of the same craft, he did remain with them, and was working, for they were tent-makers as to craft;* (Aquila (Eagle - the standard of the Romans) with his brother Niceta is in the Clementines, both being illegitimate twins of the Emperor's family adopted by Helena, Mary Magdalene's mother, "wife of Zebedee" (Simon Magus) being John and James in the Gospels, step-uncles of Mary Magdalene's child Tamar-Phoebe. Implied is that John Aquila and his wife Priscilla are chaperones of Paul and Phoebe's betrothal.)
Acts 18:2b *because of Claudius having directed all the Jews to depart out of Rome.* (Suetonius, Life of Claudius, 25:4 "Since the Jews constantly made disturbances at the instigation of Chrestus, he expelled them from Rome." (Orosius Book 7.6 choosing 51AD) "In the ninth year of his reign (49AD), Claudius expelled the Jews from Rome.")

# Chapter 100 (March 52AD)
## Paul (35) is betrothed to Phoebe

*Jesus, Luke, Phoebe, and Paul arrive in Corinth from Athens. They greet Aquila and Priscilla with a kiss.*

Jesus says, "John Aquila and Priscilla, how are things since you were expelled from Rome by Claudius due to Simon's misuse of Church funds?"

John replies, "The people in Corinth have been very receptive. I guess we are tentmakers again and no longer carpenters, since our Mission to the Diaspora has to move from place to place. My group of five thousand, that you began in that miraculous feeding, has continued to grow exponentially."

Priscilla says, "Christianity has been extremely popular with women who believe their husbands to be too involved in materialistic and carnal things. This has caused problems for the monastic mission when husbands retaliate." Paul smiles, "And I have the scars to prove it!" She continues, "However, by allowing the married couples to embrace the Faith, all have deepened their relationship to the divine within each other."

Jesus says, "So Phoebe, my dearest daughter, who comforted me from Magdalene's womb when I was suffering on the cross, are you prepared to be betrothed to Paul and joined in marriage this November?"

Phoebe answers, "Since I heard Paul speak on that rock in Athens last autumn, I could not imagine being with a more perfect man. His words to me were as melodic as a chorus made up of the seven dominions of angels. My answer is yes."

Paul says, "My love for Jesus is great and yet, for his daughter, it is greater still. I cannot imagine a more perfect union than with by dearest Phoebe."

*Antiq 20.7.2 While Felix was procurator of Judea, he saw this Drusilla, and fell in love with her; for she did indeed exceed all other women in beauty; and he sent to her a person whose name was Atomos one of his friends; a Jew he was, and by birth a Cypriot, and one who pretended to be a magician (following in Simon Magus' footsteps), and endeavored to persuade her to forsake her present husband, and marry him; and promised, that if she would not refuse him, he would make her a happy woman. Accordingly, she acted ill, and because she was desirous to avoid her sister Bernice's envy, for she was very ill-treated by her on account of her beauty, was prevailed upon to transgress the laws of her forefathers, and to marry Felix;*

*Excerpts from The Acts of Philip (52AD)*
*(There was a dispute between Philip and Ananias, the High Priest when Ananias son of Nedebaios (Antiq 20.5.2, called "Ananias ben Nebedeus") was brought to trial before Claudius in 52AD. He officiated as high priest from about 47 to 52AD. Quadratus, governor of Syria, accused him of being responsible for acts of violence between the Jews and the Samaritans which also caused the recall of the Procurator Ventidius Cumanus. The writer has given Philip supernatural power to accomplish this. Ananias was acquitted by emperor Claudius and would later preside over the trial of Paul at Jerusalem and Caesarea. Much of these Acts of Philip are insignificant and have been deleted, however, the passages that are included give interesting insights about the apostles and their assigned locations.) When Philip entered into the city of Athens which is called Hellas, 300 philosophers gathered and said: Let us go and see what his wisdom is, for they say of the wise men of Asia that their wisdom is great. For they supposed Philip to be a philosopher: he traveled only in a cloak and an undergarment. So they assembled and looked into their books, lest he should get the better of them. Philip said: 'May the veil of unbelief be taken from you, and thou learn who is the deceiver, thou or I." Ananias' address: 'How Jesus destroyed the law and allowed all meats and was crucified. How the disciples stole his body, and did many wonders, and were cast out of Jerusalem. And now go all about the world deceiving everyone, like this Philip. But I will take him to Jerusalem, for the king Archelaus (Agrippa II, but more likely the Sanhedrin) seek him to kill him.*
*Philip seeing him grieved, and said to Ananias: 'This is through your folly: if I raise him will you believe?' Ananias: I know you will raise him by your magic, but I will not believe. Philip was wroth and said: Catathema (cursed thing), go down into the abyss in the sight of all. And he was swallowed up: but the high-priestly robe flew away from him, and therefore no man knows where it is from that day. The people cried out, believing in God, and the 500 were baptized. And Philip stayed two years at Athens, and founded a church and ordained a bishop and a presbyter, and departed to Parthia to preach.*

# Chapter 101. (52AD)
## Procurator Felix marries Drusilla;
## The Acts of Philip

*(Perished in the eruption of Mount Vesuvius in AD 79)*

*Philip takes his turn to speak at Ares Rock*

Paul is off to the side with Atomos, "Hail Atomos, esteemed Magian replacement for Simon. I hear you have encouraged the new procurator Felix to marry Herod Agrippa's youngest daughter Drusilla. I think it is a mistake as people will think of him as one of us, but he will surely act corruptly."
"Or it will bind him to us."

A philosopher yells at Philip, "Get on with this speech and let it be on new subjects."

Philip says "I am glad to hear that you desire something new. You must cast away the old constructs. The Lord said: 'We cannot put new wine into old bottles'."

The philosophers ask, "Who is this Lord?"
Philip replies, "Jesus Christ."

Conferring with the High Priest, they say "This is a new name to us. Tell us, Ananias, who is this Jesus Christ?"

Ananias says, "Are these followers of this deceiver in Athens also? He should be arrested."

Philip says, "You should not listen to this man, I prophesy he will soon be defrocked by Claudius for causing friction with Judeans and Samaritans. People, confess now with a pure heart that Jesus is Lord, and you will be saved. As for this man, little by little by his own evil actions, he will surely be swallowed up by the earth."

*Acts 18:7 And having departed thence, he went to the house of a certain one, by name Titius Justus (Titus, tutor of Jesus Justus), a worshipper of God, whose house was adjoining the synagogue,*

*Acts 18:8 and Crispus, the ruler of the synagogue did believe in the Lord with all his house, and many of the Corinthians hearing were believing, and they were being baptized.* This aligns with Paul's epistle: 1Cor 1:14 which shows that he only baptized Crispus and Gaius in Corinth and salutes Sosthenes as a brother in the Church. Paul had strong connections with the Corinthians as evidenced by two detailed epistles to them.

*Acts 18:9-11 And the Lord said through a vision in the night to Paul, 'Be not afraid, but be speaking and you may be not silent; because I am with you, and no one shall set on you to do you evil; because I have important people in this city;' and he continued a year and six months, teaching among them the word of God.*
Here again is the vision, instead of Luke speaking for Jesus it is Jesus is talking directly to Paul encouraging Paul and Phoebe in their marriage. Since it is April and one and a half year shows that Paul and Phoebe were unsuccessful to conceive in the first winter, but succeeded the next winter. The hope is that it will be a boy and thus "the Word of God".

*Acts 18:12-17 And Gallio (Gallio is the brother of Seneca, his new found friend) being proconsul of Achaia, the Jews made a rush with one accord upon Paul, and brought him unto the tribunal, saying -- 'Against the law this one does persuade men to worship God;' and Paul being about to open his mouth, Gallio said unto the Jews, 'If, indeed, then, it was anything unrighteous, or an act of wicked profligacy, O Jews, according to reason I had borne with you, but if it is a question concerning words and names, and of your law, look you yourselves to it, for a judge of these things I do not wish to be,' and he drove them from the tribunal; and all the Greeks having taken Sosthenes, the chief man of the synagogue, were beating him before the tribunal, and not even for these things was Gallio caring.* (Claudius Delphi Inscription places Gallio as proconsul in 51-52AD, which is the most valuable time point in Paul's life their betrothal in March 52AD.)

## Chapter 102. (March 52AD)
## Objections to Paul's marriage;
## Gallio releases him

Phoebe says, "I am disappointed that we did not conceive this past winter, but we still have two years to try. I was hoping for a girl that I will call Paulina after my grandmother Helena real name."

Paul says, "Yes that is a perfect name, but you know I would prefer a boy to carry my work forward."

Jesus says "Do not be discouraged. In my first marriage, it took me three years to conceive my beautiful Phoebe and now look at my first son, Jesus Justus, almost fifteen and going to be tutored by Titus. Phoebe has already proved that a woman can rival any man and so would her daughter."

Jesus Justus says, "I am so glad you are family now and, Uncle Paul, I hope to be as learned as you."
Paul says, "Thank you for your compliment. I hope my letters to my followers such as the Corinthians and the Ephesians can contribute to the Church doctrine."

Simon-Silas comes rushing in, saying to Paul, "There is a faction of Jews who are objecting to your wedding saying that you are not of the David dynasty and not really a Jew."

Paul says, "This must be the work of Simon Magus. My father Herod Antipas has always been considered to be an honorary Jew and I was circumcised. Even if they try to arrest me, the proconsul Gallio will free me as he is the brother of Seneca the Younger, of whom I am now friends."

Winter 53AD Having failed to have a child with Phoebe in the Winter 52AD, Paul tries again:

Acts 18:18 And Paul having remained yet a good many days, having taken leave of the brethren, was sailing to Syria -- and with him are Priscilla and Aquila -- having shorn his head in Cenchera, for he had a vow;

(Cenchera is a port of ancient Greece, on the Saronic Gulf, east of Corinth. It is a convent as shown in in his letter from later on in 57AD:

Rom16:1-2 I commend unto you Phoebe our sister, which is a servant of the church which is at Cenchrea: That you receive her in the Lord, as becomes a saint, and that you assist her in whatsoever business she hath need of you: for she hath been a helper (prostatis) (KJV succourer) of many, and of myself also. Greet Priscilla and Aquila, who work with me in Christ Jesus, and who risked their necks for my life, to whom not only I give thanks,) This is the most important proof that Paul is betrothed and about to enter the sexual part of his marriage in the winter time. Jesus did the same thing when he was Tempted by Satan in the Wilderness. Although it was presented there as Jesus' preparation of his ministry, its real purpose was to prepare himself for sexual relations with Mary Magdalene. Priscilla and Aquila are chaperones preparing Tamar-Phoebe.

March 54AD Once Phoebe had reached her three months pregnant milestone in March, Paul took her with him to Ephesus where she stayed until the birth. The plan was to leave her in care of her grandmother Mary Magdalene in at the convent of Hierapolis near the Church of Laodicea (one of the Seven Churches).

Acts 18:19 and he came down to Ephesus, and did leave them there, and he himself having entered into the synagogue did reason with the Jews:

## Chapter 103. (March 54AD)
## Paul's Nazarite vow; 2nd year results in conception; Phoebe 3 months pregnant is left with Magdalene in Hierapolis

*Magdalene opens the door of the convent in Hierapolis to Paul and Phoebe. Phoebe kisses her.* "Hello mother, you will never believe: I am three months pregnant with Paul's child!"

Magdalene says, "Great news! It was so long ago that I was three months pregnant with you at the cross"

"Yes, I always wonder if I have a memory of that event. It certainly feels like I do."

Magdalene kisses Paul and says, "I never thought of you as the marrying type."

Paul says, "I believe that being more serious about my Nazarite vow, having this time stayed 40 days and nights in the desert, is the reason for our successful outcome. While there, I would think of Jesus' struggle when he was told by Jonathan Annas that he must take the poison. Measured to that, I feel unworthy of Phoebe's love."
Phoebe says, "Oh, my dearest, not you but me."

Magdalene, welling up with tears, says, "Phoebe I have missed so much you since the divorce."

Paul says, "Thank you for agreeing to take care of Phoebe. It is important to finish my Second Journey with Silas and to start my Third. Already seven years have gone by."
Magdalene says, "It is my pleasure."
*Paul and Phoebe kiss each other and Paul leaves. Magdalene wipes a tear from Phoebe's eye.*

# SECTION 18 (September 54 to May 58AD)
# Paul's Third Missionary Journey

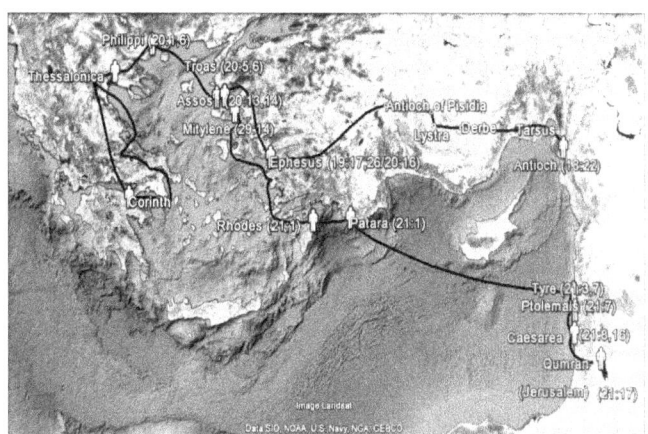

(Antioch .. Galatia .. Phrygia .. Ephesus .. Assos .. Troas .. Philippe .. Thessolonica .. Corinth .. backtrack to Assos .. Mitylene .. Rhodes .. Patara .. Tyre .. Ptolemais .. Caesarea .. Qumran .. Jerusalem)

*(The inserted section Revelation 12:01 Jesus' Bar Mitzvah in 6AD and ending at Rev 14:05 being just prior to the Ascension in 33AD can be assigned to John Aquila. The next part in its different abbreviated style starts with this year 54AD (when Nero becomes emperor) to 74AD (The fall of Masada (Rev 14:06 to Rev 19:17) can be assigned to Tychicus, the younger brother of Timothy, having been mentioned by Paul in his Second Epistle to Timothy 4:12 : "Tychicus I have sent to Ephesus", starts with this year 54AD (when Nero becomes emperor) and ends in 74AD (The fall of Masada (Rev 14:06 to Rev 19:17). In two sets of seven years assigned to specific angels (leaders) who were important (54-60AD); then to vials of blood: the factors during (61-67AD) leading to the Fall of Jerusalem (70AD). (Tychicus writes:)*
Rev 14:6,7 And I saw another angel flying in mid-heaven, having good news everlasting to proclaim to those dwelling upon the earth, and to every nation, and tribe, and tongue, and people, saying in a great voice, 'Fear you God, and give to Him glory, because come did the hour of His judgment, and bow you before Him who did make the heaven, and the land, and sea, and fountains of waters. (This first angel is Jonathan who at Jesus' Bar Mitzvah was 'flying from east to west', but now 'another': his brother Matthew. The year 54AD that would also be designated as the first year of Nero's reign, having become Emperor in October of 54AD (Claudius having been poisoned by Agrippina the Younger whose memoirs inspired the Clementines).

Phoebe, who gave birth to a girl in September in Ephesus, begs him to stay: Acts 18:20-28 and they having requested him to remain a longer time with them, he did not consent, but took leave of them, saying, 'It behooves me, by all means, to keep the coming feast at Jerusalem, and again I will return unto you, God willing.' And he sailed from Ephesus, and having come down to Caesarea, having gone up, and having saluted the assembly, he went down to Antioch, staying for a while.

And a certain Jew, Apollos by name, an Alexandrian by birth (a Therapeut like Theudas), a man of eloquence, being mighty in the Writings, came to Ephesus, this one was instructed in the way of the Lord, and being fervent in the Spirit, was speaking and teaching exactly the things about the Lord, knowing only the baptism of John (code for follower of Simon Magus and Jonathan Annas: Sceva); this one also began to speak boldly in the synagogue, and Aquila and Priscilla having heard of him, took him to them and did more exactly expound to him the way of God, and he being minded to go through into Achaia, the brethren wrote to the disciples, having exhorted them to receive him, who having come, did help them much who have believed through the grace, for powerfully the Jews he was refuting publicly, showing through the Writings Jesus to be the Christ.

Cor 1:12 One of you says, 'I follow Paul'; another, 'I follow Apollos'; another, 'I follow Cephas (Peter)'; still another, 'I follow Christ.'

## Chapter 104. (September 54AD) Paul attends Paulina's birth; prepares for his Third Journey

*At Ephesus, Matthew Annas and Paul are talking together.*

Paul says, "Phoebe and other members of the congregation begged me to stay, but I think my skills are better used as a missionary. Having been tied down with the conception of my daughter for two years, I am anxious to get back to missionary work. I hope that I have your approval."

Matthew says, "With Nero becoming Emperor after Claudius, rumored to have been poisoned by Agrippina the Younger, who is the mother of Nero and the sister of Caligula, I have a bad feeling that we will see another outbreak of the family madness. As long the riots are contained, you should be safe."

"I plan to return to Antioch and then follow a similar route as my Second Journey that I took seven years ago. These congregations are now well established resulting in less confrontation. It important to show that we still care about our converts."

Matthew says, "Unfortunately, Apollos has changed his alliance to Simon Magus and Jonathan Annas. John Aquila and Priscilla have suggested, when you return to Ephesus, that you challenge him with your powerful oration skills."

"Next to letter writing, my joy is talking to the crowds and debating with them. I would certainly accept this challenge."

*Acts 19:1-10 Paul having gone through the upper parts, came to Ephesus, and having found certain disciples, he said unto them, 'The Holy Spirit did you receive -- having believed?' and they said unto him, 'But we did not even hear whether there is any Holy Spirit;' and he said unto them, 'To what, then, were you baptized?' and they said, 'To John's baptism.' And Paul said, 'John, indeed, did baptize with a baptism of reformation, saying to the people that in him who is coming after him they should believe -- that is, in the Christ -- Jesus;' and they, having heard, were baptized -- to the name of the Lord Jesus, and Paul having laid on them his hands, the Holy Spirit came upon them, they were speaking also with tongues, and prophesying, and all the men were, as it were, twelve. And having gone into the synagogue, he was speaking boldly for three months, reasoning and persuading the things concerning the reign of God, and when certain were hardened and were disbelieving, speaking evil of the Way before the multitude, (John Aquila having departed from them.) He (Paul) did separate the disciples, every day reasoning in the school of a certain Tyrannus. And this happened for two years (Paul as bishop) so that all those dwelling in Asia did hear the word of the Lord.*

*Rev 14:9 And a third angel (Agrippa II) did follow them, saying in a great voice, 'If anyone the beast does bow before, and his image, and does receive a mark upon his forehead (archaic Tau: X - that had been used for protection of initiates since the 6th century BC: CD 19:12 quotes Ezekiel 9:4)), or upon his hand, he also shall drink of the wine of the wrath of God, that has been mingled unmixed in the cup of His anger, and he shall be tormented in fire and brimstone before the holy angels, and before the Lamb, and the smoke of their torment does go up to ages of ages; and they have no rest day and night, who are bowing before the beast and his image, also if any does receive the mark of his name.*

*Letter 3. SENECA TO PAUL, greeting I have arranged some writings in a volume, and given them their proper divisions: I am also resolved to read them to Caesar, if only fortune be kind, that he may bring a new (an interested) ear to the hearing.*

## Chapter 105. (March 55AD)
## Paul is bishop of Ephesus; Apollos is removed

John Aquila speaks to Paul, "What I feared has come true that Apollos has set us on a dangerous course. I convinced him to leave for Corinth. It would be good for our mission if you could be bishop of Ephesus for two years while I am gone."

Paul says, "I will be honored to do this. I understand that I will need three months of preparation, building up a rapport with the twelve leaders of the married group, that Jesus assigned to you in the miracle of the Feeding of the Five Thousand."

"I have heard word that Peter and Jesus will be going to Rome to stay at my younger brother Clement's house in Rome. Bernice, who has a house on Tiber Island nearby, is now angry at her brother Agrippa II for rejecting the Zealot requests for money."

"In the recent letter from Seneca the Younger, who tutors Nero whose 18th birthday is this year, holds my letters in high regard, saying, 'I am also resolved to read them to Caesar, and if only fortune be kind, he may bring an interested ear to their hearing.' Although I wish he had not done this, it does give us hope that Nero will be kind to our Church."

*Paul is bishop of Ephesus for two years, being well loved by his congregation and increasing in stature to become equal with Peter. As promised to John Aquila and Matthew, he made several trips to Cenchrea, near Corinth to debate with Apollos and visit Phoebe and his daughter.*

*Antiq 20.8.5 Felix also bore an ill-will to Jonathan, the high priest, because he frequently gave him admonitions about governing the Jewish affairs better than he did (i.e. his marriage to the divorced Drusilla, the younger sister of Bernice and Agrippa II), lest he should himself have complaints made of him by the multitude, since he it was who had desired Caesar to send him as procurator of Judea. So Felix contrived a method whereby he might get rid of him. Wherefore Felix persuaded one of Jonathan's most faithful friends, a citizen of Jerusalem, whose name was Doras, to bring the robbers upon Jonathan, in order to kill him. Certain of those robbers (sicarii) went up to the city, as if they were going to worship God, while they had daggers under their garments, and by thus mingling themselves among the multitude they slew Jonathan.*

*Acts 19:13-16,19 And certain of the wandering exorcist Jews (James the Just), took upon them to name over those having the evil spirits the name of the Lord Jesus, saying, 'We adjure you by Jesus, whom Paul does preach;' (Epistle of James shows he is an exorcist: James 2:19 You believe that God is one; you do well. Even the demons believe—and shudder!) And certain seven sons of Sceva, a Jew, a chief priest*
*(Jonathan has stayed on the side of Simon Magus with his Seven leaders chosen in June 37AD. Since his stoning as Stephen, being thought dead, he took a different name: 'Sceva' (Latin 'scaevus' meaning 'on the left' being such as Simon Magus' levite)*
*; and the evil spirit (Jonathan), answering, said, 'Jesus I know, and Paul I am acquainted with; and you -- who are you?' And the man (James the Just), in whom was the evil spirit, leaping upon them, and having overcome them, prevailed against them, so that naked and wounded (Jonathan - again excommunicated like a "young man similar to the arrest of Jesus (Mark 14:51,52)) they did flee out of that house, and many of those who had practiced the curious arts, having brought the books together, were burning them before all (organization was discredited); and they reckoned together the prices of them, and found it 50 thousand pieces of silver*

*After their betrothal renewal in March 57AD, Paul sends Phoebe with Jesus carrying a copy of 1 Corinthians with added parts by Jesus. In it also is Paul's coded plea in Aramaic: 'Maranatha' for "Come' Lord (1Cor 16:22) asking Jesus to come back with Phoebe, fearing his implication in the murder of Jonathan. He also sends some other Epistles to give to Seneca.*
*Rom 16:1,2 "I commend to you our sister Phoebe, a deacon of the church in Cenchreae. I ask you to receive her in the Lord in a way worthy of his people and to give her any help she may need from you, for she has been the benefactor of many people, including me."*

## Chapter 106. (57AD)
## Felix kills Jonathan; Paul sends Phoebe to Rome

Burning the books of the Magian mission

Phoebe visits Paul at Ephesus holding Paulina, their daughter aged two, saying, "I was concerned for you, as it is rumored that Procurator Felix was the one who had the Sicarii murder Jonathan Annas and many believe you had a part in it, but I know you are innocent."
Paul kisses both he says, "Phoebe and my little Paulina, how beautiful you look. I did incriminate myself when I wrote that I wanted the 'thorn' from my flesh removed, cleverly referring to Jonathan's crown of thorns as a Sadducee (2Cor 12:7)"
Phoebe says, "The Zealots of West Manasseh having been started in 44BC would be celebrating their 100th birthday in this year 57AD and with annual fees would be worth 50,000 pieces of silver."

"And how much will I be worth on my 40th birthday this year?" "That is easy: the price of a son."

Paul says, "Yes, our next betrothal is tomorrow. I look forward to it. I have a favor: would you accompany Jesus and Peter to Rome taking a copy of my epistles to the Corinthians with Jesus' additions and give a set of them to Seneca. Then returning in time, I hope, to be in each other's arms in Troas."

Phoebe says, "Already trying to get rid of me! Of course, I will do it! Does this have to do with your Peter envy?"
"I suppose, but you know how much I want to go to Rome!"

Justin Martyr (died 165AD) in his First Apology, 26: "After Christ's ascension into heaven the devils put forward certain men who said that they themselves were gods. There was a Samaritan, Simon, a native of the village called Gitto, who in the reign of Claudius Caesar, and in your royal city of Rome, did mighty acts of magic, by virtue of the art of the devils operating in him. He was considered a god, and as a god was honored by you with a statue, which statue was erected on the river Tiber, between the two bridges, and bore this inscription, in the language of Rome, 'Simoni Deo Sancto', 'To Simon the holy God'.

*Simon Magus has made great progress in Rome having gone there probably in the previous year 56AD: THE VERCELLI ACTS OF PETER IN ROME IV. Now after a few days there was a great commotion in the midst of the church, for some said that they had seen wonderful works done by a certain man whose name was Simon, and that he was at Aricia, and they added further that he said he was a great power of God and without God he did nothing. Is not this the Christ? And the brethren were not a little offended among themselves, seeing, moreover, that Paul was not at Rome, neither Timothy nor Barnabas, for they had been sent into Macedonia by Paul. **(Jesus talks to Peter, encouraging him and goes to Rome with him.)** V. The Lord Christ showed in a vision, saying unto him: Peter, that Simon the sorcerer whom thou did cast out of Judaea, convicting him, hath again come to harass our Church at Rome. Delay you not: set forth on the morrow, and there shalt thou find a ship ready, setting sail for Italy. XVI. Now when the night fell, Peter, while yet waking, beheld Jesus clad in a vesture of brightness, smiling and saying unto him: 'Already is much people of the brotherhood returned through me and through the signs which thou hast wrought in my name. But thou shalt have a contest of the faith upon the sabbath that cometh, and many more of the Gentiles and of the Jews shall be converted in my name unto me who was reproached and mocked and spat upon. For I will be present with you when thou ask for signs and wonders, and thou shalt convert many: but thou shalt have Simon opposing you by the works of his father; yet all his works shall be shown to be charms and contrivances of sorcery. And when all had prayed, the hall wherein they were shining as when it lightens, even with such a light as cometh in the clouds, yet not such a light as that of the daytime, but unspeakable, invisible, such as no man can describe, even such that we were beside ourselves with bewilderment, calling on the Lord and saying: 'Have mercy, Lord, upon us your servants: what we are able to bear, that, Lord, give thou us; for this we can neither see nor endure'. And as we lay there, only those widows stood up which were blind; and the bright light which appeared unto us entered into their eyes and made them to see. Unto whom Peter said: 'Tell us what you saw.' And they said: 'We saw an old man of such comeliness as we are not able to declare to you;' (Jesus is 63 years old: 57+6.); others, 'We saw a young man;' others: 'We saw a boy touching our eyes delicately, opening our eyes.'*

# Chapter 107. (57AD)
## (Vercelli) Acts of Peter; Travel to Rome

*Jesus, Phoebe, Peter, & Luke board a ship for Rome.*

Jesus says, "Peter, You have a hard task ahead of you because Simon Magus is well known in Rome. He even claims that a statue on the Tiber Island bridge, which says 'Simoni Deo Sancto', is dedicated to him."

Peter says, "I am not afraid of him. He may appear to make dogs talk or broken statues to walk or be restored, but I will unmask all of his tricks. The people are constantly wanting me to perform magic tricks so I have even learned how to make a herring come to life with a numbing potion."

Jesus says, "You should not stoop to his level. If you preach the Gospel with a true heart, you will find that people will see miracles because they want them to be. People need hope."

Phoebe asks, "Father, but why do people need lies?"

Jesus answers, "People have grown up with stories of gods that have survived death like Osiris, Mithras, and Dionysus. Reality, however good it is, can appear to be a letdown. This is why Simon Magus told everyone that I was resurrected."

Luke says, "In the New Testament and the Acts of the Apostles, I have to embellish because people want larger than life stories."

Phoebe says, "Already I see that people are better off not knowing that I am Jesus' daughter; otherwise, in their envy, they will call me a child of a bastard and a whore and a temptress to Paul, who lured him from his sworn celibacy."

Sept 57AD Acts 19:20-22 *so powerfully was the word of God increasing and prevailing. (Jesus Justus - age 20 and Joseph (2nd son of Jesus) - age 13) And when these things were fulfilled, Paul purposed in the Spirit, having gone through Macedonia and Achaia, to go on to Jerusalem, saying -- 'After my being there, it behooves me also to see Rome;' and having sent to Macedonia two of those ministering to him --* Timothy (Timothy (Herod) - father: Aristobulus son of Herod of Chalcis and mother: Salome daughter of Herodias and Herod Thomas - disciple) *and* Erastus (Christian name for Herod Saul grandson of Costobar, the second husband of Salome, the sister of Herod the Great. (An associate of Paul's in his Romans Epistle: "the city's director of public works") *-- he himself stayed a period in Asia.*(Paul renews sexual relations with Phoebe in Troas November 57AD)

Mary Magdalene dies. Acts 19:23-34 *And there came, at that time, not a little stir about the way, for a certain one,* Demetrius *by name, a worker in silver* (tithe collector of silver coins - Simon Magus) ), *making silver statuettes of Artemis* (icons of Mary Magdalene), *was bringing to the artificers great gain, whom, having brought in a crowd together, and those who did work about such things, he said, 'Men, you know that by this work we have our wealth; and you see and hear, that not only at Ephesus, but almost in all Asia, this Paul, having persuaded, did turn away a great multitude, saying, that they are not gods who are made by hands; and not only is this craft in danger of declining, but also, that of the great goddess Artemis and her temple may be reckoned for nothing, whom all Asia and the world does worship.'* (Simon is rejecting 'Lydia, the second wife of Jesus, as more important than Magdalene.') *And they having heard, and having become full of wrath, were crying out, saying, 'Great is the Artemis of the Ephesians!' and the whole city was filled with confusion, they rushed also with one accord into the theater, having caught* Gaius (Herod Costobar - older brother of Erastus above) *and* Aristarchus (Aristobulus), *Macedonians, Paul's fellow-travellers. And on Paul's purposing to enter in unto the populace, the disciples stopping him.* (Actually, Paul is in Troas with Phoebe!), *and certain also of the chief men of Asia, being his friends, having sent unto him, were entreating him not to venture himself into the theater. Some indeed, therefore, were calling out one thing, and some another, for the assembly was confused, and the greater part did not know for what they came together; and out of the multitude they put forward* Alexander *-- the Jews thrusting him forward -- and* Alexander (Apollos- Therapeuts in Alexandria, Egypt) *having beckoned with the hand, wished to make defense to the populace, and having known that he is a Jew, one voice came out of all, for about two hours, crying, 'Great is the Artemis of the Ephesians!'*

## Chapter 108. (December 57AD)
## Mary Magdalene, having died, Simon Magus
## *(Demetrius)* sells silver icons of her

Simon Magus calls out, "Get your icons of Artemis here! Made by Demetrius, the finest silversmith in Ephesus."

Apollos joins him, "Commemorate Mary Magdalene's ascension, Great is the Artemis of the Ephesians!" *The crowds join in.*

Simon says, "Thank you for your help Apollos. This is especially important as Mary Magdalene's mother Phoebe was a priestess in the temple of Artemis. When I rescued her, I gave her the name Helena for Helen of Troy. I miss her."

"I see that Paul is ignoring this event; still angry at Magdalene's divorce and not too pleased with Jesus remarrying Lydia."

Simon Magus says, "People say he influenced his cousin Felix to kill Jonathan. Ever since the people of Lystra declared him to be Mercury, Paul has been flying on his winged feet pretending to be the thirteenth disciple."

Apollos says, "You must join us in the celebration of God's Restoration when I lead Therapeuts to bring down the Walls of Jericho, next year."

Simon says, "You must not trust Felix, he is a friend not to be trusted; he will act with violence as Florus did with Theudas."

*Antiq 20.8.6 tells how Apollos leads an abortive reenactment of the 'Walls of Jericho': "At this time (Pentecost, 58AD) there came to Jerusalem from Egypt (Therapeuts have their center in Alexandria, Egypt) a man who declared that he was a prophet (Apollos) and advised the masses of the common people to go out with him to the mountain called the Mount of Olives, which lies opposite the city at a distance of 5 stadia. For he asserted that he wished to demonstrate from there that at his command Jerusalem's walls would fall down, through which he promised to provide them an entrance into the city. When Felix (the Roman governor) heard of this he ordered his soldiers to take up their arms. Setting out from Jerusalem with a large force of cavalry and infantry, he fell upon the Egyptian (Apollos) and his followers, slaying 400 of them and taking 200 prisoners. The Egyptian himself escaped from the battle and disappeared."*

*Paul writes his Epistle to Titus to help Apollos in his escape: Titus 3:13 "Do everything you can to help Zenas the lawyer and Apollos on their way and see that they have everything they need."*

*Acts 20:1-6 And after the ceasing of the tumult, Paul having called near the disciples, and having embraced them, went forth to go on to Macedonia; and having gone through those parts, and having exhorted them with many words, he came to Greece; having made also three months' stay -- a counsel of the Jews having been against him -- being about to set forth to Syria, there came to him a resolution of returning through Macedonia. And there were accompanying him unto Asia, Sopater of Berea, and of Thessalonians Aristarchus (Aristobulus) and Secundus, and Gaius of Derbe, and Timothy, and of Asiatics Tychicus and Trophimus; these, having gone before, did remain for us in Troas, and we sailed, after the days of the unleavened food, from Philippi, and came unto them to Troas in five days, where we abode seven days.*

*Acts 20:7-12 And on the first of the week, the disciples having been gathered together to break bread, Paul was discoursing to them, about to depart on the morrow, he was also continuing the discourse till midnight, and there were many lamps in the upper chamber where they were gathered together, and there was sitting a certain youth, by name Eutychus, upon the window -- being borne down by a deep sleep, Paul discoursing long -- he having sunk down from the sleep, fell down from the third story, and was lifted up dead. And Paul, having gone down, fell upon him, and having embraced him, said, 'Make no tumult, for life is still in him;' and having come up, and having broken bread, and having tasted, for a long time also having talked -- till daylight, so he went forth, and they brought up the lad alive, and were comforted in no ordinary measure.*

# Chapter 109. (March 58AD)
## Joyous reunion of John Mark *(Eutychus)*

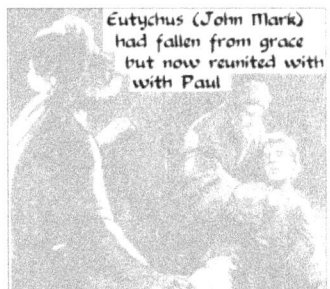

*In Troas Paul meets with Phoebe, having returned from Rome, and three months later is assured that the pregnancy is viable. In the evening Paul, standing on the third story of the Church, is giving a sermon:*

> *"If I speak in the tongues of men or of angels, but do not have love, I am only a resounding gong or a clanging cymbal. If I have the gift of prophecy and can fathom all mysteries and all knowledge, and if I have a faith that can move mountains, but do not have love, I am nothing. If I give all I possess to the poor and give over my body to hardship that I may boast, but do not have love, I gain nothing." (1Cor 13:1-3)*

*Paul talked on into the midnight. Eutychus was sitting in the congregation and, having fallen asleep after his long trip, fell off his pew, making a loud racket.*

Paul calls out, "Is that person hurt?"

John Mark answers, "No, my dear friend, I know that I once did fall from the place on which you are standing and was as if dead. Now that Magdalene has passed on, I have returned."

Paul comes down from the upper floor and embracing him, says, "It a joyous event to have you back. Yes, you still have life and can begin again as an initiate."

John Mark says, "I was always torn by the decision to leave you, as I could have had Philip watch over Magdalene."

Phoebe runs forward from the back pews and embraces John Mark saying, "I have missed you."

*Acts 20:13-16 And we (plural: Jesus and Luke note that "we" does not include Paul, but also Phoebe) having gone before unto the ship, did sail to Assos, thence intending to take in Paul, for so he had arranged, intending himself to go on foot; and when he met with us (plural: Jesus and Luke) at Assos, having taken him up, we came to Mitylene, and thence having sailed, on the morrow we (plural: Jesus, Luke, and Paul) came over-against Chios, and the next day we arrived at Samos, and having remained in Trogyllium, on the following day we came to Miletus, for Paul decided to sail past Ephesus, that there may not be to him a loss of time in Asia, for he quickly, if it were possible for him, on the day of the Pentecost to be at Jerusalem. Paul requests the ministers of Ephesus to come to Miletus as he is in a hurry to get to Jerusalem. He resigns his ministry in Ephesus April 58.*

*Paul continues his Third Mission: Acts 21:1-7 ... and did land at Tyre, for there was the ship discharging the lading. And having found out the disciples, we (plural: Jesus, Luke, and Paul) tarried there seven days, and they (Phoebe) said to Paul, through the Spirit (Jesus in person), not to go up to Jerusalem but when it came that we completed the days, having gone forth, we went on, all bringing us on the way, with women and children, unto the outside of the city, and having bowed the knees upon the shore, we prayed, and having embraced one another, we (plural: Jesus, Luke, and Paul - Phoebe left behind) embarked in the ship, and they returned to their own friends. From Tyre came down to Ptolemais, and having saluted the brethren, we remained one day with them;*

*Acts 21:8,9 and on the morrow Paul and his company having gone forth, we came to Caesarea, and having entered the house of Philip the evangelist -- who is of the seven -- we remained with him, and this one had four daughters, virgins, prophesying (Philip had originally been the superior of Mary Magdalene: daughter at level 4).*

*Acts 21:10-14 And we remaining many more days, there came down a certain one from Judea, a prophet, by name Agabus (Matthew), and he having come unto us, and having taken up the belt of Paul, having bound his own hands and feet, so shall the Jews in Jerusalem bind, and they shall deliver you up to the hands of nations.' And when we heard these things, we called upon him -- both we, and those of that place -- not to go up to Jerusalem, and Paul answered, 'What do you -- weeping, and crushing mine heart? for I, not only to be bound, but also to die at Jerusalem, am ready, for the name of the Lord Jesus;' and he not being persuaded, we were silent, saying, 'The will of the Lord be done.'*

# Chapter 110. (May 58AD)
## Jesus and Phoebe try to persuade Paul not to go to Jerusalem

*At Tyre are Jesus, Luke, Paul, and Phoebe.*

Phoebe says, "Jesus, I do not have a good feeling about Paul going to Jerusalem. Matthew has warned that as soon as he sets foot there, he will be arrested."

Jesus says, "I have tried to convince him not to go, but he has insisted; you know how stubborn he is. He is like Saul of old."

Paul tries to comfort her, "Your weeping and crushing my heart with sorrow does not help. I am willing to die in Jerusalem if need be. To not do so, will make me look guilty of Jonathan's death. And besides Simon-Silas is betrothed and he needs me. He will be taking his Nazarite vow for marriage and joining him are the three sons of Aristobulus and Salome: Timothy, Tychicus, and Trophimus They are important for our mission and Timothy is Agrippa II's adopted heir."

Phoebe says, "But what if you are imprisoned, then you will not get to see your child in September."

Paul kisses Phoebe and says, "The ship awaits. I promise to do everything to speed my return."
*He walks forward to the dock and boards the ship. Jesus and Luke follow. Phoebe is in tears. Paulina runs after him and Phoebe grabs her before she falls.* "We will see him soon, do not worry."

Paul kneels on the bow of the ship, saying, "May God's will be done."

# SECTION 19 (June 58AD to 61AD)
## Paul imprisoned in Jerusalem

*Acts 21:23-26, 28-34; 22:1,24; 23:1-3* **Nazarite vows:** *'We have four men having a vow on themselves, these having taken, be purified with them, and be at expense with them, that they may shave the head, and all may know that the things of which they have been instructed concerning you are nothing, but you do walk -- yourself also -- the law keeping.' (Simon-Silas is 36 years old and prepares for marriage using the Nazarite principles and sons of Aristobulus: Timothy, crown prince and heir of Agrippa- age 24, and his two brothers: Tychicus- age 22 and Trophimus- under 21 joined him and* **Entered the Temple**; *having followed the rules for Gentiles agreed at the Council of Jerusalem) Then Paul, having taken the men, on the following day, with them having purified himself, was entering into the temple, announcing the fulfillment of the days of the purification, till the offering was offered for each one of them.* **Uproar at the Temple** *The people crying out, 'Men, Israelites, help! this is the man who, against the people, and the law; and here he is teaching everywhere; and further, also, Greeks he brought into the temple, have defiled this holy place'; having seen before Trophimus, the Ephesian, in the city with him, whom they were supposing that Paul brought into the temple. All the city also was moved and there was a running together of the people, and having laid hold on Paul, they were drawing him out of the temple and they seeking to kill him. A rumor came to the chief captain of the guard, having taken soldiers and centurions, ran down upon them, and they seeing them, did leave off beating Paul.* **The Rescue** *Paul says, 'Men, brethren, and fathers, hear my defense now unto you ...' then the chief captain in the commotion commanded him to be brought into the castle.* **The Sanhedrin** *Paul, having earnestly beheld the Sanhedrin, said, 'Men, brethren, I in all good conscience have lived to God unto this day;' and the chief priest Ananias commanded those standing by him to smite him on the mouth, then Paul said unto him, 'God is about to smite you, you whitewashed wall, and you, you sit judging me according to the law, and, violating law, you order me to be smitten!'*

*Acts 23:11,16,17 And on the following night, the Lord, having stood by him, said, 'Take courage, Paul, for as you did fully testify the things concerning me at Jerusalem, so it behooves you also at Rome to testify.' And the son of Paul's sister, having heard of the lying in wait, having gone and entered into the castle, told Paul, and Paul, having called near one of the centurions, said, 'Lead this young man unto the chief captain, for he has something to tell him.'*

*Acts 23:16 And* **the son of Paul's sister** *.... told Paul, (This sister would be Salome, the daughter of Herodias (Antipas' 2nd wife). Her three sons with Aristobulus are Herod (Timothy), Agrippa (Tychicus), and Aristobulus (Trophimus-this son). Paul is the son of Herod Antipas and his 1st wife who is Paul's father and Salome's step-father.)*

## Chapter 111. (June 58 AD to July 60AD
## Paul enters the Temple, beaten by the Jews,
## saved by the guards

*Paul is in chains at the Fortress of Antonia, Jesus & Salome, his step-sister are there.*

Paul says to Salome, "Thank your son Trophimus for discovering the plot against me. I cannot believe those idiots claim he was unclean. They all followed the rules for Gentiles agreed by the Council of Jerusalem and they were clean by Nazarite rules. Clearly, that whitewashed wall, Ananias the High Priest, is corrupt. Philip said he had buried him in the ground, but here he is, returning like a zombie."

Salome says, "My brother Paul, calm down. Their anger is misplaced, they have lost two of their most precious leaders. Felix has just slaughtered the Therapeuts led by Apollos. They know Felix is part of our Church by marriage and still suspect him and you for Jonathan's murder, so they lash out at you."

Aristobulus says, "Since Felix's removal is imminent, I have persuaded him to have you moved from here, to be protected by two hundred soldiers and taken to Felix's palace in Caesarea. Soon you will have a chance to go with Jesus, to Rome for Felix's trial and yours and to be free again."

Salome says, "As a witnesses for Felix, we will certainly be invited. Besides, Drusilla wants to move to Naples next to that volcano Mount Vesuvius. Agrippa II and Bernice have assured me that they will support your request of wanting to be judged by Caesar when the new procurator Festus arrives."

*Acts 23:23; 24:23-27* having called near a certain two of the centurions, he (chief captain) said, 'Make ready soldiers two hundred, that they may go on unto Caesarea' ... (Felix) having given also a direction to the centurion to keep Paul, to let him also have liberty, and to forbid none of his own friends to minister or to come near to him. And after certain days, Felix, having come with Drusilla his wife, being a Jewess, he sent for Paul, and heard him concerning the faith toward Christ, and he reasoning concerning righteousness, and temperance, and the judgment that is about to be, Felix, having become afraid, answered, 'For the present be going, and having got time, I will call for you;' and at the same time also hoping that money shall be given to him to release him, therefore, also sending for him the oftener, he was conversing with him. and two years having been fulfilled, Felix received a successor, Porcius Festus; Felix also willing to lay a favor on the Jews, left Paul bound. (Felix, needing Paul to a be a witness at his trial in front of Nero, keeps him imprisoned for two years, However, he is perfectly willing to let Paul travel to Tyre to be at his second daughter's birth in September if Paul offers him money.)

*Acts 25:10,13;26:32* And Paul said, 'At the tribunal of Caesar I am standing, where it behooves me to be judged; to Jews I did no unrighteousness, as you do also very well know; for if indeed I am unrighteous, and anything worthy of death have done, I deprecate not to die; and if there are none of the things of which these accuse me, no one is able to make a favor of me to them; to Caesar I appeal!' And certain days having passed, Agrippa the king, and Bernice, came down to Caesarea saluting Festus. And Agrippa said to Festus, 'This man might have been released if he had not appealed to Caesar.'

*Acts 27:1-3* And when our (plural: Jesus and Luke) sailing to Italy was determined, they were delivering up both Paul and certain others, prisoners, to a centurion, by name Julius, of the band of Sebastus, and having embarked in a ship of Adramyttium, we (plural: Jesus, Luke, and Paul), being about to sail by the coasts of Asia, did set sail, there being with us Aristarchus (Aristobulus), a Macedonian of Thessalonica, (The procurator Felix is being brought to Rome to stand trial before Nero for the death of Jonathan Annas. Paul and Aristobulus are going as witnesses. Luke and Jesus are also going.) on the next day also we touched at Sidon, and Julius, courteously treating Paul, did permit him, having gone on unto friends, to receive their care. (In Sidon, Paul picks up Phoebe and his two daughters and will drop them off at Myra to travel on to Philippi:
*Phil 4:2,3* "I beseech Euodia (Eunice=Salome in 2Tim 1:5) and Syntyche (Lydia, having married Jesus in Philippi), that they be of the same mind in the Lord. And I entreat thee also, true yokefellow (Phoebe), help those women which labored with me in the gospel, with Clement also, and with other my fellowlaborers, whose names are in the book of life.")

# Chapter 112. (July 60AD)
## Paul leaves with Jesus for Felix's Trial in Rome

*The new procurator Festus arrives; Felix, Paul, & Jesus set sail for Rome, stopping at Sidon where Paul runs to meet Phoebe & his two daughters.*

Paul kisses Phoebe and the youngest daughter in her arms saying, "Little daughter, you have grown so big since I saw you in September, two years ago." *He stoops down and kisses Paulina.* "And Paulina, my first born; almost six years old!"

Paulina says, "I missed you, Father. She then runs up to Jesus and hugs him, saying, "Grandfather, you came, too." Jesus hugs her, "How is my special granddaughter?" Jesus turns and hugs Phoebe, "And how are you, my only daughter?"

Aristobulus kisses Phoebe, "Salome, sends her love."
Phoebe says, "I am indebted to your son, Trophimus, for alerting Paul of the threat on his life."
Aristobulus says, "He is, after all, the son of Paul's sister, Salome, my wife!"

Phoebe says, "Paul, are you sure that I cannot go with you to Rome?"

Paul replies, "My true yoke-fellow, it would be too dangerous now as I have many adversaries even in Rome. From Myra, you can get a ship to Philippi in Macedonia. Clement can watch over you there and you can be deaconess again. Don't worry, Felix's brother Pallas surely will intercede with Nero and Seneca has Nero's ear as his tutor."

Jesus says, "Phoebe, please give my love to your step-mother Lydia in Philippi, and wish your brother happy ninth birthday from me. I do miss her."

*Acts 27:4-8 And thence, having set sail, we sailed under Cyprus ... the wind not suffering us, we sailed under Crete and came to a certain place called 'Fair Havens'.*

The storm is symbolic of the failure of the Restoration to come in 60AD.

*Acts 27:13-15 And a south wind blowing softly, ... they sailed close by Crete, and not long after there arose against it a tempestuous wind and the ship being caught, and not being able to bear up against the wind, having given her up, we (plural: Jesus, Luke, and Paul) were borne on.*

Paul uses this opportunity to convert the crew attributing their safety to Jesus, crediting their fasting for the purpose of baptism.

*Acts 27:26 And there having been long fasting, then Paul having stood in the midst of them, said, 'It behoved you, indeed, O men -- having hearkened to me -- not to set sail from Crete, and to save this hurt and damage; and now I exhort you to be of good cheer, for there shall be no loss of life among you, except the ship; for there stood by me this night an angel of God (Jesus) -- whose I am, and whom I serve -- saying, 'Be not afraid, Paul; before Caesar it behooves you to stand'; and, lo, God has granted to you all those sailing with you; therefore be of good cheer, men! for I believe God, that so it shall be, even as it has been spoken to me, and on a certain island it behooves us to be cast.'*

*Acts 27:33-38 And till the day was about to be, Paul was calling upon all to partake of nourishment, saying, 'Fourteen days to-day, waiting, you continue fasting, having taken nothing, therefore I call upon you to take nourishment (the sacrament), for this is for your safety, for of not one of you shall a hair from the head fall;' and having said these things, and having taken bread, he gave thanks to God before all, and having broken he began to eat; and all having become of good cheer, themselves also took food, (and we were -- all the souls in the ship -- 276) (a triangular number larger than the 153 converts after the Resurrection), and having eaten sufficient nourishment, they were lightening the ship, casting forth the wheat into the sea. (Wheat is symbolic of the mission planting the wheat who are converts)*

*Acts 28:1-6 And having been saved, then they knew that the island is called Malta, and the foreigners were showing us no ordinary kindness, for having kindled a fire, they received us all, because of the pressing rain, and because of the cold; but Paul having gathered together a quantity of sticks, and having laid them upon the fire, a viper, having come out of the heat, did fasten on his hand. And when the foreigners saw the beast hanging from his hand, they said unto one another, 'Certainly this man is a murderer, whom, having been saved out of the sea, the justice did not suffer to live;' he then, indeed, having shaken off the beast into the fire, suffered no evil, and they were expecting him to be about to be inflamed, or to fall down suddenly dead, and they, expecting it a long time, and seeing nothing uncommon happening to him, changing their minds, said he was a god.*

# Chapter 113. (December 60AD)
## Shipwreck and a Viper

*After the storm, Jesus, Paul, Luke, and Aristobulus exit from the wrecked ship on Malta. They are welcomed by Seneca and Apollos.*

Seneca says, "We were anxiously awaiting your arrival. The storm was ferocious. Please come to the fire and warm up."

Paul says, "Seneca, I am so glad to see you again. It has been a long time since we first met in Athens."

Luke says, "Paul was an amazing force, giving comfort to all. In fact, he baptized 276."

Apollos says, "What Church did he baptize them into? Jonathan Annas' Church or the Church of Paul?"

Jesus says, "There is but one God and one Church. Paul follows my instructions."

Apollos says, "Then why did Paul kill Jonathan?"

Paul defends himself, "Apollos, why do you, with your poison skills, set your viper teeth on me. True, I have never liked Jonathan because he had a high opinion of himself and he always seemed to be a thorn in my side, but I did not kill him. And what of your foolish attempt to cross the River Jordan? This had already failed with my great-uncle Theudas. Did you ever have compassion for all those who died, after you escaped?"

Apollos says, "Was not your shipwreck a message that God does not recognize your Eschaton also!"

Aristobulus says, "You both need to reconcile! If Felix is found guilty, you both will die." *They nod.*

## Paul's Journey to Rome (60AD to 61AD)

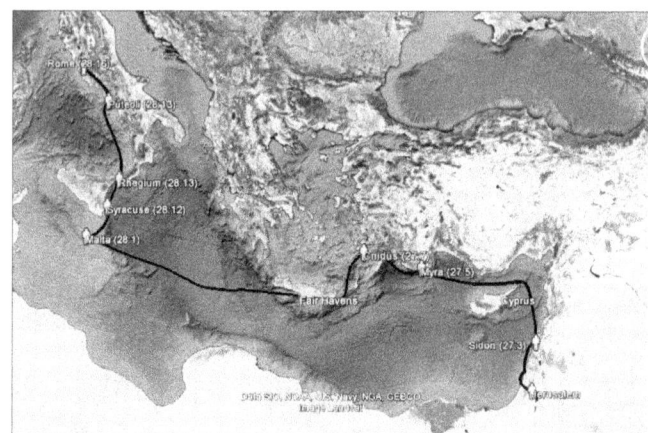

(Jerusalem .. Sidon .. Cyprus .. Myra .. Cnidus .. Fair Havens .. Malta .. Syracuse .. Rhegium .. Puteoli .. Rome)

# SECTION 20 (61AD to 65AD)
## *Jesus, Paul, and Peter in Rome*

Legend: Nero fiddles while Rome burns in 64AD

*Acts 28:11-16 And after three months, we (plural: Jesus, Luke, and Paul) set sail on a ship, on another ship that had wintered at the island: Alexandrian ship with the twin gods as its figurehead, and having landed at Syracuse, we remained three days, thence having gone round, we (plural: Jesus, Luke, and Paul) came to Rhegium, and after one day, a south wind having sprung up, the second day we (plural: Jesus, Luke, and Paul) came to Puteoli; where, having found brethren, we (plural: Jesus, Luke, and Paul) were called upon to remain with them seven days, and thus we (plural: Jesus, Luke, and Paul) came to Rome; and thence, the brethren having heard the things concerning us, came forth to meet us, unto Appia Forum, and Three Taverns, whom Paul having seen, having given thanks to God, took courage. And so we came to Rome, but Paul was suffered to remain by himself, with the soldier guarding him.(Paul arrives in Rome under house arrest.)*

## ACTS OF PETER 61AD

### Simon performs his Magic Act of Flying with Peter present

*For tomorrow I shall forsake you, godless and impious that you are, and fly up unto God whose Power I am, though I have become weak. XXXII. And already on the morrow, a great multitude assembled at the Sacred Way to see him flying. And Peter came unto the place, to see the sight, that he might convict him in this also; So then Simon, standing on a high place, beheld Peter and began to say: 'Peter, at this time when I am going up before all these people that behold me, I say unto you: 'If your God is able, whom the Jews put to death, you that were chosen of him, let him show that faith in him is faith in God, and let it appear at this time, if it be worthy of God. (Jesus is there with Peter and Simon taunts him to reveal himself.) For I, ascending up, will show myself unto all this multitude, who I AM.' (like GOD himself) And behold when he was lifted up on high, and all beheld him raised up above all Rome and the temples thereof and the mountains, the faithful looked toward Peter.*

### An assistant of Peter sabotages the pulleys and Simon falls to the ground

*And Peter seeing the strangeness of the sight cried unto the Lord Jesus Christ: 'If thou suffer this man to accomplish that which he hath set about, now will all they that have believed on you be offended, and the signs and wonders which thou hast given them through me will not be believed: hasten your grace, O Lord, and let him fall from the height and be disabled; and let him not die but be brought to naught, and break his leg in three places.'*

*And Simon fell from the height and brake his leg in three places.*

### Simon dies from his injury

*But Simon in his affliction found some to carry him by night on a bed from Rome unto Aricia; And there he was sorely cut, and so Simon the angel of Satan came to his end.*

## Chapter 114. (61AD)
## In Rome Paul in Prison; Simon Magus on the Ropes

*Simon Magus is on the rooftop about to begin his flying trick. Peter and Jesus are watching it below.*

Simon Magus shouts to Peter, "Where is your buddy Paul: locked in prison?"

Peter shouts back, "When you fall to the ground and break your leg in three pieces, the people will see that the Resurrected One is more powerful."

Simon shouts, "I am the Standing One, show me this Resurrected One."
Peter shouts, "He is the Holy Spirit."
Simon shouts, "He looks pretty material to me with no holes. Hello, Jesus."

*The crowd starts to cheer as Simon appears to be flying. Then suddenly the thin wires that hold him break and he falls to the ground.*

Jesus runs over to him, "Are you all right?"
Simon replies, "I think my legs are broken, but they have been broken before."
Jesus says, "That they were; and you recovered then and will again."

Simon says, "I guess I am too old for this. I leave you my Church, my dear step-son-in-law."
Jesus kisses his forehead, "Goodbye my dear father; peace be with you."

*A bystander picks him up and puts him in a stretcher.*

Turning to Peter, "Tell me you did not sabotage him?" Peter says. "Not with my own hands."

*Josephus 20.9.1 - James is murdered by Ananus the Younger 62AD*
*And now Caesar, upon hearing the death of Festus, sent Albinus into Judea, as procurator. But the king deprived Joseph of the high priesthood, and bestowed the succession to that dignity on the son of Ananus, who was also himself called Ananus. Now the report goes that this eldest Ananus proved a most fortunate man; for he had five sons who had all performed the office of a high priest to God, and who had himself enjoyed that dignity a long time formerly, which had never happened to any other of our high priests. But this younger Ananus, who, as we have told you already, took the high priesthood, was a bold man in his temper, and very insolent; he was also of the sect of the Sadducees, who are very rigid in judging offenders, above all the rest of the Jews, as we have already observed; when, therefore, Ananus was of this disposition, he thought he had now a proper opportunity [to exercise his authority]. Festus was now dead, and Albinus was but upon the road; so he assembled the Sanhedrin of judges, and brought before them the brother of Jesus, who was called Christ, whose name was James, and some others; and when he had formed an accusation against them as breakers of the law, he delivered them to be stoned: but as for those who seemed the most equitable of the citizens, and such as were the most uneasy at the breach of the laws, they disliked what was done; they also sent to the king [Agrippa]. Some went also to meet Albinus, as he was upon his journey from Alexandria, and informed him that it was not lawful for Ananus to assemble a Sanhedrin without his consent, whereupon Albinus wrote in anger to Ananus, and threatened that he would bring him to punishment for what he had done; on which king Agrippa took the high priesthood from him, when he had ruled but three months,*

*(Paul is released by the intercession of Pallas 63AD and travels north to Lugdunum Convenarum on the border of Spain where his father Antipas Herod's family lives.)*
**Vercelli Acts of Peter** *I. At the time when Paul was sojourning in Rome and confirming many in the faith, it came also to pass that one by name Candida, the wife of Quartus (Simon who was married in was the fourth in line of descent from Jesus and his youngest brother and mentioned in Paul's Epistle to the Romans as "the brother") that was over the prisons (having ministered to Paul when under house arrest), heard Paul and paid heed to his words and believed. And when she had instructed her husband also and he believed, Quartus suffered Paul to go whither he would away from the city: to whom Paul said: 'If it be the will of God, he will reveal it unto me.' And after Paul had fasted three days and asked of the Lord that which should be profitable for him, he saw a vision (Jesus, residing in Rome, speaks directly to Paul), even the Lord saying unto him: 'Arise, Paul, and become a physician in your body (i.e. by going there in person to visit his father Antipas who is 82 and ailing) to them that are in Spain.'*

## Chapter 115. (62AD)
## Ananus kills James; Paul visits Lugdunum Convenarum on the border of Spain

*Paul, having been freed by Felix's brother Pallas' intercession, visits Antipas Herod in Lugdunum Convenarum on the border of Spain where he was exiled in 39AD by Caligula. Jesus and his brother Simon and wife Candida traveled with him. Paul knocks on the door.* Herodias answers, "Greetings Paul. Antipas will be so glad to see you." Paul says, "Greetings mother" and kisses her.

Herodias says, "Welcome Jesus of Pilate's crucifixion folly, you are looking well. Come in Silas and your wife." *Antipas starts to rise, but falls back in his chair.*

Paul says, "Father, it has been a long and frustrating time in prison in Rome being implicated in Jonathan Annas' death. Thank God for Pallas' intercession to Nero or I would still be in prison."

Antipas says, "This story of Jonathan Annas, having accused Felix of having violated Jewish law with Drusilla's divorce and remarriage seems like a replay of John the Baptist with my Herodias' divorce."

Jesus says, "And like your situation, it was more complex. Ananas the Younger, whom you call Demas, must have suspected that my brother James was responsible. Being tired of just being the bishop of Jerusalem, James had started attacking the followers of Simon Magus and persuaded Felix that Jonathan Annas death would allow him to confiscate the Church money."

Antipas says, "Jonathan was, after all his brother. The opportunity for justice would be too easy, being High Priest with the new Procurator on route."

Herodias says, "Paul, where are Phoebe and the two daughters, you should move here with us."
Paul says, "Thank you. Nero's Rome will not be safe with the Eschaton expected next year."

*(Tychicus writes:)* Rev 16:4-7 *And the third angel did pour out his vial to the rivers, and to the fountains of the waters (baptism), and there came blood (martyrdom), and I heard the angel of the waters, saying, 'righteous, O Lord, are You, who is, and who was, and who shall be, because these things You did judge, because blood of saints and prophets they did pour out, and blood to them You did give to drink, for they are worthy;' and I heard another out of the altar, saying, 'Yes, Lord God, the Almighty, true and righteous are Your judgments.'*

Nero Accuses the Christians of Setting the Great Fire of July 18-19 64AD (Tacitus Annals 15.38) "But all human efforts, all the lavish gifts of the emperor, and the propitiations of the gods, did not banish the sinister belief that the conflagration was the result of an order. Consequently, to get rid of the report, Nero fastened the guilt and inflicted the most exquisite tortures on a class hated for their abominations, called Christians by the populace. Christus, from whom the name had its origin, suffered the extreme penalty during the reign of Tiberius at the hands of one of our procurators, Pontius Pilate, and a most mischievous superstition, thus checked for the moment, again broke out not only in Judaea, the first source of the evil, but even in Rome. Accordingly, an arrest was first made of all who pleaded guilty; then, upon their information, an immense multitude was convicted, not so much of the crime of firing the city, as of hatred against mankind. Mockery of every sort was added to their deaths. Covered with the skins of beasts, they were torn by dogs and perished, or were nailed to crosses, or were doomed to the flames and burnt, to serve as a nightly illumination, when daylight had expired."

*ACTS OF PETER - MARTYRDOM OF PETER (QUO VADUS) (near the Catacombs of St Callistus are the supposed footprints of Jesus Christ.) XXXV And as he went forth from the city, he saw the Lord entering into Rome. And when Peter saw him, he said: 'Domine, Quo Vadis?' (Lord. whither goest thou thus?)' And the Lord said unto him: 'I go into Rome to be crucified.' And Peter said unto him: 'Lord, art thou being crucified again?' He said unto him: 'Yea, Peter, I am being crucified again.' And Peter came to himself: and having beheld the Lord ascending up into heaven, he returned to Rome, rejoicing, and glorifying the Lord, for that he said: 'I am being crucified', which was about to befall Peter. XXXVI. He went up therefore again unto the brethren, and told them that which had been seen by him: and they lamented in soul, weeping. And while Peter thus spoke, and all the brethren wept, behold four soldiers took him and led him unto Agrippa (Nero) commanded him to be crucified on an accusation of godlessness (failure to honor the Roman gods). And Peter, when he came unto the place, stilled the people and said: 'You men that are soldiers of Christ! you men that hope in Christ! remember the signs and wonders which you have seen wrought through me, remember the compassion of God, how many cures he hath wrought for you. Wait for him that cometh and shall reward every man according to his doings. And now be you not bitter against Nero; for he is the minister of his Father's working. XXXVII. I beseech you the executioners, crucify me thus, with the head downward as a baby at birth.*

## Chapter 116. (64AD)
## Jesus meets Peter fleeing from Rome (Quo Vadis?)

Near the Catacombs of St Callistus, Peter says, "Lord where are you going?"

Jesus says, "I go to Rome to be crucified." Peter says, "Would you really be crucified again?"

"Yes, I am willing to be crucified again."

Peter says, "No, Lord, I will go instead. You have corrected my cowardly actions and have shown me the true path."

Jesus says, "Although we may think that we have no power against evil, God has promised us that to be martyred is now the greatest proof of faith. The blood of saints and prophets is poured out and, in the Communion, we become worthy to be born again in the Resurrection to come."

Peter says, "As you suffered on a cross, it is time that I also shed that blood of the Resurrection. Let me drink of the blood which brings eternal life after this life. Lord, you should stay hidden in the catacombs as your blood has already been shed for our sins."

Jesus says, "Thank you, Peter, I will pray that God will show you the path that he has planned for you"

Peter says, "Let me be first to the Resurrection as when I ran to your tomb and was the first to see you risen. If crucified, I will ask to be upside down, head first, as a baby born into the next world."

Jesus, "I will see you then at the Gates of Heaven."

*X ACTS OF PAUL - THE MARTYRDOM OF PAUL 65AD II.* And *"Barsabas Justus"* (Joses-Barnabas-Matthias) (The Acts of Barnabas shows that he was martyred by fire), and Caesar's chief men: Urion the Cappadocian (probably Timothy being the adopted heir of Agrippa II), and Festus the Galatian (this is clearly Felix the Procurator recalled to Rome, having traveled to Rome with Paul, and having been replaced by Festus.) said: We also are soldiers of the king of the ages (Christ). And he shut them up in prison, having grievously tormented them, whom he loved much, and commanded the soldiers of the great king (Christ) to be sought out, and set forth a decree to this effect, that all that were found to be Christians and soldiers of Christ should be slain. III. And among many others, Paul also was brought, bound: unto whom all his fellow-prisoners gave heed; so that Caesar perceived that he was over the camp. And he said to him: Thou that art the great king's man, but my prisoner, how did you think well to come by stealth into the government of the Romans and levy soldiers out of my province? But Paul, filled with the Holy Ghost, said before them all: O Caesar, not only out of your province do we levy soldiers, but out of the whole world. For so hath it been ordained unto us, that no man should be refused who wishes to serve my king. And if you desire to serve him, it is not wealth nor the splendor that is now in this life that shall save you; but if thou submit and entreat him, thou shalt be saved; for one day (in the Resurrection) he shall fight against the world with fire. And when Caesar heard that, he commanded all the prisoners to be burned with fire, but Paul to be beheaded after the law of the Romans. (Paul was buried on the second mile on the Via Ostiensis, on the estate owned by a Christian woman named Lucina.) VII. And as Paul charged them, Longus and Cestus the centurion went early in the morning and approached with fear unto the grave of Paul. And when they came thither they saw two men praying, and Paul betwixt them, so that they beholding the wondrous marvel were amazed, but Titus and Luke being stricken with the fear of man when they saw Longus and Cestus coming toward them, turned to flight. But they pursued after them, saying: We pursue you not for death but for life, that you may give it unto us, as Paul promised us, whom we saw just now standing betwixt you and praying. And when they heard that, Titus and Luke rejoiced and gave them the seal in the Lord, glorifying the God and Father of our Lord Jesus Christ

*1Clement Epistle to the Corinthians, Ch. 5 - The Martyrdom Of Peter And Paul.* Owing to envy, Paul also obtained the reward of patient endurance, after being seven times thrown into captivity, compelled to flee, and stoned. After preaching both in the east and west, he gained the illustrious reputation due to his faith, having taught righteousness to the whole world.

## Chapter 117. (65AD)
## Phoebe hears that has Paul been beheaded

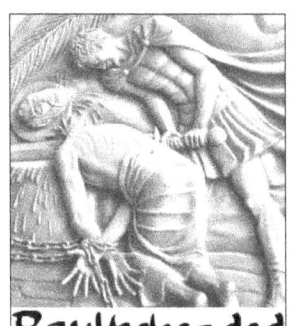

*At Herodias' house in Lugdunum Convenarum, Jesus knocks on the door.*
Paulina opens it and calls to Phoebe, "Grandfather is here." Phoebe comes rushing to the door asking, "What is the news?"
Jesus says, "Let us go into the other room away from the girls." Phoebe starts to sob, "I know what you are about to tell me."
Paulina says, "What is the matter, mother?" "It is nothing," says Phoebe, "Let me talk to Jesus in private. You go play with your sister."

Jesus tells the story, "Timothy, Paul's favorite and heir to the Herods was found to have sent money to the Zealots. Barnabas tried to intercede, but was caught in the middle. Nero ended up burning them alive on crosses. But for Paul, being the grandson of Herod the Great, he delegated that he be given a more humane death by decapitation. The witnesses say that Paul prayed on his knees for a time and then put his head on the block and died quickly."

Phoebe cries, "Oh my dear husband, the Christian soldier, patiently enduring the seven times he was thrown into captivity, and the many times he was compelled to flee the stones that were thrown at him and now to die on the Appian Way alone."

Jesus says, "Surely he has not died alone for his epistles will guide many to interpret the Gospel: that all men can be saved from sin by grace. He will always be in our hearts."

# SECTION 21 (70AD to 112AD)
## Church survives the death of Peter and Paul

Last Judgement, Church of Cypress

(Tychicus writes:) Rev 16:19 And the great city split into three parts, and the cities of the nations did fall, and Babylon the great *(Rome)* was remembered before God, to give to her the cup of the wine of the wrath of His anger. (3 Emperors: Galba by the Spanish Legions (Jun 8, 68AD-Jan 15, 69AD); Otho (Jan 15, 69AD-Apr 16, 69AD) by the Praetorian Guard and Vitellius Apr17, 69AD-Dec 20, 69AD) by German Legions. Vespasian defeats him; is emperor as son Titus continues the War.)

*Rev 17:1-6 And there came one of the seven angels, who were having the seven vials, and he spoke with me, saying to me, 'Come, I will show to you the judgment of the great whore, who is sitting upon the many waters (Bernice who allows females to be priests - many waters referring to their monthly periods that require cleansing), with whom the kings of the earth (her affair with Titus, son of the Emperor Vespasian) did commit whoredom (for like Jezebel, she had abandoned the Jews in favor of the false gods of Rome); and made drunk with the wine of her whoredom were those inhabiting the earth.' And he carried me away to a wilderness in the Spirit, and I saw a woman sitting upon a scarlet-colored beast (Bernice, having declared herself a cardinal as the sister of Agrippa II), full of names of evil-speaking, having seven heads and ten horns, (like the "dragon" Joazar Boethus at the Bar Mitzvah of Jesus: the head of the seven leaders and the ten provinces of the Diaspora) and the woman was arrayed with purple and scarlet-color (purple as the Queen of Judea as sister of Agrippa II and scarlet as cardinal), and gilded with gold, and precious stone, and pearls, having a golden cup in her hand (the cup of the Sacrament) full of abominations and uncleanness of her whoredom, and upon her forehead was a name written: 'Mystery, Babylon the Great, the Mother of the Whores, and the Abominations of the earth.' (intending to become Empress of Rome as the wife of Titus) And I saw the woman drunken with the blood of the saints, and from the blood of the witnesses of Jesus, and I did wonder, having seen her, with great wonder (metaphor of the sacramental wine being the blood of the martyrs that she is betraying). Rev 17:9-11 'Here is the mind that is having wisdom; the seven heads are seven mountains, upon which the woman does sit, and there are seven kings, the five did fall (Caligula, Nero, Galba, Otho, & Vitellius), and the one (Vespasian), the other did not yet come (Titus), and when he may come, it behooves him to remain a little time (Titus died two years after becoming Emperor); and the beast that was, and is not, he also is eighth, and out of the seven he is, and to destruction he does go away. (Eleazar ben Simon, head of East Manasseh - the previous "beast" was Simon Magus of West Manasseh.)*

*Cassius Dio Roman History Epitome of Book LXV Bernice was at the very height of her power and consequently came to Rome along with her brother Agrippa. The latter was given the rank of praetor, while she dwelt in the palace, cohabiting with Titus. She expected to marry him and was already behaving in every respect as if she were his wife; but when he perceived that the Romans were displeased with the situation, he sent her away.*

## Chapter 118. (January 70AD)
## Bernice almost saves Jerusalem

*Titus, son of the Emperor and soon the conqueror of the Jews, is in bed with Bernice drinking wine.*

Titus says, "So are we to decide the fate of Jerusalem in this bed? My father Vespasian ordered me to sack the city and bring the Zealots in chains to Rome."

Bernice says, "I would say that your success depends on whether you think I am more beautiful than Cleopatra."

Titus says, "Let me look at your bust again. *She puts down her wine, allowing the sheets to fall away to expose her breasts.*
"Yes, Cleopatra was a hag compared to you!"

Bernice takes his wine away and reaches under the sheet and says, "But are you more of a man than Julius Caesar and Mark Antony?" Titus flips her over and on top of her, says "Let's test it out."

"As queen of Jerusalem, I grant you entry to the temple." Titus says, "I already took it." Bernice groans, "Yes, yes, take all my treasure."

Vespasian pounds on the door, saying "Are you cavorting with that whore of Babylon again?"

Titus says, "She is not a whore, but Queen of the Jews. I want her to be my queen."

"Do you expect the people to allow you to march in triumph through the streets of Rome holding the unfettered hands of the conquered queen?"

Titus says, "Father, would this not solidify the new union of Rome and the vanquished Jewish nation?" Vespasian says, "Under the covers, but not in public."
*In 70AD The Jerusalem temple goes up in flames. Titus becomes emperor in 79AD, but dies in 81AD*

*(Tychicus writes:) Rev 18:16-23 And saying, Woe, woe, the great city, that was arrayed with fine linen, and purple, and scarlet, and gilded in gold, and precious stone, and pearls -- because in one hour so much riches were made waste! (The failure of Queen Bernice's affair with Titus, that would have led to her being the Empress of Rome and thus her leadership in the Church, having been dissolved.) 'And every shipmaster (priests), and all the company upon the ships, and sailors (apostles), and as many as work the sea (Bernice's Church on Tiber Island, Rome), far off stood, and were crying, seeing the smoke of her (Babylon: Bernice's Church like Jerusalem) burning, saying, What city is like to the great city? and they did cast dust upon their heads, and were crying out, weeping and sorrowing, saying, Woe, woe, the great city! in which were made rich all having ships in the sea, out of her costliness -- for in one hour was she made desolate. (The failure of Bernice's plan to become Titus' wife leaves Agrippa II and Bernice with no power in Jerusalem or Rome. Rome that was supposed to fall by prophecy is now Bernice representing the Jewish Babylon which ironically had fallen instead). 'Be glad over her, O heaven, and you holy apostles and prophets, because God did judge your judgment of her!' And one strong angel (John II, born in 46AD now 25 years old, to John Aquila and Priscilla, descendant of the Emperors) did take up a stone as a great millstone (the converts were the wheat and the millstone is now replaced with that of Jesus - and also the requirement of circumcision), and did cast it to the sea, saying, 'Thus with violence shall Babylon be cast, the great city, and may not be found anymore at all; and voice of harpers, and musicians, and pipers, and trumpeters, may not be heard at all in you anymore; and any artisan of any art may not be found at all in you anymore; and noise of a millstone (grinding the wheat: converting initiates) may not be heard at all in you anymore; and light of a lamp may shall not shine in you any longer (double negative: the light of Christianity in the abbey churches having replaced the Herodian system will surely continue); and voice of bridegroom and of bride may not be heard in you (double negative: the monasteries and generations of Jesus shall surely prosper rather than the Jewish monarchy); because your merchants (apostles) were (once) the great ones of the earth because in your sorcery (reference to Simon Magus) were all the nations led astray, Jesus Justus (age 35) and his bride are betrothed which thus Jesus' apostles ("merchants") and those of Jesus' family ("great ones") like his brothers and son-in-law Paul are now better sources ("lamps") than the Magi like Simon Magus and Atomos, who give false prophecies.*

*Rev 18:24 and in her (Babylon: Rome) the blood of prophets and of saints was found, and most of all those who have been slain on the earth.' (Martyrs were found in clergy and congregation, but the greatest of all was Jesus (the Slain One), who is now dead in June 72AD at age 78)*

## Chapter 119. (72AD)
## Paulina makes a promise

*It is 71AD, in Lugdunum Convenarum. Jesus gets up from Antipas' favorite red velvet chair decorated with gold leaf and beckons Paulina to sit next to him.*

Jesus smiles and says, "I remember the strong-willed Peter and the patient-loving Paul that my Father in Heaven had sent me. Clearly, you also possess your mother Phoebe's strength and courage! Now that they are gone in my old age, He has blessed me with my granddaughter Paulina, the sum total of both!"

"You only say that because I am your granddaughter! My feet are too small for their footsteps!"

Jesus looking at her kindly, "I see so much of your father Paul in you. It seems only yesterday that I placed on his shoulders my mission to the Gentiles. He was only twenty-two, and he never failed me. Now you are seventeen and, though I know that women grow up faster than men, I should not be placing my burden on your shoulders."
"It is all right, Grandfather. What do you need?"

Jesus explains, "My biggest regret is that I allowed Paul to preach my Resurrection when it was a lie.
Paulina says, "But it was like a resurrection and it was amazing that you survived."

"That is true, but a lie is a lie. I want you to promise to tell the world the truth. People need to know that life on this earth is precious and that death is merely a door to a heaven that you create on earth, not a fictitious place that I resurrected to."
"Of course, you are right. I promise."
*(Jesus dies in June 72AD at the age of 78)*

I, John III - (In Rev 22:8,9 "I, John" has been added in some versions but not in Vaticanus: grandson of John Aquila and Priscilla writes:) Rev 21:1-3 And I saw a new heaven and a new earth, for the first heaven and the first earth did pass away, and the sea is not any more; and I saw the holy city -- new Jerusalem -- coming down from God out of the heaven, made ready as a bride adorned for her husband; and I heard a great voice out of the heaven, saying, 'Lo, the tabernacle of God is with men, and He will tabernacle with them, and they shall be His peoples, and God Himself shall be with them -- their God, ( Jesus Justus (Jesus' first son) was betrothed in 72AD at the age of 35 and now in 111AD his son is betrothed, In 112AD Jesus IV is born.)

Rev 21:9-17,22-27 And there came unto me one of the seven angels, who have the seven vials that are full of the seven last plagues, and he spoke with me, saying, 'Come, I will show you the bride of the Lamb -- the wife,' and he carried me away in the Spirit to a mountain great and high, and did show to me the great city, the holy Jerusalem, coming down out of the heaven from God, having the glory of God, and her light [is] like a stone most precious, as a jasper stone clear as crystal, having also a wall great and high, having twelve gates, and at the gates twelve angels, and names written thereon, which are [those] of the twelve tribes of the sons of Israel, at the east three gates, at the north three gates, at the south three gates, at the west three gates; and the wall of the city had twelve foundations, and in them names of the twelve apostles of the Lamb.
And he who is speaking with me had a golden reed, that he may measure the city, and its gates, and its wall; and the city lies square, and the length of it is as great as the breadth; and he did measure the city with the reed -- furlongs twelve thousand; the length, and the breadth, and the height, of it are equal; and he measured its edge (χεῖλος italicized form of χιλος not wall), a hundred forty-four cubits, the measure of a man, that is, of the angel; and the building of its wall was jasper, and the city [is] pure gold -- like to pure glass; And the twelve gates are twelve pearls, each several one of the gates was of one pearl; and the broad-place of the city is pure gold -- as transparent glass. (glass ceiling and stain glass) And a sanctuary I did not see in it, for the Lord God, the Almighty, is its sanctuary, and the Lamb, and the city has no need of the sun, nor of the moon, that they may shine in it; for the glory of God did lighten it, (many candles) and the lamp of it is the Lamb; and the nations of the saved in its light shall walk, and the kings of the earth do bring their glory and honor into it, and its gates shall not at all be shut by day, for night shall not be there (always open); and they shall bring the glory and the honor of the nations into it; and there may not at all enter into it any thing defiling and doing abomination, and a lie, but -- those written in the scroll of the life of the Lamb.

# Chapter 120. (111AD)
## Betrothal of Jesus' grandson; 6 Sacraments

*Pope Alexander, sitting on the throne, has taken his name from Alexandria showing he is a Therapeut and thus he will steer the Church away from the monastic Essene influences.*

Pope Alexander says, "Today we are here to witness the betrothal of Jesus' grandson. Jesus' first son Jesus Justus was betrothed in 72AD at the age of 35 and now in 111AD his son is betrothed."

Pope Alexander preaches, "The Holy Spirit imparted to me six sacraments for the Church:

- *In the Baptism to wipe away every tear from your eyes*
- *Confirmation because death shall be no more*
- *Eucharist for in the sorrow is hope*
- *Penance because crying is the necessary cure*
- *Matrimony that two can bear the pain of life as one*
- *Holy Orders as the first thing of importance"*

The Pope continues, "God makes all things new. His words are faithful and true for as Paul said, 'We are justified by faith' and Christ's truth of selfless love connects us all in the fellowship that is our Church forever and ever."

| Aaron's breastplate (KJV:Exodus 28:17-21) | New Jerusalem (KJV:Rev 19,20) | Assumed stone |
|---|---|---|
| 1.1 sardius | jasper | sardius |
| 1.2 topaz | sapphire | topaz |
| 1.3 carbuncle | chalcedony | chrysoprase |
| 2.1 emerald | emerald | garnet |
| 2.2 sapphire | sardonyx | lapus lazuli |
| 2.3 diamond | sardius | opal |
| 3.1 ligure | chrysolite | rubellite |
| 3.2 agate | beryl | agate |
| 3.3 amethyst | topaz | amethyst |
| 4.1 beryl | chrysoprase | chrysoberyl |
| 4.2 onyx | jacinth | beryl |
| 4.3 jasper | amethyst | sardonyx |

(John III writes:) Rev 22:10-17 And he said to me, 'You may not seal the words of the prophecy of this scroll, because the time is near; he who is unrighteous -- let him be unrighteous still, and he who is filthy -- let him be filthy still, and he who is righteous -- let him be declared righteous still, and he who is sanctified -- let him be sanctified still: And lo, I come quickly, and my reward is with me, to render to each as his work shall be; I am the Alpha and the Omega -- the Beginning and End -- the First and the Last. 'Happy are those doing His commands that the authority shall be theirs unto the tree of the life, and by the gates they may enter into the city; and without are the dogs, and the sorcerers, and the whoremongers, and the murderers, and the idolaters, and everyone who is loving and is doing a lie. 'I, Jesus (son of Jesus Justus announcing the birth of his son) did send my angel to testify to you these things concerning the assemblies; I am the root and the offspring of David, the bright and morning star! And the Spirit and the Bride say, Come; and he who is hearing -- let him say, Come; and he who is thirsting: let him come; and he who is willing: let him take the water of life freely.
The lineage of Jesus is intact as my child is a male. Jesus' great grandson!

# Chapter 121. (112AD)
## Jesus IV is born in 112; First & Last

Jesus III comes to the podium and says, "I, Jesus the grandson of Jesus Justus did send my angel to testify to you these things concerning the assemblies; I am the root and the offspring of David, the bright and morning star!"

And the Spirit (Jesus III) and the Bride say, "Come; and he who is hearing, let him say, 'come'; and he who is thirsting, let him come; and he who is willing, let him take the water of life freely. The lineage of Jesus is assured in our son! Jesus will live on in his great-grandson and within our hearts!"

The Pope says "It has been done! God declares 'I am Alpha and Omega, the Beginning and the End'. No longer will it be required to pass through grades from beginning to end. From this point, even the clergical positions can be attained by all. He who overcomes with strength brought under control, although meek, shall inherit the earth and be born again in the kingdom. The first shall be last and the last first. We are sons of the Father in heaven."

"As for the fearful, the unsteadfast, the abominable, the murderers, the whoremongers, the sorcerers, the idolaters, and all the liars, their part is in the lake that is burning with fire and brimstone, they will go to Hell, which is the second death." (Rev 21:4-8)

\*\*\*\*\*\*\*\*\*\*\*\*\*\*\*\*\*\*\*\*\*\*\*\*\*\*\*\*\*\*\*\*\*\*\*\*\*\*\*\*\*\*\*\*\*\*\*\*

Rev 22:21 The grace of our Lord Jesus Christ be with you all the holy ones.
Amen.

\*\*\*\*\*\*\*\*\*\*\*\*\*\*\*\*\*\*\*\*\*\*\*\*\*\*\*\*\*\*\*\*\*\*\*\*\*\*\*\*\*\*\*\*\*\*\*\*

*Front cover:* Portrait of Jesus
The only live portrait of Jesus from Mandylion (or "holy towel") brought to King Abgar by Simon Magus. (St. Catherine's Monastery, Sinai) (See start of Section 11)

*Notes on Back cover:* New Jerusalem
Astrological signs: Leaders (Numbers 2) are at
the centers of the Zodiacal Cross
Barnabas is Matthias, Simon Magus is replaced by Paul,
Theudas by Simon-Silas, Clement replaces Jonathan Annas

*Major characters in order of appearance:* Joseph (Jesus' father)* Theudas (Nicodemus, Barabbas, Therapeut leader, Jesus' Uncle Cleopas, of 12)* Ananas (High Priest)* Jesus* Herod Antipas (son of Herod the Great, Paul's father)* Mother Mary (Tabitha)* Simeon & Anna (Essenes)* Father Jonathan (son of Annas, James of Alphaeus, of 12)* Simon Magus (Pope, Lazarus, Ananias, of 12)* John the Baptist* Philip(of 12)* Andrew (of 12)* Peter (of 12)* Helena (consort of Simon, mother of Magdalene, Martha, Sapphira)* Herodias (mother of Salome, brother of Agrippa, wife of Aristobulus)* Salome (12yrs, wife of Aristobulus)* James Niceta (of 12)* John Aquila (of 12)* Herod Agrippa (grandson of Herod the Great, later King)* John Mark (Eutychus, Bartholomew, of 12)* Thomas (son of Herod the great, disinherited, father of Salome, of 12)* Judas Sicarii (Iscariot, of 12)* Matthew (son of Ananas, of 12)* Mary Magdalene (Jesus' wife)* Joses (Barnabas, Matthias, son 3 of Mary)* James the Just (son 1 of Mary)* Titus (Marsyas, Fish 2)* Priscilla (wife of John Aquila, mother of John the presbyter)* Zacchaeus (Ananus, the youngest son of the High Priest Ananas)* Caiaphas (High Priest)* Pontius Pilate* Luke (Cornelius, centurion)* Susanna (daughter of Uncle Cleopas)* Caligula* Paul (Saul)* Tamar (Phoebe, child; Paul's wife)* Blastus (Nicolaus)* Agrippa II (son of King Agrippa, twin brother of Bernice)* Simon (Silas, son 5 of Mary)* Aristobulus (father of Timothy & Tychicus)* Jude (son 4 of Mary)* Timothy (designated heir of Agrippa II)* Lydia (Jesus' 2nd wife)* Paulina (daughter of Phoebe and Paul, young & age 22)* Apollos (Therapeut leader replacing Theudas)* Titus (son of the Emperor Vespasian)* Pope Alexander* Jesus III*

# Other books this author:

*Paulina's Promise to her Grandfather, Jesus*
*The story is told by Paulina who is the daughter of Phoebe and St.Paul. Her mother Phoebe is the daughter of Jesus and Mary Magdalene. From her vantage point, she reveals all the secrets with full documentation. Among these secrets is that Jesus survived the Crucifixion by taking poison on the cross that made him to appear to be dead. He lived to the age of age of 78.*
*Paulina's grandfather Jesus agonized about the lie that he allowed his son-in-law Paul to tell about the Resurrection and on his death bed begged her to write this tell-all book, that later was discovered by Bernadette of Lourdes when Paulina appeared to her in a vision.*

*The Seven Sisters of the Apocalypse A novelette imagining a time when a forward-thinking Pope (almost like Pope Francis, but going further!) allows 7 select young women and 6 select young men to form the School of the Pesher of Christ™ in secret.*
*When the Pope is assassinated and the bomb blows up the world, these students of Father Stephanos go back a second in time to create a Second Coming by visiting characters that lived in the time of Jesus and gathering the twelve jewels to the new City of Jerusalem. Using their knowledge of the Pesher of Christ™ and of Gurdjieff's enneagram, they solve the puzzles and return. The world is saved but their true quest to define the Three Mysteries and establish the New Jerusalem on earth. All this is accomplished while decoding the verses of Revelation.*

*Author's Web Sites:*
*pesherofchrist.com - main site for Pesher of Christ*
*gurdjieff.justwizard.com - Gurdjieff Demystified*
*buffalorising.infinitesoulutions.com - oldiesbutdillies (songs)*
*peshertechnique.infinitesoulutions.com - Dr. Barbara Thiering's site*

www.ingramcontent.com/pod-product-compliance
Lightning Source LLC
Chambersburg PA
CBHW021143160426
43194CB00007B/665